"The Hungarian government shocks or offends you, you're [...] over other people. If on the [...] exactly the sort of country you'd be grateful to live in, read this book."

Tucker Carlson
Political Commentator, Host of the Tucker on X

"Balázs Orbán's latest book is devoted to the contemporary international situation, that is characterised by the collapse of the Western world, and the development of a new multipolar, even anarchic order. His ambition is to locate Hungary within this order, and more specifically, to define a specific Hungarian strategy. The author explores how Hungary rejects dogmatic liberalism, refusing to accept freedom as an unrestricted force that runs without any sense of responsibility. Balázs Orbán demonstrates how and why, on this fundamental point, Hungary is at odds with the European elite, who have moved from socialism to dogmatic liberalism in the space of just a few decades. He believes that Hungary, 'which is headed towards the West but comes from the East,' has a certain ideal of liberty that could pave the way from one era to the next. We may not always agree with Hungary's policies – whether domestic or foreign. Yet in these turbulent times, it would be in our best interest to listen to contrarian views instead of rejecting them on principle."

Chantal Delsol
Philosopher and Professor at Marne-la-Vallée University

"In this impressive and original book, Balázs Orbán has set forth timely and timeless political lessons for readers in Hungary and beyond. Situated between East and West, and steeped in deep historical currents arising from the heart of Europe, a nation and region once dismissed by Westerners as the 'periphery' in fact exemplifies essential new forms of connectivity. As one of the architects of Hungary's extraordinary rise from the devastation wrought during the twentieth-century, Orbán is an able, perceptive, and judicious guide amid these tumultuous yet promising times."

Patrick J. Deneen
Professor of Political Science at the University of Notre Dame

"In the Hussar Cut, *Balázs Orbán offers an insightful analysis of the state of the world and a compelling case for a group of countries, Hungary among them, that are rising to fulfil a much needed role to preserve and further connectivity in this fragmenting era. Globalization as we know it is being torn apart by the very Western powers that propelled it in the beginning. But we are at precisely the moment increasing connectivity is much needed for the developments of so many countries, Western ones included, and for solving the myriad global problems. Balázs Orbán's prescription and Hungary's strategy point a way forward."*

Eric Li
Political Commentator, Founder and President of the Guancha.cn Media Platform, and Member of the Advisory Council of the International Institute for Strategic Studies

"Hungary has infuriated European elites by maintaining an independent immigration and foreign policy. Now Balazs Orban lays out an equally independent economic vision that transcends traditional bloc-based thinking and that will ensure that his country continues punching above its weight on the international stage."

Heather Mac Donald
Thomas W. Smith Fellow,
The Manhattan Institute for Policy Research

*"*Hussar Cut *identifies Hungary's present and future success as drawing maximal leverage from its geographical, cultural, and economic circumstances to champion a bold 'connectivity-based strategy' to widen its network of relationships beyond the narrow confines of its EU partners and NATO allies. Dr. Orbán argues forcefully—and convincingly—that the embrace of Hungary's singular potential to become Central Europe's middle power or, as he puts it, a regional 'keystone state', is the key to sustainably (and proudly) enhance its material and spiritua achievements in the decades to come.* Hussar Cut *is an original and forceful argument for questioning the contemporary mainstream European intellectual and political climate, and, ultimately, makes the case for a moderate sort of nationalism that is rooted not so much in the soil but rather in what can become of the soil; it should thus be understood as falling within the Enlightenment tradition of Montesquieu's towering political science. In short,* Hussar Cut *deserves the widest possible audience and is to be considered indispensable reading for our geopolitically and geo-economically transformational times."*

Damjan Krnjević Mišković
Senior Diplomat and Advisor to the Former President of the Republic of Serbia, Professor of Practice at ADA University

Balázs Orbán

Hussar Cut

The Hungarian Strategy for Connectivity

MCC PRESS

Budapest, 2024

ISBN 978-963-644-052-7

Published by MCC Press Kft.
Responsible manager: Tamás Novák
Translator: Thomas Sneddon
Responsible editor: Anikó Gorácz
Editing and proofreading: The Pro Book Editor
Figures: Gábor Fodor
Cover design: Attila Futaki and Péter Haragos
Printing preparation: Péter Somos

Printing works: Prime Rate Kft.
Responsible manager: Péter Tomcsányi

CONTENTS

INTRODUCTION

What is a hussar? *"Equites levis armaturae, quos hussarones appellamus"*—"lightly armed cavalry, which we call hussars." This is the answer given in a document written in 1481 by the legendary King Matthias Corvinus. There are indications that hussars existed even before the time of Matthias, but this document provides the first textual evidence that these legendary Hungarian soldiers already formed a part of the famous Black Army—the most feared force in Europe at the time. It not only halted but even single-handedly defeated the much more powerful Ottoman Empire on its own soil. And were this not evidence enough of its superiority, during the same period Hungarian armies conquered Bohemia and Moravia, as well as Upper and Lower Austria. This was the key characteristic of Matthias's army: it knew how to use quality and ingenuity to win against overwhelming odds. Indeed, the Hungarian hussar stands as the very embodiment of quality and ingenuity. The task of the hussars was to strike first, typically against a much larger enemy, using speed and initiative to constantly disrupt the enemy's ranks, ambushing, cutting off, and grinding down its opponents.

This military innovation not only comprised the backbone of Hungarian armed forces for centuries, but it even became an international innovation. Seeing the Hungarian successes, Prussian, Russian, French, British, and even American hussar regiments were recruited. Hungarian hussar officers traveled to major Western states, passing on their knowledge and experience to help train light cavalry regiments. Of these, perhaps the most famous is hussar Colonel Mihály Kováts, who fought on the battlefields of the American War of Independence, where he also served as a training officer. He wrote the first regulations for the American Cavalry. Along with his Polish friend Kazimierz Pułaski, he is known as the "Father of the US Cavalry."

If there is single motif that best encapsulates the hussar ethos, the essence of hussar virtues, it is the so-called hussar cut. One dictionary of the Hungarian language defines it as follows: "A fast, decisive, surprising, and at the same time reckless enterprise; an initiative or action that risks everything." The hussar's success depends on whether there is an opportunity for a hussar cut. If not, superior force and the fortunes of battle will eventually grind him down. But if it is possible, then—despite all rational calculations, military conventions, or numerical superiority on the opposing side—the hussar will surely win and his opponents lose.

It is no accident that I chose the idea of the hussar cut as the title of this book. Hungary needs just such a maneuver. Today's world is most reminiscent of a vast battlefield on which great armies are milling in confusion, and the opposing generals are trying to rearrange their ranks to meet the changed circumstances. The United States of America, having won the Cold War, attained brief global dominance as a superpower, but has now lost its dominance due to the strengthening of its rivals and its own internal insecurities. A new game is beginning, and there are so many unknown factors that the outcome of the game is unpredictable. The whole world is looking on with fear and anxiety at this growing disorder, and speculating about what may come next. By waiting patiently or failing to act, individual countries essentially subordinate their own destiny to the machinations of the great powers. Smaller nations that want to take their destiny into their own hands have no choice but to face matters with boldness and creativity. The hussar cut offers Hungary a strategy that allows us to respond to the great challenges of the present while building on our own special strengths—to surprise others with bold action and seize the initiative. Over the past decade, Hungary has reached a point where it has the potential to become a fully developed country. It was able to achieve this favorable initial state even without a particularly large population, territory, economic or military power, or even valuable raw materials. We have been able to count on only two things: our talent and our diligence. It worked: in the second decade of the second millennium, the size of the Hungarian economy tripled. We have closed the gap with the western half of Europe by more than ten percentage points. Full employment has been achieved. Everything that reaches Hungary leaves more valuable than when it arrived. And Hungary has become the world's ninth most complex economy, not merely an "assembly plant." Thanks to improving economic performance, the tax burden has been reduced even while overall tax revenue has increased, making it possible to accelerate the expansion of the middle class, protect the real value of pensions, and reduce poverty. Hungarian companies are becoming increasingly successful in regional and now even global markets. Industry, energy, and infrastructure investments of an unprecedented scale are taking place all over the country. Meanwhile, in Europe, relative to the size of the economy, we are among the highest spenders in terms of supporting young people and families, as well as on higher education and culture. So far so good. However, deep down we do not feel we have yet achieved our potential. According to the World Bank's methodology, we have long since left behind the upper-middle development bracket. But what if the World Bank's scale is not refined enough to show small but important differences? Moreover, there are examples of countries slipping back from previously promising positions. The most common causes of backsliding include factors such as reduced productivity, diminishing returns on existing means of production, poor infrastructure, poor access to public and financial services, weak political institutions, lack of innovation capacity, and high levels of income inequality. For a country to maintain its position among the developed nations of the world, it has to keep working on these factors. Moreover, to be truly developed, it also needs to break through an invisible but very real glass ceiling, increase the size of its own economy, strengthen its own national economic champions, and become a center of innovation. This is the economic dimension of the task before us.

At the same time, there is also an international political dimension. Hungary is the most populous country in the central Carpathian Basin, has been a participant in and shaper of the European political space for more than a millennium, has traditionally been one of the leading states of the Visegrád Group, and is one of the protectors of the Balkan region. How is this role to be described in the language of international politics? The classical system of categorization recognizes superpowers, great powers, middle powers, regional powers, and small states. But this does not cover the entire spectrum of possible roles in international politics. Regional middle powers are emerging as a new, independent category. Essentially, a regional middle power is a state capable of exerting power outside its territory, and of meaningfully shaping regional processes, though it lacks a surplus of power covering all areas. These characteristics make it the driving force behind the organization and operation of regional cooperation and stability. In addition, the region has to be in a geopolitical and cultural situation that makes it—and thus also the regional middle power—globally significant. Hungary possesses exactly these attributes and exactly this level of ambition.

This is the double goal that Hungary can set for itself: to permanently join the camp of the most developed countries and become a regional middle power. It turns out that we have clear goals as well as the opportunity to attain them. This is important to know. According to the well-known aphorism of the great Hungarian poet Sándor Weöres, "There is only one thing to know, the rest is just details: Beneath you is the earth, above you the sky, and within you the ladder." We have no doubt that Hungary will be able to harness its inherent potential and achieve the goals it has set itself—not, however, by repeatedly trying to climb the ladder in the same way. We must look out with a knowing eye for changes to the earth below us, the sky above us, and the ladder before us that we seek to climb.

For this reason, I also think it vital that in this book we discuss at length the international processes currently taking place in the world. In Hungarian public life, too many people discuss these processes in a merely descriptive way, without any apparent awareness of the in-depth data and results of the international scientific debates necessary for a comprehensive examination. I would like this book to fill the resultant gap. My other excuse is that this is the part most likely to be of interest to foreign readers. Likewise, looked at from the other side, foreign readers may never have had the chance to see how the world is perceived in a country as "exotic" as Hungary.

In all honesty, we are witnessing the end of the world as we knew it. This is not a cry for help, but a harsh statement of reality. Still, such initially shocking statements are easier to accept if they are clearly explained. Here is what I mean. The institutions established after 1945, organized according to Western principles, first brought the Cold War to a successful conclusion, and then offered the rest of the world the following deal: In exchange for investment and developmental resources to help them become successful countries, they would be expected to adopt a certain model of neoliberal economic policy, a concept of the role of the state, and, in a certain sense, a certain ideal of humanity.

Well, that is all over now, as is the idea that anyone would consider it the only way a country could succeed. The story no longer holds together, its validity having been challenged by time, geopolitical realignment, and resurgent superpower rivalry. The international institutions still remain, as do the developmental resources and investment they dole out, together with elements of the economic models they developed and promoted, but no one today seriously claims that these represent the only path to salvation or to ensure the peaceful development of a country over the coming decades. Too many countries have achieved success without basing their development on these principles, or at least not exclusively, and it is already too obvious that in the coming years, international institutions will be organized outside the West, creating new sources of developmental resources and investment. It is equally clear that any country that shuts its doors to them will lag behind those who, in spite of outside pressure, are able to keep all doors open. It has become quite clear that all countries will have to write their own recipes for success. Borrowed recipes will not work. The world of "the grass is always greener on the other side" is gone.

It is also important to talk honestly about how and why the former model ceased to function, and how the world order it sought to create fell apart, so that no one misunderstands my key claims here. After all, at bottom it was not a silly idea. Many countries—including, it must be said, our Central European region—can thank it for much of their upward trajectory to date. But in the end, it was built on a flawed premise. The idea was that thanks to accelerating globalization and the unprecedented post-Cold War peace dividend, a world order based on economic connectivity, cultural exports, and US military leadership would be able to permanently ensure the supremacy of the leading countries, within a framework simultaneously capable of elevating the rest of the world. All states would thus have an interest in maintaining the system. This meant that, in addition to globalization as fact, we also witnessed the rise of globalism as ideology. You might compare this to the conquests of Alexander the Great, who sought to Hellenize the ancient East from Alexandria and named a city named after himself. But the results of Alexander's efforts were not at all what he intended. While some of the barbarians were Hellenized, not a few Hellenes were in turn somewhat "barbarized."

Processes similar to those in antiquity have been taking place before our eyes from the early 2000s until the present. At the beginning of the millennium, fundamentalist terrorists attacked the headquarters of the World Trade Center in New York, at that time the symbol of this entire globalist edifice. It should be noted, however, that the disintegration of the previous order can be seen not only in such horrible events, but also in economic terms. Today, for instance, it has become clear that although China has become part of the international free trade system, thereby strengthening itself, it has not adjusted its own country's operations to Western rules. This means that, after a hiatus of several centuries, it once again occupies the position of a great power and is the only great power that continues to nurse superpower aspirations—thereby challenging the United States. But it was not only the rise of both China and fundamentalist Islam that has contributed to the disintegration of the post-1990 global system. Dozens of countries on all continents, including the oil-rich states of the Middle East, as well as India and several East Asian nations, have found key roles for themselves by exploiting their raw materials and technological innovations, or through a population explosion (thus expanding their internal market), or by finding a particular niche (a role in the supply chain, military power, or geopolitical importance, for example). Moreover, in order to protect its positions, the West has often fragrantly disregarded the world order it created—I am thinking here, for example, of the military interventions launched without the authorization of the UN. Any challenger could reasonably suppose that if the institutions of the international order are of so little consequence to the West, then there is no need to take them particularly seriously.

The story of how events turned out this way is a long one, but some Western thinkers and political strategists are now convinced that the current international order no longer serves the interests of their countries. In other words, if things continue like this, there will be trouble. The plan to connect the world and promote free trade, thus acquiring a dominant economic and geopolitical position and enabling existing dominance to be maintained and strengthened, has backfired. A change of strategy is therefore underway. Countries are again being divided into "good" and "bad," where the good are morally superior and must vanquish the bad. So far as possible, the good must organize themselves into an ever more closely cooperating camp against the bad. The task is therefore not to strengthen connections, but to divide economies, infrastructure networks, and institutional systems into those inside and those outside the camp. It is ironic that this process is accelerating the collapse of the existing world order, but that is exactly what is happening. It is telling that five scenarios for the character of the next world order can be imagined, and in three of them, bloc formation—i.e., return to Cold War logic—can be seen as a realistic consequence.

There are many tell-tale signs that we are moving in this direction. On the one hand, many Western, primarily American, political leaders want to make the coming decades (perhaps the next century?) a struggle between democracies and autocracies and have made this dichotomy part of their rhetoric. In practice, this means that the USA no longer aspires to the role of world hegemon but wants to strengthen its position within the Western world. This goes hand-in-hand with claiming the right to determine which country is a sufficiently "pure" democracy. On the other hand, it is exerting increased pressure on its allies, attempting to shape their foreign policy positions according to its own taste.

From Hungary's perspective, this looks like a terrible strategy. It is just as hypocritical as the previous one, since it is clear to everyone that behind the mask of ideology lie hard geopolitical interests, and attempts to deny this appear repellent to many countries. It is also feared that this strategy will in time backfire, since the USA has many non-Western allies that are not even nominal democracies. If enough non-Western countries decide to distance themselves from the leading Western power, the geopolitical formula will be fatally simplified. It will not be a question of a confrontation between democracies and autocracies, but rather of a minority of countries turning against an increasingly united majority.

And this does not bode well. Let us take just a few important indicators. In economic terms, the non-Western states are already ahead of the of the West in terms of production capacity, and they have much larger reserves of raw materials. Technological progress, meanwhile, is essentially a dead heat—in this world, few innovations can be kept secret for long. In terms of global population, the West accounts for only about one-seventh of the total. The only area in which the West excels is military power. And this looks like good news only at first. Because what it really means is that the West can win a possible conflict only by military means. A military conflict is a thinly veiled admission that the power in question has no other means at its disposal. Everyone has known since the days of the ancient sages that the highest level of excellence is to break the enemy's strength without a fight. Today, however, this wisdom has been lost, which unfortunately presages a bloody future for us all.

In light of all this, it would be self-evidently suicidal for the entire Western world to narrow its scope and arbitrarily divide the world into blocs. Doing so would alienate its own potential allies and generate unnecessary points of conflict. And, if this were not enough, economic "decoupling" or "de-risking" (that is, the severing of economic relations) comes at a significant cost, while simultaneously the long term effect will be to weaken rather than strengthen the West in the global economic space.

What is most important for us is that such bloc-forming processes do not serve Hungary's interests either. The Western world is preparing for such an outcome, even if it makes its own position worse. Because Hungary is part of the Western world, it shares Europe's destiny. In addition, over the past decade our country has attained success as an export-oriented open economy. Accordingly, the more difficult we make it to build economic, political, and cultural relations, the more we seriously endanger everything we have achieved, as well as the method by which that success was gained. The problem is, therefore, at least from this point of view, almost unsolvable—the threads cannot be disentangled.

If it is, in this sense, genuinely unresolvable, then let us consider the matter from another angle. What is needed is a quick, inventive solution, a radical re-evaluation of the context of the problem, a cutting of the Gordian Knot, or in Hungarian, a hussar cut! The hussar cut is my term for the Hungarian strategy based on connectivity, as the special Hungarian perception of the appropriate role for our country. We see that the previous world order, which tried to exploit the advantages of connectivity, did help Hungary catch up with the West. At the same time, we also saw how this concept failed during crises, and how the promotion of free trade did not lead to the expected geopolitical dominance of the West—quite the contrary.

To understand why this happened, we need a better understanding of the concept of connectivity and the consequences of its impact to date. In the world order that emerged after the collapse of the Soviet Union, connectivity was a fashionable Western buzzword. However, the kind of deep reflection that should have been devoted to the possible drawbacks of this approach never took place. The Western world threw itself wholeheartedly into connectivity so long as it could enjoy the advantages, then discarded it with the same fervor when its disadvantages became apparent. But, as with most things, lurching between extremes only leads to making the same mistake again, just in the opposite direction. As Hungarians say, it is no use falling off the other side of the horse—you have to learn to sit on it.

In this book, with reference to the international literature I am most familiar with, I go through what connectivity—that is, a strategy based on connectivity in the third decade of the twenty-first century—means in practice. Its starting point is that in a globalized world, interdependencies necessarily develop to such a degree that states must manage them. The principle underlying this process is that the relative advantages of each dependency must outweigh the relative disadvantages. Network theory adds to this by pointing out that the ability to exploit relative advantages increases if the given state has more connections, but decreases if it has fewer. If we represent the system of interdependencies using the tools of network science, we may say that a given node plays a more important role in a network when it has more connections. Or, translating this theoretical description into practical terms: building relationships helps boost the Hungarian economy and strengthens our country's international position. These are precisely the twin goals (becoming a securely developed country and a regional middle power) that we have set for Hungary. I also argue that exploiting the possibilities inherent in connectivity backfired on the Western world because it concentrated on obtaining the benefits to such an extent that it forgot to make its own system of dependency resistant and resilient. This may have been because a system that can protect itself, but is nevertheless based on connectivity, has to reconcile mutually contradictory goals in a harmonious unity, and today's rationalized Western thinking has difficulty coping with such contradictions. This is also indicated by the fact that the West was once fond of, but now shuns, connectivity.

However, laying down the principles of modern connectivity is only half the job. That is, even if we have interpreted the concept of connectivity correctly, we still have to apply it in practice. What is more, this knowledge only becomes specifically applicable in the Hungarian context if we successfully work out a role that our country can take advantage of in terms of connectivity. As I wrote in my previous book, foreign ideas only work when they are molded to fit our own features.

I am convinced that Hungary's position in this new world can best be described by imagining the world as a huge building made up of all the countries of the world, with our country as a small keystone of the largest and most beautiful arch. It is widely understood that the keystone has a special role in the integrity of a structure. Despite its potentially small size, it is of vital importance. The forces generated by arches act against each other, and an arch would collapse if the keystone were not there to transform what would otherwise be destructive forces into mutually reinforcing, strengthening pressures. In a certain sense, the keystone encapsulates the essence of the arch. Without the keystone there is no arch, just as without the arch the keystone has no meaning. The keystone is both part and yet not part of the arch, yet it can also be interpreted independently. The keystone is at once decorative, central, and indispensable.

The keystone is therefore truly the key to the arch and thus the entire building, and the country that plays the keystone role can become the key state of the new world. Such a state maintains relations in all directions, is a member of complex federal systems, is open, innovative, and integrates effectively into the world economy, while remaining able to exert significant political, military, economic, and cultural power. The narrower region of such a state may itself straddle geopolitical fault lines and major international trade routes, thereby allowing the key state to use its connections to organize its own region, increase its importance, and exploit its potential. Without such a key state, the region would fall prey to competing forces, but with its help, it can be stabilized.

Hungary is perfectly suited to play such a keystone-state role thanks to its geographical characteristics, cultural ties, economic connections, and characteristics of state operation. It is well positioned to aim for the position of developed, regional middle power position. In addition, such a role perception would allow the country to take advantage of the opportunities inherent in connectivity even in an increasingly bloc-based world.

The essence of the Hungarian connectivity-based strategy is therefore to use our own geographical situation, cultural characteristics, and economic features to our greatest possible advantage, and to achieve this we must try to build the widest possible network of relationships. The first condition for this is to be aware of our own values. We must build upon Hungarian culture, which contains elements of both East and West, yet remains distinct from both. This is the most important condition of connectivity because what is similar to yet different from others has the ability to act as a connecting force. From this fundamental position, we must find the connection points through which we can cooperate with other countries. An important element of cooperation is the inflow of foreign direct investment, since no country can become fully developed without substantial working capital. We have to achieve all this in such a way that, in addition to foreign players entering the Hungarian market with investment capital, more and more Hungarian players are able to enter the international market. These are the national champions whose growth and development the state should support. Sectors that become breakout points are also needed for success. In the case of Hungary, the obvious choices include the defense sector, which requires high-tech research and knowledge transfer, the energy and food industries, which increases security of supply and resilience, information communication, which is conceived from the outset in the spirit of connectivity, the vehicle manufacturing industry, which has the most extensive supply chains, and the banking sector, which excels in financing and profitability. Adequate infrastructure is also needed: trade, passenger transport, and energy connection points through which Hungary can take part in the global movement of goods and people, and an internal infrastructure network that has no "dark spots," allowing all parts of the country to be reached equally quickly and straightforwardly. And since the Hungarian connectivity strategy builds strongly upon the advantageous features of our own region, we must also play our part in the development of that region. Hungary must support regional trade and economic partnerships and contribute to joint undertakings and infrastructure development projects.

These goals can be achieved only if the Hungarian people are partners in the task and can see the benefits of connectivity. This means that the task facing the Hungarian state is also to literally invest in future generations: in a broader sense through public spending on education and talent development, and, more narrowly, by training a civil service that speaks the language of both the state and the market, and also understands both the global good and the Hungarian national interest. Closely related to all this is the fact that Hungary must emphatically be made an international meeting point, in the fields of culture, sport, and tourism. This is unquestionably made easier by the fact that Hungary is one of the safest countries in the world. Without security, there is no connectivity. Therefore, the task of the state is to guarantee both external and internal security. This also shows how the potential of connectivity and the question of peace are closely related. Without the latter, the former cannot exist; therefore, Hungarian foreign policy must always support the cause of peace. And even more importantly, Hungarian foreign policy must always be based on the national interest.

At this point, the reader might be forgiven for thinking that if this is the case, then Hungary is in a tight spot: recent world developments do not exactly seem to favor such a strategy. But it may be more useful to look at it the other way around: if a country, in our case Hungary, is able to invent and implement its own connectivity strategy, then that country will be a real winner in the coming decades. We only need a Hungarian *coup de foudre*, a strategic hussar cut. We must turn unfavorable circumstances to our advantage. As this book shows, the work in all these directions has already begun.

In Hungarian history, there is no shortage of hussar stories. Here is one example from the 1848/49 War of Independence: it was toward the end of the war, when the Russian Tsar's troops had joined the fight against the Hungarian revolutionaries at the Habsburgs' request. Even as a combined force, however, the two great empires had trouble dealing with the Hungarian hussars. Such was the case at an engagement near Somos. The Hungarian military leadership decided not to deploy the hussars against the more numerous Russian light cavalry, but rather to rely on artillery and preserve their manpower. In the event, some hussars were even assigned to the artillery as gunners. Difficult times often give rise to emergency solutions. However, the hussars were in no mood for this, and leaped into their saddles at the first opportunity. They were joined by a first lieutenant of artillery by the name of Lukács, who was so "taken by" this sudden change in fighting style that he took a slain Russian's uniform and horse from the battle as prizes. His superiors held him accountable despite his success, as his place was, after all, with the artillery. "But what of hussar bravura." cried out hussar Captain József Szomjas, who had single-handedly killed three Russians. This is the essence of the hussar cut: the brilliant move that changes the logic of the whole game and turns defeat into victory.

However, the question arises: how can connectivity be made a guiding principle in everyday political tasks? Nothing could be simpler. I once read a piece of wisdom from the head of the American firm GE: "Strategy is straightforward—just pick a general direction and implement like hell." So it is with us. We have to stay focused and not let ourselves get side-tracked. I hope this book will help us see the path, recognize the goal, and strengthen us to press on as others suggest.

I am profoundly grateful to everyone who contributed to the writing of this book. First, the fundamental idea for the book did not appear from nowhere. Marcus Aurelius, one of the sages of antiquity, also argues that we must learn to understand the world order of which we are a part and the governing principles of which we are the emanating rays; we must not waste the time allotted us for this task. I take this to mean that the world around us is going through amazing changes at a tremendous speed, and because of that the need for thinking is greatest. This realization prompted me to publish my ideas on Hungary's connectivity strategy in the columns of the Hungarian current affairs weekly magazine *Mandiner*, and also in

English on the website of the European Council of Foreign Relations. These articles made significant domestic and international waves, and so achieved their goal.

It is due to the very intensity of those reactions that the publication of *Hussar Cut* was preceded by many discussions. Professors, analysts, journalists, politicians, and businesspeople from all corners of the globe shared their opinions with me, and after the articles were published, I received plenty of both supportive comments and scathing criticism—in both Hungarian and English. Fortunately, this meant that my thought process had a place to start from. In my previous book, *The Hungarian Way of Strategy*, I attempted to enumerate the fundamental principles that must be considered in Hungarian strategic thinking at any given time. In this sense, the subject of my book was not so much strategy as meta-strategy. This term may seem pretentious at first, but there is a concrete idea behind it, and the history of Western thought understands the distinction. There is a very great difference between the study of fundamental principles and the study of how to apply contingent principles in a particular, often rapidly changing situation. However, it is easy to see that the latter requires the former.

That is why the previous volume covered the absolute, noncontingent principles of Hungarian strategy—the value commitments that must be adhered to in all circumstances. I felt, however, that it was necessary to be able to show, and even demonstrate, so to speak, how the noncontingent principles enumerated in the previous book could be applied to the specific situation in which we currently find ourselves. One of the main claims of the previous volume is that now is the time to create a strategy, because the world is changing, our room for maneuver is expanding, and those who fail to act are making a historical mistake. Today, I claim that it is not only possible but, in some cases, even mandatory to create a strategy, because events have accelerated in recent years and the world has been almost completely transformed.

Everything we once knew to be true is no longer true, or not as true as it was. In the meantime, a new truth is discovered. It is difficult to adapt to unexpected situations, but it is easy to get tangled up in problems. Those who do not adapt to this will fail, while those who overcome the obstacles in their path will succeed.

However, I am grateful not only for the inspiring criticism, but also for the supportive environment around me. First, of course, to my family, who still put up with me. As I am writing these lines, on a warm summer's day, the whole family is playing outside in the sun, splashing around in the water, while I am inside working. And I miss them a lot, but they let me work. Not to worry though—later we played a ball game together. Secondly, I owe a debt of gratitude to my outstanding colleagues—especially Attila Palkó, Márton Ugrósdy, and Gladden Pappin—with whom I have spent long days discussing these issues and who carried out the indispensable research work. Thirdly, I have many people to thank for thought-provoking conversations, among whom I would especially like to highlight Jeffrey Sachs and Professor John Mearsheimer, as well as Ivan Krastev, who provided me with much useful inspiration during the work. I also owe a debt of gratitude to Prime Minister Viktor Orbán, who allows me to occupy myself with such things while, as usual, he is at once my biggest critic and my greatest inspiration. For all the statements in the book, all possible glory, but also full responsibility, rests with me. I wish everyone pleasant reading and a fruitful search for ideas!

Porec, 12 August 2023

1 WORLD/ORDER: WHAT WILL THE COMING DECADES BRING?

"Time drives swiftly on—runs its course—if we mount, it moves us on; if we stay behind, it will not wait; the world changes; what is strong grows weak; and what was weak grows strong."
(János Arany)

According to tradition, in the village of Cinkota—which in olden days was supposedly farther from Pest than today—the *icce* (an old Hungarian unit of measure) was twice as large as elsewhere, so twice as much wine was measured out per unit. Mór Jókai noted why this is so in his anecdote about King Mathias. According to the story, the resourceful cantor of Cinkota was able to answer Mathias's typically riddling questions so skillfully that the king rewarded the churchman. The cantor—because he loved wine—asked that the standard measure at Cinkota be made precisely double the size of the previous one. So it came to be, and Mathias enshrined the double-size measurement unit in law.

But, as usual, there was a twist in the tale. A double measure also meant double the price, and in the end the good cantor was no better off. He was clever enough to answer riddling questions, but King Mathias ultimately outsmarted him. The mistake made by the otherwise shrewd cantor was that, although he was able to formulate his own goals precisely (a supersized *icce*), he did not pay sufficient attention to the circumstances related to his goals (the price), and specifically to the fact that changing the unit of measure can and will influence prices.

To put it more technically: if we change one factor in a dynamic system, the other factors will also change. This is why we can never focus exclusively on our goals but must also examine the circumstances in which we seek to achieve them. Therefore, before we start thinking about planning a Hungarian strategy, we must

Figure 1: The evangelical church in Cinkota,
some elements of which still bear traces
of its Romanesque iteration, dating from the eleventh century.
Who knows? Perhaps the cantor in the anecdote served here.
Source: Wikimedia Commons

carefully examine the international environment in which Hungary has to thrive in the coming decades. A thorough analysis is required, so the entire first chapter is dedicated to a detailed explanation and justification of the following line of thought.

Our starting point is that the international order created at the end of the Cold War is currently in a state of flux and will not last long in the form we know it. Moreover, for the first time in centuries, there is a real chance that a change in the international order will also end of dominance of Western civilization. Whether or not that comes to pass, how the West reacts to the changed situation is of the utmost importance.

I do not know whether you have noticed, but it gives us an uneasy feeling when we observe how the peaceful panda has been replaced by a fire-breathing dragon in the pictorial sketches of today's mainstream Western political weeklies, and the bald eagle no longer looks down on the landscape below with as peaceful an eye as it did in former decades. Historical experience shows that these changes, which are also perceptible at the level of public opinion, are not accidental, and reflect changes in the general public mood quite accurately.

In our opinion, the return of Cold War rhetoric and the increasingly rapid slide toward a world of economic blocs—even if these may appear logical at first glance—do not serve the interests of the Western world. They alienate the West's allies and generate unnecessary points of conflict within the West itself, as well as increasing the chances of a military conflict by leaving military power as the West's sole competitive advantage. And as though this were not enough, economic decoupling or de-risking comes at a significant cost, with no guarantee that it will not cause a more significant economic downturn in the West than outside it. Moreover, the East, rich in human and raw material resources and technologically catching up, would certainly overcome such an obstacle more easily. Finally, and most importantly of all from our point of view, such a process of bloc formation is not in Hungary's interests either.

But every journey begins with a single step. The big picture outlined in the lines above can be truly understood only if we go through the individual problems step by step. Our first conclusion was that the world order as we have known it until now is breaking down. To clarify this statement, one must first explain what this world order is.

1.1. Anatomy of a Global Order
on the Brink of Collapse

Biographers tell us that Charles Dickens was a superstitious man, with a compulsive need for cleanliness and tidiness. There is a curious ambivalence in this. Superstition, after all, is elusive: for every rule there is another that counteracts or overrides it. Even if we do as we believe should be done, we cannot determine with certainty afterward that it had any efficacy. For example: I did not let the black cat cross my path, and I missed the bus. But then it turns out that the bus ended up in an accident, so what seemed like bad luck, an offense against the rules of superstition, turned out to be good luck, an expression of a "greater good" that exists on some higher plane. Or perhaps there was a chimney sweep nearby who brought good luck? A black cat means bad luck, a sooty chimney sweep means good luck. If there is one thing we cannot count on in a world dominated by superstition, it is predictability.

In stark contrast to this is the mania for order. This is predicated on the notion that a useful or decorative object, whether man-made or natural, can exist correctly in one way only. Under a particular set of circumstances, it exists correctly if it occupies the point in space and time assigned to it. All else is decline, decay, entropy. Time degrades, and the order-obsessed person is born to put things right (crazy talk: "But there's an inner logic to it"). The world of the order-obsessed, where clarity reigns, is in stark contrast to the world of the superstitious, where all is interpretation.

And yet, in Dickens, the two are closely related. There is a motif that connects the two properties: namely, the need for control over our lives. Just as in superstition, in the mania for order the demand is expressed that if we pay close attention to the correct order of our actions and are aware of what surround us, we can limit the unpredictability of our lives—i.e., forestall unexpected trouble—while at the same time being more likely to achieve our goals, because the way in which actions lead to these goals can be seen and understood.

In a strange way, from this perspective, Dickens was not only right, but also correctly perceived the connection between order and control: There are necessities in our world that are as unambiguous as the correct place of things for the order-obsessed. At the same time, there are contingencies that can be as unpredictable, as dependent on interpretation, as the laws of superstition. So there is room for both. It is no different when it comes to the world order, which is also a world of necessities and contingencies. It has its defining actors, whom we can in turn define and describe, and even specific rules, but the application of those rules often depends on how the individuals involved interpret them. That is why there are several ways to grasp what the world order is all about.

In a study by the famous RAND Corporation, the "international order" is defined as "the body of rules, norms, and institutions that govern relations among the key players in the international environment."[1] However, the situation is more complicated than that. The concept of the world order also goes through continuous transformations, and different phenomena are understood by it from age to age, just as the world order itself is constantly changing.[2]

All the same, it makes sense to begin with the RAND definition, and from there to move on to explore the many other ways the

---

[1]   Mazarr et al. 2016: 7.

[2]   A very good and readable summary of the problem is provided by Henry Kissinger, who draws attention not only to the fact that the term world order has been interpreted differently in different historical epochs of Western civilization, but also to the fact that the meaning of the word differs in other civilizations, for example, in the Chinese or Islamic worlds (Kissinger, 2014a: 2–8).

concept can be interpreted. On the one hand, it is therefore worth examining existing power relations, which primarily originate from political, economic, military, cultural, and geographical factors.[3] On the other hand, any concept or description of the world order includes the normative rules on which the actors in the international system base their actions in a given situation.[4] From these descriptions of power relations and normative rules, it is possible to determine such factors as whether the actors in the international order interact within a structured or unstructured framework, or whether they prefer cooperative or confrontational solutions. In addition, the validity of explanations for the norms and subjects of the international order is further nuanced by the fact that in recent years the importance of non-state actors in the international order has also increased, so we must understand the totality of normative rules as also embracing the rules applicable to them.[5]

What is more, some schools of international relations also interpret the international order according to quite different metrics. The realist school makes the existence or absence of order a function of the balance of power, especially military power.[6] According to John J. Mearsheimer, this may be the reason for the widespread view that associates realism with war, saying that if supporters of the theory that interprets the world as a competition for power are placed in a decision-making position, they will quickly resort to the

---

3   This division of power relations into political, economic, military, cultural, and geographical factors is Joseph S. Nye's method (Nye, 2011).

4   For more on the role of normativity, see Schmidt-Williams, 2023; Gorobets, 2020; Jovanović, 2019; Shelton, 2006.

5   Two fundamental problems can arise in connection with the appearance of non-state actors: First, the rise of these actors may limit the sovereignty of individual state actors. This, in turn, leads to the second problem: they demand the construction of a normative system that clearly stipulates the rights and responsibilities of these non-state actors (Ben-Ari, 2012: 32).

6   Morgenthau, 1972. The most important realist authors are Niccolò Machiavelli, Hans Morgenthau, Reinhold Niebuhr, Raymond Aron, George F. Kennan, Martin Wight, Barry Buzan, John Mearsheimer, Barry Posen, Kenneth Waltz, and Stephen Walt.

Figure 2: Busts of the fathers of the post-1990 world order: George Bush, Helmut Kohl, and Mikhail Gorbachev in front of the Berlin building of the Axel Springer newspaper publisher.
Source: Wikimedia Commons, photograph by Dick Osserman

use of military force.[7] However, in practice, supporters of the realist school tend not to belong to the pro-war camp.[8]

In the liberal interpretation, "international order" means the totality of international organizations and norms, to which states are naturally also subject; these norms and institutions help to establish mutually beneficial cooperation, and to avoid zero-sum games.[9] Thus—in contrast to the realist school—those evaluating the liberal

---

7   Mearsheimer cites several studies to support his view. These include Carr, 1962; Gilpin, 1996; Mearsheimer, 2005a; Mearsheimer, 2005b.

8   The reason for this can be found in the fact that realists do not aim to spread their ideas in the world, while idealists with a sense of mission do not shy away even from war in their efforts to shape the political system of a given country in their own image (Mearsheimer, 2022: 346).

9   The most important liberal authors include Immanuel Kant, Robert Keohane, Joseph Nye, Andrew Moravcsik, Robert Gilpin, and Peter J. Katzenstein.

school often suppose that conflicts can be resolved peacefully by following its principles.[10]

The basic starting point of the constructivist school, meanwhile, is that the shared values of individual societies determine the interests and ultimately the actions of international actors.[11] In this context, constructivists see the international order first and foremost as an arena of ideological competition.[12]

This also shows that there is no shortage of analytical means by which we can describe the post-1990 world order. The easiest element to determine is that of power centers. It is a widely accepted view that the world order after 1990 was unipolar, predicated on the hegemony of the United States.[13] From an ideological point of view, we can say that the world order was based on the primacy of Western civilization. This idea was presented in its most refined form in Francis Fukuyama's theory of the "end of history." As is well known, Fukuyama predicted the global spread of Western liberal democracy at the dawn of the post-Cold War era.[14] That is,

---

10   This belief can be traced all the way back to Immanuel Kant (Kant, 2016: 117–142). In his work "Perpetual Peace" ("Zum ewigen Frieden"), Kant argues in defense of the idea that democratic states never go to war with each other, and instead settle their conflicts within institutional frameworks. This view formed the basis of the modern liberal school's aspiration to confine conflict resolution to institutional frameworks by strengthening international institutions. In a peculiar way, the Kantian idea is embedded in the idea of democracy export, which—based on the experiences of the past decades—is in most cases far from a peaceful process.

11   The most important constructivist authors: Kathryn Sikkink, Peter Katzenstein, Elizabeth Kier, Martha Finnemore, and Alexander Wendt.

12   Wendt, 1999.

13   Ikenberry, 2012; Kagan, 2012: 7–9. Partly following these scholars, some Hungarian authors have also argued that the hegemony of the United States can be seen as an exception only in international relations theory. In essence, what is exceptional is that "the United States could become so strong in the international system without a challenger that it was able to pursue a purely liberal foreign policy, the goal of which was to spread the liberal order according to its interests, stemming from internal values." At the same time, the two authors insist that such an exceptional state cannot long endure (Rada-Stepper, 2023: 3).

14   Fukuyama stated not only that liberal democracy has no alternative, but also that this political system will be adopted by more and more states in the world: "It is against this background that the remarkable worldwide character of the current liberal

he believed that in time the non-Western half of the world would also adopt the Western institutional system, as well as its political and economic principles of organization. This would lead to the end of major civilizational conflicts, and at the end of the process, the whole world would become like the West and its leading power, the United States. Therefore, it was unsurprising that the norms of the international order were primarily determined by the West and the United States, mostly through the significant influence accumulated in international organizations.[15]

revolution takes on special significance. For it constitutes further evidence that there is a fundamental process at work that dictates a common evolutionary pattern for *all* human societies—in short, something like a Universal History of mankind in the direction of liberal democracy." (Fukuyama, 1992: 39–55). This "liberal revolution" assumes that the course of history is rational, can be understood by reason, and that if the adoption of the most advanced political and economic system is, rationally, the best option for non-Western countries, a significant number of countries will do so. Fukuyama is just one among many authors proclaiming the final victory of the Western world. Similar arguments are also put forward by Krauthammer, 1990; Muravchik, 1991; Ikenberry, 2012; Kagan-Piccore, 2014; and Beckley-Brands, 2022.

15 We have already covered this topic in *The Hungarian Way of Strategy*: A lively debate developed concerning the unipolarity of the international system in the decade following the end of the Cold War. The debate primarily revolved around whether the unipolar world order and the hegemony of the United States could be sustained over many decades, or whether it is necessarily doomed to failure. These ultimately coalesced into three broad positions. As early as 1990, during the last days of the Soviet Union, in the periodical *Foreign Affairs*, Charles Krauthammer entered into a sharp debate with the camp of those predicting the rise of a multipolar world order, such as, for example, the legendary British liberal historian Paul Kennedy. In his book *The Rise and Fall of the Great Powers*, published in 1987, Kennedy argued that a permanently stabilizing multipolar world order would emerge within roughly two decades. In Krauthammer's view, by contrast, unipolarity would characterize the post-Cold War international system. With the fall of the Soviet Union, only one superpower, the United States of America, would remain, alongside a number of second-rank powers such as Germany or Japan. The USA would be able to claim the mantle of international hegemonic superpower because it is the only country possessing sufficient political, economic, and military power simultaneously. Even Krauthammer admitted that the hegemony of the United States could not last forever, but he argued that a multipolar world order would emerge only after many decades (Krauthammer, 1990). In 1993, the neorealist Kenneth Waltz argued that, although several powers within the Western alliance system had grown stronger, the United States would be the world's number one power for some considerable time. The only question was, what strategy would the USA choose? Would it be isolationist, perhaps allowing considerable freedom to other countries while still actively participating in

The Role of Neoliberalism in a Globalizing World

The above description is, of course, rather general, but it covers many important points. Since a key ideological element of the post-1990 world order was a unifying, increasingly connected world, public opinion often tends to closely connect it to the phenomenon of globalization, and even identify the latter with the world order itself. And since the neoliberal model of economic organization favors economic connectivity, we tend to identify this with globalization. Still, any partial or complete conflation of these two concepts—globalization and neoliberalism—will only worsen, or at least certainly will not improve, our chances of describing the current world in precise conceptual terms. In what follows, we will therefore attempt to clarify the relationship between the two concepts and then show how they are related.

Globalization—as András Lánczi described it as early as 2002—is a development that follows organically from the logic of Western modernization.[16] It almost resembles a natural force, and as such, it

---

shaping the international system, or would it become expansive? (Waltz, 1993). In an article published in 2000, Waltz argues that a unipolar world order had indeed emerged after the Cold War, but that this was the most unstable system in the history of mankind, and that it would shortly come to an end. This was primarily because the United States, as the world's number one power, has taken on too many tasks in the international system, and there was no other power to counterbalance American aspirations. Other states, meanwhile, fearing this unipolar system, were trying to increase their own power and, independently or as part of alliance systems, to counterbalance the United States (Waltz, 2000). As a counterpoint to the neorealists, G. John Ikenberry gave a liberal reading of the unipolar international system. According to the Princeton University professor, the United States would be able to maintain the unipolar international system by employing a strategy that gave potential challengers an interest in upholding it. In other words, it would be necessary to persuade other states that international organizations dominated by the USA would bring them more benefits than if they created alternative systems that sought to counterbalance the hegemony of the United States. Put more crudely, unipolarity based partly on the actual power of the USA and partly on the illusion of equal participation (Ikenberry, 1998).

16   "Globalization is not a matter of choice or a conscious decision, but a consequence of the internal logic of Western culture. With the power almost of natural law, the West binds the world together economically, politically, and culturally."

possesses no intrinsic moral value. As a phenomenon, is has more the character of a trend, even a law, like the sun rising in the morning—the world would have to completely transform to reverse this. For us, the consequences of this phenomenon can be both positive and negative. How we relate to it is up to us. Sticking to our most recent metaphor, we can regret that the time for rejuvenating sleep is over or look forward to getting up and beginning another productive day.

Neoliberalism, by contrast, is more difficult to define. It is a fundamentally elusive phenomenon that adapts well to changing circumstances, and its precise content changes as times change, making it resistant to essentialist definitions.[17] It is worth examining it historically in order to more precisely understand its nature and the how it relates to the phenomenon of globalization. Neoliberalism emerged as a distinct worldview in the 1970s. By this time, the economic policy approach that had come to prominence after 1945, commonly referred to as Keynesianism, and based on welfare provision, active state involvement, and a belief that the key to growth lay in accelerating the state's capacity for mass production, was in crisis. In addition to high inflation, economic growth had stalled, key budgetary indicators were negative, and public debt was increasing. The Western economic system, which had worked so well until then, was no longer sustainable.

In the first instance, neoliberalism therefore emerged as an economic response to this crisis, a kind of promarket turn. Moreover, in a certain sense, it marked a return to the economic liberalism typical of the late nineteenth and early twentieth centuries.[18]

---

17   "Neoliberalism is anything but a concise and clearly defined political ideology" (Plehwe-Mirowski, 2009: 1). "Neoliberalism is clear, but incredibly elusive when it comes to defining its essence" (Peck, 2010: 8).

18   One important difference, however, is that while the watchword of early twentieth-century liberalism was free competition, the watchword of neoliberalism is greater competitiveness. Milton Friedman formulates this as a criticism of classical ninteenth-century liberalism, in that by prioritizing free competition, it was in practice encouraging the creation of monopolies. On the other hand, he suggests that

So, neoliberalism mainly means limiting the role of the state, strengthening free trade, pushing deregulation, simplifying the tax system and preferably reducing its progressive elements as far as possible, and privatizing industry as far as practicable.[19] Still, neoliberalism in the 1970s remained primarily a theoretical (i.e., not a practical political) position, so in this era it was economists—the most prominent names being Milton Friedman and the Chicago School—who played the most important role, and it only really entered the political mainstream in the following decade.

That is why the 1980s are often called the golden age of neoliberalism. By this time, politicians had taken over from the theoreticians as its most prominent exponents. The two iconic leaders of the Western world during that decade, Margaret Thatcher and Ronald Reagan, began to put neoliberal principles into practice, and these genuinely represented a way out of the economic crisis and stagnation of the 1970s.[20] Moreover, this marked advantage in

---

a state following neoliberal economic policy principles should consider sharpening competition to be its key task (Friedman, 1951: 89–93).

19 Taking a broad view, David Osborne and Ted Gaebler highlight the following features of neoliberal economic policy: a government that sees its key task as catalyzing economic growth and increasing competitiveness, a market-oriented, customer-oriented, entrepreneurial approach (generating more income and spending less), and decentralized governance. Osborne-Gaebler (1993) as cited by Denhardt, 2008: 145–146.

20 Neoliberal principles were already present in Reagan's 1981 inaugural address. These were the words the president addressed to the people of the United States: "In this present crisis, government is not the solution to our problem; government is the problem. From time to time we've been tempted to believe that society has become too complex to be managed by self-rule, that government by an elite group is superior to government for, by, and of the people [...] Now, so there will be no misunderstanding, it's not my intention to do away with government. It is rather to make it work—work with us, not over us; to stand by our side, not ride on our back. Government can and must provide opportunity, not smother it; foster productivity, not stifle it." Similar principles were formulated by Margaret Thatcher in a 1984 speech: "I came to office with one deliberate intent: to change Britain from a dependent to a self-reliant society—from a give-it-to-me, to a do-it-yourself nation. A get-up-and-go, instead of a sit-back-and-wait-for-it Britain." Both speeches clearly show how neoliberal economic philosophy differs from the laissez-faire liberal capitalism of the early twentieth century. In the former, the state has many roles,

economic performance helped bring an end to the Cold War: the Soviet Union's collapse can be traced to its economic problems, and the crisis of the Soviet regime was only intensified by the strong economic and arms competition initiated by the West.

The third phase of neoliberalism dates from the end of the Cold War in the 1990s, which led to the global spread of neoliberal principles.[21] In this era, neoliberalism was a cornerstone of the development program put forward by the West, fresh from its victory in the Cold War, and primarily by the United States, to the non-Western world, including Latin America, Asia, Africa, and the former Soviet Bloc. One characteristic of this period is that the Bretton Woods institutions and agreements, established in 1945, became the means of spreading neoliberal economic principles: the World Bank (WB), the International Monetary Fund (IMF), the

---

primarily in terms of creating opportunities and maintaining equal competition. It is also peculiar how the principles of neoliberalism are interwoven with conservative ideas in the thinking of the two Anglophone politicians. Both Reagan and Thatcher expected free competition in its fully realized form to strengthen self-sufficient individuals who live off their work and take responsibility for themselves. The uniquely conservative populism we perceive in Reagan's words is also an important conservative motif. The president equated strong, centralized government with an elitist bureaucracy, but saw government operating by neoliberal principles— thanks to its self-imposed limits—as an operating model of governance closer to the people. However, it is by no means certain that neoliberalism could ever have fulfilled the hopes of conservatives. In fact, it appears that quite the opposite has happened. Roger Scruton recalled how in the 1980s he understood the principles by which Thatcher was spearheading neoliberalism, but even then, he saw its flaws. According to Scruton, the two great Anglophone conservative leaders of the day failed to see that the free market they believed in and preferred over managerial, bureaucratic governance did not exist. It did not exist because large companies and multinational corporations operated according to precisely the same managerial, bureaucratic principles, in the same elitist way, using the same central planning as the government sector that conservatives so loved to criticize (Scruton, 2023: 21). And indeed, there are few such technocratic entities today as a multinational corporation. If a modern remake were to be made of what was (in a broad sense) the quintessential late-Reagan-era movie, *Working Girl* starring Melanie Griffith, the heroine would not be able to climb the career ladder thanks to her superior business ideas (as in the film), but by optimizing the processing of Excel tables, and thus her job title could be changed from "accountant" to "subject matter expert."

21 Jamie Peck calls the 1990s the "roll-out" phase of neoliberalism (Peck, 2003: 195).

International Bank for Reconstruction and Development, IBRD), the General Agreement on Tariffs and Trade (GATT), and then the World Trade Organization (WTO).[22] This is the so-called Washington Consensus, which was originally intended to promote the economic development of Latin America and, by extension, other regions of the world.[23] As part of the consensus, the abovementioned institutions typically made the adoption of neoliberal economic principles a precondition for receiving development resources.[24]

It follows from the above that the history of neoliberalism can be divided into at least three eras, and the concept itself had different meanings in each era. This historical overview shows why it is difficult to give a single definition of neoliberalism, since we can approach it as a "package of economic policy measures," a "system of government," and an "ideology."[25] The neoliberal policy package typically includes the abovementioned measures. By "system of government"—following Michel Foucault—we mean the hidden premises, value propositions, and specific logic on which governance is based.[26] According to the principles of neoliberal governance, the state functions well and effectively if it uses the self-regulating free market as its model of operation, and at the same time promotes the enforcement of free market principles throughout the state. Thirdly, neoliberalism is also an ideology that proclaims that

---

22 "The Bretton Woods institutions were meant to facilitate the rapid spread of the Washington Consensus recommendations throughout the developing world" (Phillips, 2020: 261).

23 The Washington Consensus meant the adoption of the following principles: budgetary discipline—meaning in this context a reduction in public expenditure—tax reform, interest rate liberalization, trade liberalization, FDI liberalization, privatization, deregulation, and priority protection of property rights (Phillips, 2020: 256).

24 By stipulating the adoption of Western principles of economic governance, Western institutions did in fact lead Fukuyama's prediction or expectation of the adoption of the Western model towards fulfillment.

25 Steger-Roy, 2010: 11.

26 The concept of governmentality (French: *gouvernementalité*) was first introduced by the French philosopher Michel Foucault in a series of lectures held at the Collège de France in 1978 and 1979.

Figure 3: Aristotle instructs his student, Alexander the Great.
The Greek philosopher was a teacher and advisor of the Macedonian ruler
until he set off on his Eastern campaigns. However, he did not agree with
Alexander's Hellenization program, believing that the process would ultimately lead
to the erosion of Hellenic culture, so he left Alexander the Great's court
at the beginning of the campaign. Just as Aristotle was proved right,
so the downsides of global Westernization have now become obvious.
Source: Getty Images, Ann Ronan

a global economy based on the free market and interwoven with interdependencies brings prosperity to humanity, and accordingly, that the ideal image of humankind is a society of individuals who profess market values and find personal realization in production, consumption, and free exchange. Thus, it essentially accords with the ideal promoted by Western civilization.[27]

---

27 Manfred B. Steger and Ravi K. Roy conceptually summarize neoliberalism as an ideology that has become the organizing principle of globalization: "For example, one of these neoliberal claims presents the creation of globally integrating markets as a rational process that furthers individual freedom and material progress in the world. The underlying assumption here is that markets and consumerist principles are universally applicable because they appeal to all (self-interested) human beings regardless of their social context. Not even stark cultural differences should be seen

The cornerstones of an international order established on this basis are interdependence, and the idea that, through free trade regimes and the adoption of a neoliberal political institutional system, the risk of war can be reduced and faster economic growth can be achieved, both internationally and at the level of individual Western states. It is important to emphasize that this fundamental Western position meant both the need to deepen economic relations and spread political values and organizing principles. Behind this was also the consideration that interdependencies bring benefits to all states involved, but ultimately Western states would be at a greater relative advantage.[28] These greater benefits would strengthen existing economic asymmetries, and this surplus of economic power would eventually be translated into a surplus of political power. That is, thanks to its stronger economic performance, the Western powers would be able to dictate political expectations toward the non-Western states of the world.[29] This relationship to the world has been a conscious Western strategy for the last thirty years, and it was not until US President Donald Trump took office that the West had a leader inclined to question the correctness of the strategy.[30]

---

as obstacles in the establishment of a single global free market in goods, services, and capital. A related neoliberal claim states that the liberalization of trade and the global integration of markets will ultimately benefit all people materially. This assertion is designed to enhance the global appeal of neoliberalism because it seeks to assure people that the creation of a single global market will lift entire regions out of poverty." (Steger-Roy, 2010: 53).

28 The theory of democratic peace, which flourished again in the 1990s, was inspired by Immanuel Kant's essay "Perpetual Peace." According to Kant, perpetual peace can be achieved if all countries transition to a system of republican constitutionalism; if these countries sign treaties of peace; and if the necessary framework of international law can be established, taking the form of a sort of cosmopolitan constitution. The modern exponents of the concept of democratic peace include, for example, Doyle (1983), Maoz-Russet (1993), and Russet (1993).

29 Consider, for instance, how the development resources provided by the institutions of the Washington Consensus have been tied to specific policy measures.

30 According to Clarke-Ricketts (2017), the election of Trump as president marked the return of so-called Jacksonian foreign policy, the main goal of which is to safeguard

To summarize the above: globalization is a "natural process" that has been going on for centuries, while the term "neoliberalism" refers to a specific set of economic policy measures, principles of government, and ideological commitments. The reasons for the frequent conflation of the two phenomena are to be found primarily in the fact that the Western powers, through their own international institutional system, began to impose neoliberal principles on non-Western parts of the world. In practice, this meant that after 1990, neoliberalism became the organizing principle and essential model for those processes of globalization that had already been going on for centuries. And since the phenomenon can be defined in numerous ways, the model came to be associated with the spread of the economic measures, principles and methods of governance, and ideological tenets of neoliberalism. This is also the reason why

---

and protect the virtues of republicanism, and above all the well-being and happiness of one's own national political community, rather than shaping the world in one's own image—as liberal internationalism does. The foreign policy aspect of the "America First" program therefore consists of an essentially unilateral strategy: from this arose, among other things, skepticism towards NATO at the alliance-system level, and it led to the American president voicing the expectation that all members of the defense alliance comply with military spending obligations. In Wright's (2017) assessment, "Trump is the first post-World War II president to oppose the liberal order [based on alliances, an open global economy, the primacy of rules and institutions, and the spread of democracy and human rights]." Brands (2021) makes a similar case. Although it is often said in Washington that realists have regained their influence over American foreign policy thinking over the last ten years, according to Roa (2023), editor-in-chief of *The National Interest*, this is far from the case. American realist thinking looks back on a centuries-old tradition: the country has proven in countless cases that it is able to properly assess its opportunities and capabilities, choose the right tactics, and thereby assert its national interests. All of this was organically connected to national self-image—this was also the case with the export of democracy or, later, the Washington Consensus. In the last decade, however, realists have not been able to do the same. They refuse to consider that the USA is struggling with countless internal economic, institutional, and political problems, or the fact that its relative strength is no longer sufficient to maintain its hegemony. In this way, American realists often end up buying into liberal foreign policy ideas. For more on this, see Kirschner, 2008; Daalder-Lindsay, 2003: 288; Feulner, 1996.

neoliberalism became the globalization model for the era of the *Pax Americana*, which ushered in the hegemony of the United States, the force shaping the rules of the world order.[31]

The End of a World Order: Nails in the Coffin

As we all know, nothing lasts forever. That which has been created must eventually pass away.[32] Every existing system, including the current world order, has its drawbacks, and these inevitably lead to

---

31 Any discussion of the concept of *Pax Americana* will tend to lead towards the classic question: "What have the Romans ever done for us?", or at least many like to use the analogy of Rome in relation to the USA (see Bender, 2003). The *Pax Romana* refers to the approximately two-hundred-year-long period when the Roman Empire, as hegemon, determined the rules and operating principles of the international order. Its overwhelming gravitational force as a civilization meant that the Roman world was characterized by relative peace and economic prosperity. *Pax Americana*, by analogy, refers to the hegemony of the United States after the Second World War, the operation of globalization along the lines of the Washington Consensus, the resultant relative prosperity, the liberal international order, and the absolute—diplomatic, economic, and military—preponderance of the USA, which enabled it to maintain the global balance of power. For further interpretations of *Pax Americana*, see Brzezinski, 1997; Nye, 1990; Cox, 2005; Ferguson, 2005; Kennedy, 1989.

32 Nair (2023) draws attention to five major changes in the international system, each of which led to a decline in the relative power of the West and thus to its loss of status as a major power. First, the Western narrative is no longer dominant when it comes to the interpretation of world history. The narrative of the non-Western world is now firmly established at the academic level, while the non-Western view of history is also affecting political action and self-confidence. Secondly, the balance of power has been upset, and the non-Western world has sufficient power to counterbalance Western geopolitical pressure. Thirdly, the West has also lost much of its credibility. In recent decades, it has promoted peace-building initiatives, while at the same time the eight largest "democratic" states have sold weapons to 124 countries, of which 74 do not qualify as "free and democratic," even in the assessment of the vendor states (Hartman-Béraud-Sudreau, 2023). Fourthly, the economic weight of the West has also decreased significantly, and the non-Western world is beginning to think about alternative monetary systems. This is clearly indicated by the fact that the dollar now accounts for 47 percent of global currency reserves, compared to 73 percent in 2001. Fifthly, faith in the reliability of Western press and news services, which were previously considered impartial points of reference, has also crumbled, further eroding the cultural influence of the West.

a change in the status quo.[33] The post-1990 unipolar world order was no exception.[34] As early as the mid-2000s, the symptoms of crisis

---

33 The history of the Roman Empire as a former hegemon is an instructive parallel in understanding these processes. With reference to Edward Gibbon's six-volume work *The Decline and Fall of the Roman Empire* (1776–1789), it is fashionable, and by no means futile, to compare the current tribulations of the West with those of Rome. The thesis of Heather and Rapley (2023) fits into this line, arguing that the Roman Empire was at the peak of its power at the beginning of the fifth century and was seen as the unquestionable hegemonic power of the world as it was then known to Westerners, but collapsed in under a century. The West is now in exactly the same situation: it won the Second World War and the Soviet Communist system was never a true full-spectrum rival; then, following the Cold War, the world was characterized by indisputable Western dominance. However, since the 2008 crisis, the West's advantage in terms of economic performance and technology has been squandered, while it continues to struggle with serious social problems. Again, drawing parallels with the Roman Empire, the authors emphasize that the end of hegemony was basically attributable to the empire, for two reasons. First, during in the golden age that lasted until the fifth century, Rome had a stable, only moderately unequal society. Secondly, it succeeded in giving the world outside the empire an interest in maintaining the status quo through negotiations and agreements. In this way, it enjoyed systemic security, economic advantages, and, in addition—typical of the modern world—the advantage of influence and cultural hegemony going beyond its territorial frontiers. The West acted similarly until quite recently. It reduced social inequalities while skillfully negotiating within the Washington Consensus system, and it attained widespread acceptance of the Western model of globalization. However, thanks to its embrace of neoliberal economic policy, inequality once again widened, the technological advantage was lost, and energy was no longer invested in securing engagement by the non-Western world in the Washington Consensus (see, for example, WTO reform, which has been postponed for decades), so the West began to opt instead for disconnection. To change course, Heather and Rapley propose, first, that the West should abandon disconnection and bloc formation. In addition, it should come up with some essentially left-wing policies to maintain social balance, the central element of which would be an increase and expansion of the global minimum tax. True, it is still not clear here how the global minimum tax could be made truly global, and in the absence of this, how the remaining competitiveness problems could thus be resolved.

34 One way to ask the question is: "Who Killed the New World Order?" Putting it that way, we immediately find ourselves at the climax of an Agatha Christie novel, with Hercule Poirot revealing one by one how everyone present had a motive for the murder. We can draw this parallel, if only because it is extremely popular these days to draw conclusions about the end of the previous world order: "The Russian invasion of Ukraine has put an end to the globalization we have experienced over the last three decades," wrote BlackRock CEO Larry Fink, in a letter to company shareholders in the spring of 2022. In a peculiar way, Vladimir Putin himself had a similar opinion back in 2018 at Valdaiforum: "Thank God, the monopoly-based, unipolar world order is dying." And if that wasn't enough, even Joe Biden agreed

in the *Pax Americana* world order were visible.[35] Today, in 2023, we can trace, step by step, the events that made the unsustainability of the post-1990 world order obvious:[36]

- In 2001, China joined the WTO, paving the way for its economic rise.
- Also in 2001, al-Qaeda launched an attack on the World Trade Center in New York: an open challenge to the hegemonic power.
- The global financial crisis of 2008 shook the belief in the primacy of the neoliberal and capitalist economic model: first, by highlighting growing levels of social inequality, and also because considerable state intervention was required to stave off even greater damage.[37]

---

with the above two actors regarding the end of the world order, stating at a round-table discussion with business actors, "There's going to be a new world order out there, and we've got to lead it." Richard Haass, the former president of the Council on Foreign Relations, joined those proclaiming the end of the world order in his article on *Project Syndicate*, the title of which is arrestingly straightforward: "Liberal World Order, R.I.P." Xi Jinping, the President of the People's Republic of China, who is strengthening the already populous camp of seeking to change world order, explained in relation to the Russian-Ukrainian war: "China is ready to stand guard over a world order based on rules." So Poirot's exposition is complete. On the other hand, if all important players and most of the analysts are announcing the end of the current world order, then it is hardly likely to survive, since it depends precisely on these players. There are pistols in the pockets of too many key actors, and it is a dramaturgical cliché that if there is a pistol on the stage, it must eventually be fired. (Citations can be found here: Forbes, 2022; Reveel, 2018; Ray, 2022; Haass, 2018; Sauer-Hawkins, 2023.)

35 Brzezinski, 2012.

36 Although this list is my own compilation, it is not without precedent. John Ikenberry has already mentioned quite a few of these in his book on the future of liberal democracy. That volume is from 2020, so Ikenberry could not have included some of the events included here. In addition, there are a couple of earlier events that we added to the list. The logic of these additions lies in Nassim Taleb's "Black Swan" theory, so we were looking for unexpected, unpredicted events that could have a major impact on the development of international processes, or perhaps events that had unexpected effects (Ikenberry, 2020: 2–3; Taleb, 2010).

37 Foroohar (2022) uses the term post-neoliberalism to characterize the exhaustion of neoliberal economic organizational principles and models, and to describe the emerging new paradigm.

- The Migration Crisis of 2015 showed that the meeting of civilizations is not nearly as utopian a process as that envisioned by the ideologues of globalism. Indeed, the meeting of civilizations tends to lead instead to the strengthening of fault lines.[38]

- Brexit, in 2016—the root cause of which was, in no small part, the migration crisis—demonstrated that the model of European integration has stalled and the European project has stumbled into a legitimacy crisis.[39]

- China's economic output—measured in terms of purchasing power parity—reached that of the United States in 2016, and since then its national industrial output has risen every year.[40]

- The election of Donald Trump in 2016 indicated that there is still considerable support for national interest-based politics in the United States.

- The 2020 pandemic showed how global production chains can cause serious anomalies in national economies.[41]

- Russia's aggression against Ukraine in 2022 fundamentally changed the way Western progressive elites think about the world order. In addition, the Russian-Ukrainian war, and the

---

38 Murray (2017) sees Europe's biggest problem—a problem permeating the entire Western political environment—as being a loss of self-esteem. In Western Europe, support for mass migration among elites is so strong and so widespread because the elites do not value European culture. And without self-respect, it is impossible to stand your ground in the ever-sharpening competition of the changing international order.

39 According to German professor and Christian Democrat politician Andreas Rödder (2019), Europe's biggest mistake is that it has been operating for a very long time without a strategy of its own. In better times, there were leaders and capable crisis managers like Angela Merkel, but a strategy that could have ensured the continent's lasting sovereignty has never been developed.

40 IMF, 2023b.

41 Several works have identified 2020 as the starting point of the biggest change in globalization to date. In this, the most decisive elements were not exclusively geopolitical changes, but also economic changes (Ágh, 2023: 951). Some experts, such as Menon (2022), see the cause in the mistrust of elites peaking in the wake of the 2008 financial crisis, while others, such as Walt (2023), claim instead that the non-Western world is opposed to the USA subjectively interpreting norms.

violence that repeatedly flares up in the Middle East, also warn that the existing order is no longer capable of guaranteeing peace.

The above events do not in themselves explain the crumbling of the world order. As we have seen, the world order can be described first in terms of its subjects, then according to the logic of power centers, and finally as a system of rules defining the relationship between subjects. Therefore, if we are looking for the reasons behind the instability of the international order, it will be necessary to examine how its individual subjects relate to the rules—that is, whether the international order can be characterized chiefly in terms of rule adherence, or of rule evasion.

Rule Evasion[42]

Of course—as cynics say—the rules are there to be broken. This wisdom, though admittedly unattractive, does describe a frequently observed phenomenon. In competitive sports, for example, it is not uncommon for competitors or teams to look for new, more advantageous ways of interpreting the rules. It is especially true of more technical sports that the fairness or unfairness of a new technique or piece of equipment is the subject of lengthy debate. However, in competitive sports there are always "actors outside the competition"—i.e., judges, supervisory bodies, and

---

42   In the following, we will primarily deal with the erosion of the rules of the international order. It could be argued that we should deal equally with changes in the subjects of that order, and the ways in which the structure of the world's power centers has been transformed. However, here we follow a different conceptual path, focusing on processes instead of taking a static approach. The logic of the process is as follows: the rules have been ever less conscientiously respected by individual actors, so new centers of power have been created, and these new centres are beginning to build new, alternative institutions, which are stepping onto the international stage as new actors. However, in later sections we will present these new actors and new centers of power, such as the economic strengthening of the non-Western world and the new domains of non-Western institutional cooperation, primarily as the consequences of rule evasion.

Figure 4: There was a time when US-China relations were better.
Source: Wikimedia Commons, own edit

sporting federations—who are there to ultimately decide whether a boundary-pushing move is within the rules or not. If there were no such persons or bodies, the framework provided by the rules would be stretched over time by continuous reinterpretation. The only problem is that although the international order also has such decision-making bodies, they are themselves also a part of that order, not independent creators of it (in the way that sporting federations are for sport championships). Thus, the rules are much more exposed to the erosion caused by "inventive solutions."

In light of this, it is surely no surprise that such erosion has indeed occurred, and that both Western and non-Western actors in the international order played their part. Indeed, it has practically been a joint effort. It is easy to see that the neoliberal Western institutional model did not spread to all parts of the world with equal efficiency. While, for example, the states of Eastern and Central Europe have adopted neoliberal principles of government to a relatively comprehensive extent, today's challengers to Western power have chosen quite different approaches. China is perhaps the clearest example of this. The East Asian giant transformed its economic and trade systems in accordance with the free trade principles of the Washington Consensus, but neoliberal principles of governance were by no means fully adopted.[43] Thus, China was able to create a unique hybrid by adapting its economy to trade expectations. Because management of the economy in China remained under centralized control, this adjustment enabled the country to take maximum advantage of the possibilities provided by the rules. Party General Secretary Deng Xiaoping announced the Reform and Opening Program in 1978,[44] which enabled China to rapidly integrate both politically and economically into the globalized world. The country joined the World Bank and the International Monetary Fund in 1980,[45] and in 2001, thanks to American intervention,[46] it also joined the World Trade Organization. After that, China's exports—one of the main driving forces of growth—began to expand exponentially.[47]

---

43   Joining the globalized world but neglecting to embrace neoliberal principles of governance is not unique to the Chinese economic model. Countries such as Singapore and South Korea have based their own models of economic convergence on a very similar approach. For more, see Gewirtz, 2017; Di Maio, 2015; Santiago, 2015; Cui-Jiao-Jiao, 2016.

44   For more information on Deng Xiaoping's economic policy, the expansive economic model driven by exports, foreign investment, and technology import, see DeLisle-Goldstein, 2019.

45   Following the Chinese civil war in 1949 and the Communist takeover, Taiwan represented China in the IMF and WB, and this representation was transferred.

46   See Kissinger, 2011 for more information on the complex system of strategic goals that comprised the US-China relationship.

47   China's export volume increased by an average of more than 12 percent per year over the next twenty years, while US and European exports expanded at a rate of less than 4 percent (World Bank, 2022). Of course, economic power cannot be converted on a one-to-one ratio into power projection capacity, but the former contributes greatly to the latter. In this context, it is worth considering that, according to the IMF's calculations, in 2023, based on purchasing power parity, China accounts for 19 percent of the world's GDP, and the USA for 15 percent (IMF, 2023b).

Although the principal institutions of the Washington Consensus helped China's globalization, it became more of a "Beijing Consensus," and consequently, the expected economic liberalization did not take place—to say nothing of the hoped-for transition to liberal democracy.[48] Although China has long since abandoned the planned economy, the state continues to exercise strong control over the operation of the economy, and bolsters the competitive advantage of Chinese companies with direct state subsidies.[49] The vast majority of companies generating the largest sales revenue are state-owned, and key strategic sectors are fully state-controlled.[50] The banking system, which is also state-controlled, provides generous loans at interest rates that are typically low by international standards, likewise ensuring a significant competitive advantage.[51] As a result, China has become competitive and has acquired a dominant international position—primarily thanks to its economy—while not becoming remotely Westernized.[52] It has strengthened itself while preserving its ideological and civilizational separateness.

---

48 The term "Beijing Consensus" entered the Western political lexicon following a study by Joshua Cooper Ramo, a former foreign policy editor of *Time* magazine. Ramo's apt phrase suggests that China had always sought to join the globalized world on its own terms, with its own model, and never intended to comply with the Washington Consensus, though the strategic objective of the US had, naturally, been for it to do so. For more, see Ramo, 2004.

49 According to Chinese state estimates, each year the government gives nearly 250 billion dollars of state aid to domestic companies in the form of direct subsidies, tax breaks, loans disbursed at much lower interest rates than the international norm, and the subsidized sale of land for construction. This, incidentally, amounts to roughly 1.7 percent of China's GDP, while for United States the annual rate is only 0.4 percent of GDP, and only 0.67 percent in South Korea (DiPippo-Mazzocco-Kennedy, 2022: 2).

50 García-Herrero-Ng, 2021: 15.

51 Turner, 2017.

52 Here it is worth noting that Chinese "reinterpretation" of the Western model of competition does not necessarily represent an attempt to gain an unjustified advantage. In the first place, Chinese culture is not especially competition-oriented, but even this peculiarity may enable it to forge a competitive advantage in the field of public diplomacy and global perceptions of their country. As early as 2008, Mark Leonard noted how China was trying to counterbalance the values of the USA in its policy: harmonious cooperation instead of competition, peace instead of war,

China is not the only non-Western state that has connected to Western institutional systems. Countries in the Middle East and elsewhere in Asia also did likewise, meaning that they too began to represent their own interests from within the essentially Western-inspired institutional ecosystem. In the case of the Gulf countries, it is worth noting the Gulf Cooperation Council (GCC). This organization, established in 1981, has already been transformed economically into a customs union, and the value of internal trade is now determined jointly.[53] Of course, the international prominence of these countries was originally due to their stupendous wealth of natural resources, but the countries of the GCC now also have significant military power, and each of the member countries spends much more on defense than the 2 percent GDP level that NATO is attempting to achieve.[54] In the last two decades, the GCC has systematically opened up to Asian cooperation, especially toward India and China.[55] One clear indication of this is that it was in Beijing this year that the Saudi-Iranian rapprochement process shifted into a higher gear.[56]

India has also grown in influence. Today, it is the most populous country in the world, and the fifth largest economy in terms of nominal GDP.[57] Until the reforms of 1991, India operated a mixed but planned economy, in which industrialization played a major role, especially the development of the steel industry, supplemented by import substitution.[58] By the end of the 1980s, however, this model had reached a dead end, and thus a comprehensive transformation began in 1991, connecting India to the wider global economy.[59]

---

diversity instead of pushing uniform Western values. Establishing an alternative to the Washington Consensus is only part of this effort to present itself as a counterpoint (Leonard, 2008: 119).

53   Low-Salazar, 2011.

54   Stockholm International Peace Research Institute (SIPRI), 2023.

55   For more on this, see Janardhan, 2020.

56   Fantappie-Nasr, 2023.

57   IMF, 2023.

58   Datt-Mahajan, 2009: 179.

59   Adhia, 2015.

The above developments—namely the growing power of the emerging states, and a consequently greater ability to assert their interests—began to strain the capacities of the system they had joined. However, there is another side to this coin. The Western powers, including the United States, have themselves not always been entirely observant of the rules of the international order. While the West's challengers have excelled in finding economic loopholes, the West tended to take a more political approach to breaking the rules, primarily by challenging their authority. The military interventions engaged in periodically over the last thirty years have more than once lacked the theoretically necessary approval of international institutions (such as the UN Security Council), and some have even bypassed the UN Charter.[60] We may also note how the United States has for years been blocking appointments to WTO arbitration panels, undermining the work of these panels.[61] And if the rules of a given order are not respected by

---

60 One glaring example of this was the NATO bombing of Serbia in 1999. There was no UN Security Council resolution authorizing the strikes, but the United States and its European allies later argued that they had intervened to avert a genocide, meaning that it was a humanitarian intervention (see Latawski-Smith, 2003 for more on this). The 2003 invasion of Iraq followed the same logic. Here too there was no UN Security Council resolution granting authorization, but the US-led coalition justified the legality of military intervention by saying that Iraq had not complied with Security Council Resolution No. 1441 and was not allow UN observers to conduct inspections of its possible weapons of mass destruction. The 2011 NATO intervention in Libya also raised questions. UN Security Council Resolution No. 1973 stated that a no-fly zone should be established and that everything should be done to protect civilians. However, according to several esteemed experts (e.g., Haass, 2011), the intervention went beyond its original mandate. The United States intervened in the Syrian Civil War after 2011, with France, the United Kingdom, and other Western countries joining these efforts in 2015. The legal justification for this was predicated on UN Security Council Resolution No. 2249, which urged the international community to take action against the Islamic State, but there was no separate Security Council resolution on military intervention.

61 Since December 2019, the USA has been blocking the appointment of WTO Appellate Body judges, rendering it inoperable. The Trump administration begun blocking the appointment of judges, citing the need for comprehensive WTO reform. This position has been maintained by the Biden administration, and in February 2023

its most important actors, after a while it becomes difficult to speak of any order at all.[62]

The "Internal Erosion" of Western Values

The previous section summarized several occasions in which Western powers ignored the rules of the existing international order. We did so because these events shed light on a deeper problem. John Mearsheimer, who has already been quoted concerning the interpretation of the realist and liberal schools of international relations theory, draws attention to the fact that the spread of Western principles by violent, even military means—besides throwing the countries in question (Iraq, Afghanistan, etc.) into chaos—did not in fact contribute to the spread of Western values.[63] Even worse, however, these interventions ultimately led to the erosion of Western values in their own hinterland—i.e., in the Western states themselves.[64] The mechanism for this is as follows: states willing to spread Western ideas and the Western model even at

---

Brussels unambiguously endorsed the American position (see WTO, 2023a for more details). Last December, more than a hundred WTO members called on the United States to cease obstructing the appointment of judges.

62 Since the mid-1980s, the US State Department has been examining the proportion of countries voting with the US in the UN General Assembly. The most recent such report concluded that in no single year of the past three decades have a majority of countries voted the same way as the USA (DOS, 2022). In recent years, statistical analyses have been made (see, for example, Ferdinand, 2014; Binder-Payton, 2022), according to which the voting cohesion between the BRICS countries in the UN General Assembly is getting stronger, and they are increasingly voting against the G7 countries.

63 The reason why most interventions are doomed to failure is primarily that Western states do not embark on military interventions when costs are expected to be high, but countries in which the cost of intervention can be kept low typically do not possess the right conditions for democratization (Downes-Monten, 2013: 94). Accordingly, such interventions are typically not very successful. Based on wide-ranging research by Andrew J. Enterline and J. Michael Greig, 63 percent of the interventions between 1800 and 1994 did not achieve their goals (Enterline-Greig, 2008: 341).

64 Mearsheimer, 2022: 283. For more on how military interventions undermine liberal principles at home, see also Desch, 2007; Hendrickson, 2018; Risen, 2006; Risen, 2014; Priest-Arkin, 2011; Savage 2017.

Figure 5: Anti-war demonstration in Texas.
Source: Getty Images, photograph by Alex Wong

the cost of war find themselves involved in more and more military conflicts, and these military enterprises then provoke more and more resistance in the hinterland, meaning that the anti-war voices grow stronger. The authorities increasingly come to treat anti-war voices as enemies, and they begin limiting the freedoms of those espousing such views, including their freedom of expression.[65]

---

65 A little over a decade ago, Brzezinski (2012) outlined a plausible scenario whereby the United States would lose its hegemonic status due to its own internal problems. However, he saw that the Washington Consensus system would not be replaced by a new world order, and that instead we must prepare for anarchic conditions, because no great power will be able to become a hegemon—they will have neither the power nor the international legitimacy to do so. International disorder will therefore be characterized by continual confrontation between the great powers. Of course, Brzezinski was imbued with the optimism of the US Treasury, and he outlined this scenario only as the worst-case scenario. According to CSIS experts, the USA does best when it not only focuses on other great powers, but also strives for close relations with middle powers and regional powers (Blanchette-Johnstone, 2023).

This description encapsulates concrete, clearly delineated, and often easily identifiable processes. However, we are convinced that these processes point to even more profound phenomena.[66] There is one sense in which the ideas of Francis Fukuyama and John Mearsheimer coincide. In his book *The End of History and the Last Man*, Fukuyama also writes about the fact that there is only one threat left to the otherwise triumphant liberal democracy: namely, uncertainty about its own values.[67] The cause of this uncertainty is the egalitarian and rights-extending practice of liberalism (in the legal sense), the injudicious overapplication of which can eventually lead to cultural relativism and a questioning of community values considered fundamental. Mearsheimer likewise appears to be describing just such a process. And this process—the two theorists agree on this point—undermines the community-organizing power of liberal democracy and atomizes society.[68]

---

66 We have already written in detail about the internal contradictions of liberalism, in Chapter 2.3. of *The Hungarian Way of Strategy*, so in the following we will only briefly refer to those conclusions, and partly make use of them as well.

67 According to Holmes-Krastev (2019), liberalism suffered a defeat in the thirty years following the collapse of the Eastern Bloc in Central and Eastern Europe. The reasons for this defeat seem clear. The first is that, during the democratic transition, the countries of the region were expected to copy Western-style democratic institutions while essentially ignoring their own specific national characteristics. Thus, the West left essentially no space for the development of specifically Central and Eastern European democracy. Secondly, the economic organizing principle of the West—i.e., neoliberalism—failed, especially in the wake of the 2008 financial crisis—and did not lead to the expected rise in living standards in the region. Thirdly, although on paper they are full members of the Western institutional order, in reality the West treats Central and Eastern European countries as second-class citizens. Finally, liberalism was not compatible with the social self-image of the countries in the region, since the most reject individualism and adhere instead to a more communitarian principle.

68 The Western world's lack of faith in its own values is an old topos in the history of Western thought. In a sense, we already see it in Plato's *The Sophist*, where Plato argues that, from the perspective of atomistic (corporealist, physicalist) philosophies, the virtues cannot exist (247 b–c). In terms of our present problem, one principle worth taking from Plato's thought is that even in ancient days it was clear how a purely materialistic approach will necessarily lead to moral relativism. The reason for this was most thoroughly expostulated by G. W. F. Hegel, who remarked that when physicalists enter the realm of values, they are unable to see it in its entirety, treat values too abstractly, and in the process absolutize specific

Curiously, it was liberalism's more critical observers—and this goes beyond the international dimension of liberalism—who first perceived the relativistic tendencies hidden in the idea. German constitutional judge and legal philosopher Ernst Wolfgang

---

aspects, thereby creating internal contradictions in the foundation of values (Hegel, 1979b: §80). Those who talk about the erosion of Western values have all used this argument in one form or another. It is not from here, however, that Fukuyama takes up this particular intellectual historical thread, but very explicitly from Nietzsche, as the title of his famous work indicates: *The End of History and the Last Man*. This is a very telling title, since the term "end of history" refers to the Hegelian elements of Fukuyama's thinking, and "the last man" refers to Nietzsche, who often argued against Hegel, so we may note a strange synthesis here. Still, the synthesis is not unreasonable. Nietzsche uses the term "last man" in his work *Thus Spake Zarathustra* (*Also sprach Zarathustra*), referring to a nihilistic individual who, unsure of his own values, arrives at the end of history (Nietzsche, 2006: 9). It is interesting that this motif also appears in Hegel's *Phenomenology of the Spirit* (*Die Phänomenologie des Geistes*). In this regard, it is important to understand that in Hegel's system certain contents of consciousness appear in history, including the motif of the last man, primarily in the Greek comedies. Hegel writes that the protagonist of a Greek comedy has to face the fact that he remains on the stage alone, abandoned by the gods (thus becoming a physicalist), since the gods are all dead (1979: 379). In his view, this indicated that Greek culture had reached its peak, and in this process had ultimately become empty. Another important motif is abandonment by the gods, which also finds echoes in Nietzsche, with his famous phrase "God is dead. And we have killed him" from his book *The Gay Science* (1974: 108; in the original: *Die fröhliche Wissenschaft*). It is also important to note that, contrary to the common belief, Nietzsche did not intend his lines as gloating or celebratory, but as a warning: the physicalist and scientific tendencies of Western civilization would in time lead to nihilism. Another question is whether Fukuyama chose Nietzsche as a motif because of his critique of physicalism. In any case, if we place these figures of intellectual history side by side, their conclusions essentially point in the same direction: when a civilization reaches its peak, it is typically overthrown not by an external enemy, but by internal uncertainty. We also learn something about the nature of uncertainty, namely that it appears in parallel with the spread of materialist—or, as it is now fashionable to put it, physicalist—ideas, since the physicalist worldview undermines the values on which civilization is built. Although he does not address the connection between physicalism and nihilism, Fukuyama warns of this emptiness at the end of his work (1992: 298–299). One way in which this process may unfold is outlined by Mearsheimer in his work *The Great Delusion*: a war fought to spread liberal values results in a partial violation of those values in the very countries that spread them, since attempts are made to silence those who oppose the war, even by means that contradict the principles of liberalism (2022: 282). We would add that in this process it is not the mere act of violating the norms that has the greatest negative consequences for these values, but rather the way in which the violation of norms points out the shaky ground on which liberal values are based, since their more

Böckenförde pointed out that the modern, free, secular state operates on the basis of assumptions that it can itself no longer guarantee. That is, it can only stand as a free state if the freedom it provides to its citizens originates from within, from the moral perception of individuals, and is internally regulated through the homogeneity of society. On the other hand, it cannot itself attempt to secure these internal regulatory forces by employing the means of legal coercion and authoritative commands, as this would infringe upon the principles of freedom. Consequently, the modern, secular state had to inherit these internal regulating forces from the premodern, traditional society that preceded it.[69] If we accept Böckenförde's diagnosis that liberal democracies are incapable of reproducing the values on which they are based, it is easy to see that the values necessary for the survival of a society or political model will eventually be eroded.[70] This is because the personal acceptance of socially accepted values creates the basis for a functioning community. In other words, individual citizens make certain sacrifices for the sake of their communities because

---

violent enforcement leads to their own self-immolation as a result of their internal contradictions. By absolutizing the universal aspect, the values underpinning the particular are endangered—just as Hegel described. And that this is not merely the exaggerated alarmism of the philosophers of bygone eras; it is also well exemplified by our contemporary Thomas Nagel's observation that those who do not profess physicalist principles are nowadays considered politically incorrect (2012), and by the illuminating study by another contemporary, Sharon Street (2006), on how Darwinian evolutionary theory (as a physicalist theory) eliminates all value realism. It is important to note that this is not a criticism of evolutionary theory on Street's part, but an argument against value realism.

69 Moreover, according to Böckenförde, the operation of the modern state is not simply traditional but is nourished by religious values (1976: 66–67).

70 Patrick J. Deneen (2021) argues similarly. In his view, this self-liquidating tendency is not a mistake or an unexpected outcome, but a direct consequence of the internal logic of liberalism. According to Deneen's argument, throughout the history of Western civilization, leaders have always been raised to seek the good of a community larger than themselves. However, liberalism does not recognize this form of public good, and primarily sees individual progress as the best way of improving the social situation. However, such a logic also encourages leaders to pursue their own interests rather than the "greater good"; as such, the original objective of liberalism—a (utilitarian) political system that benefits the widest possible group of individuals—was doomed from the start.

they accept shared values and consider them important.[71] Shared values are thus the basis of social cohesion, and their disappearance leads to an extreme individualism in which the degree of individual self-assertion alone determines whether an action is right or wrong. The good of the wider community becomes incomprehensible in such a context. This phenomenon can be seen in the ever-increasing degree of material inequality within Western societies.[72] Inequality, in turn, further weakens social cohesion and at the same time undermines the conditions for further economic growth.[73]

The crisis of the world order created by the Western world is therefore not only caused by external factors, such as the strengthening of challengers. At least as large a role is played by the insecurity of the West's own values and, in this context, the contradictions inherent in the spread of Western values. And a hegemon insecure about itself rarely remains benevolent.[74]

---

71 Jürgen Habermas provided a putative solution to this dilemma, which he saw in so-called "constitutional patriotism." The essence of this is that loyalty to state institutions and, at a higher level of abstraction, to institutions of the rule of law, could take the place of religious and national values. The Israeli philosopher Yoram Hazony, on the other hand, points out that this sort of value neutrality is in itself a value proposition, i.e., an iron ring, and, moreover, that such inorganically formed liberal values are incapable of creating a functioning community (Honneth-Joas, 1991; Hazony, 2018).

72 The axiom that it is impossible to create a well-functioning state and democracy without a broad middle class is also not new, and indeed can even be found in Aristotle: "And also this class of citizens have the greatest security in the states; for they do not themselves covet other men's goods as do the poor, nor do the other classes covet their substance as the poor covet that of the rich; and because they are neither plotted against nor plotting they live free from danger. Because of this it was a good prayer of Phocylides—'In many things the middle have the best; Be mine a middle station.' " (Aristotle, 1969).

73 According to financial strategist Ruchir Sharma, a national economy can produce sustainable growth if social inequalities do not hinder growth. As a result of inequality, states tend to introduce wide-ranging redistribution mechanisms and aid systems, but this does not stimulate growth, instead shifting public finances out of equilibrium. The state will thus be unable to provide an effective response to even the smallest global financial ups and downs, and in consequence, this may even push a national economy into a long-lasting recession (2017: 126).

74 The term "benevolent hegemon" was introduced by Robert Kagan in the 1990s. The term indicates that the dominant world political role of the United States is beneficial and positive for the world as a whole (1998).

1.2. The Risk of Bloc Formation

Regardless of how we group the causes and symptoms of the crisis afflicting the post-1990 world order and, in this context, the defining model of globalization, the fact remains that the model is now in crisis. This realization has created political instability in Western states and strengthened the Eastern challengers to the Western world, primarily China. Not only the critics of the previous world order and model of globalization but also those who supported it recognize how much affairs have changed. That is why the leading theoreticians and politicians of Western states are likewise awaiting the arrival of a new model, a new international system—and indeed are working on establishing a framework for it.

That framework does not yet exist. At the time of writing, in 2023, the transformation is still ongoing,[75] so there is no way to provide an accurate description of the world order we will encounter in the decades ahead. From a theoretical standpoint, however, we can already outline several plausible scenarios.[76] As such, all we can

---

75   Grinin-Ilyin-Andreev, 2016: 77; Menon, 2022.

76   Rodrik-Walt (2022) also see the world order based on American hegemony as being in crisis, alongside great uncertainty about the future for the world order. The most important task is to formulate new rules of the game, thus hopefully minimizing the risk of great-power conflict during the transition. To accomplish this, instead of a Western-centric approach, a much more balanced system integrating multiple interests and opinions will be needed. When formulating the rules of the game, one must also take into consideration that—in contrast to the Washington Consensus narrative—there are few common interests among the great powers, and almost no common denominators in terms of values. The rules of the game for the new world order must be grouped around four main aspects. The first is the avoidance of

do is enumerate these scenarios, evaluate them, and, based on our current knowledge and the already visible signs, try to decide which outcome seems more likely.

It is increasingly apparent that the dominance of Western civilization that has to date shaped the character of global development cannot be sustained in its current form. The coming world will be characterized by a greater degree of fragmentation, while it is possible that the Western model will lose much of its appeal and the West's challengers will begin representing their own interests more boldly and independently.[77] After all, there is no shortage of challengers. In addition to the well-known East-West (China-USA) rivalry, we also have to reckon with the opposition between the global North (the developed world) and the global South (the underdeveloped world).[78] Ian Bremmer defines all these processes collectively under the sonorous moniker of "geopolitical recession."[79]

Summarizing the above, we might say that two things are beyond doubt: the center of the global economy is shifting eastward, and as a result, China's international political importance will increase.[80] In addition, the USA will naturally continue to be a key player in the

---

prohibited actions, i.e., everything that violates the UN Charter. The second is the prioritization of issues where compromise is possible. The third would encompass the fairly wide range of international affairs that the great powers are able to resolve on their own sovereign basis. And finally, there would be a very narrow range of international affairs that the great powers would attempt to resolve on a multilateral basis.

77 Kaplan, 2018: 9, Keohane-Grant, 2005; Katzenstein-Keohane, 2007: 2.

78 Rodrik-Walt, 2022.

79 Bremmer, 2023.

80 According to Tseng (2023), given deepening Russian-Chinese relations, it may appear that an anti-Western, Chinese-Russian alliance is being formed. However, he argues that this characterization is largely a mistaken appraisal of the situation that has actually developed. China is attempting by a number of means to undermine the unipolar world order represented by the United States, but it is trying to do so with the tools of multilateral diplomacy, the creation of loose coalitions based on common interests, and by embracing countries "excluded" by the West, while remaining wary of any possible armed conflict.

global order. There are also a number of ongoing trends that, while not certain, are at least highly likely to continue. An increasingly populous middle class will appear in developing countries, while the Western middle class will—largely for demographic reasons—lose much of its global significance.[81] This is an important element for our analysis, because the middle classes are the largest politically aware element of any society. Their own states must represent their interests in the global arena. In addition, it is to be assumed that climate change will continue, with all the accompanying phenomena (e.g., migration), while technological innovation to mitigate its impact will present an unprecedented challenge to states.[82]

The only question is, which model offers the best potential solutions to these new challenges. According to the literature, there are essentially five possible scenarios:

1. *Unipolarity with an unchanged hegemon.* According to this scenario, the difficulties of the 2010s and 2020s will prove temporary, and the West, led by the United States, will retain its hegemonic role.[83] Of course, this by no means implies that the West would retain the same "competitive advantage" against aspiring powers that it held in the 1990s. The possible retention of the hegemonic status of the United States can be attributed in part to the country's significant military superiority. It is telling that American defense spending remains greater than that of the

---

81 UN, 2022.

82 International Energy Agency (IEA): 2021: 21; Sachs, 2020.

83 Relatively few Western experts remain convinced that the unipolar world order will continue. The main argument of Friedman (2022) or Brooks and Wohlforth (2023), who bolster the dwindling ranks of such thinkers, is that although the power of the USA has indeed decreased in relative terms since the end of the Cold War, the absolute value of American power is still far greater than that of any other potentially pole-forming superpower. Ikenberry (2022) argues for the survival of the American-led world order, and Kagan (2021) and Sharma (2020) can also be seen as endorsing this position. There is also a view that supports America's leadership role because it sees the US as guaranteeing international security, cf. Wright (2020).

nine countries that follow it in the global ranking—China, India, the United Kingdom, Russia, France, Germany, Saudi Arabia, Japan, and South Korea—combined.[84] In this scenario, the United States would continue to act as a global leader, willing and able to determine the rules of the international political game, to abide by them, and to mobilize coalitions to maintain order.[85] This would preserve the current, rules-based international order in more or less its current form. In such a scenario, the USA would strive to reduce its political, economic, commercial, and military dependence on its main challengers—China or Russia, say—and would therefore choose a strategy of decoupling.[86]

2. *Unipolarity with a new hegemon.* The second scenario also envisages a unipolar world order, but one in which China plays the leading role, rather than the United States or the West. This is more of a theoretical possibility, and unlikely in the medium term, for several reasons:[87] First, China is still significantly behind the United States in some key areas, including military power. Even more importantly, Beijing does not seem to have any grandiose plans to seize the reins of global governance, or even to

---

84 SIPRI, 2022: 2.

85 Finnemore, 2013.

86 This issue is also dealt with by Bown-Irwin, 2019.

87 Whether or not China has superpower ambitions is a difficult question to answer. On the other hand, it clearly wishes to play a proactive role in the transformation of the international order—as opposed to continuing with the policy of the Deng Xiaoping era. This can be seen in a speech given by Party General Secretary Xi Jinping in 2017, in which he declared that China must step onto the stage of international politics (cf. Clover, 2017; Economy, 2022). China currently appears to be aspiring towards a multipolar world order, one element of which is the transformation of the institutional and normative system of the Washington Consensus, and, to a moderate, considered degree, the creation of alternative institutions. In Chinese thinking, since internal stability is of primary importance, the transformation of the international order must take place peacefully (Weng-Ai, 2023: 28). For example, China is attempting to strengthen its relations with countries that are friendly—or at least not hostile—towards it through the *One Belt, One Road* project and the 16 + 1 initiative, which aims to bring together Central and Eastern European countries (Horváth, 2022). It is a reflection of the same underlying logic that the Chinese have a fundamentally positive attitude to European strategic autonomy (Yan, 2023).

become the main provider of "global public goods" (for example, the replacement of the dollar-based financial system with its own currency or the reform of international organizations).[88] At the same time, China is engaged in certain projects that seem aimed at strengthening its great power status. Among these, the most prominent is the Belt and Road Initiative (BRI), which aids Beijing's power projection through finance, trade, human and political harmonization, and especially through large-scale infrastructure projects. In addition, it is worth noting that the BRI is essentially an umbrella project with relatively limited state supervision. The most plausible route to a Chinese-led unipolar world is through China's dramatic economic development. Chinese foreign policy has become more assertive in recent years, especially in the narrower Southeast Asian region. But this by no means suggests that the country aspires to a global hegemonic role. In the meantime, China is trying to position itself as the champion of the interests of the developing world.[89] In connection with the idea of a unipolar Chinese world order, one key question is what role Russia, increasingly isolated from the West, would play. The Russian-Chinese partnership is, at present, extremely asymmetric, but Beijing desperately needs Russian natural resources, including hydrocarbons, precious metals, and even agricultural land.[90]

3. *Bipolarity.* A third scenario is one in which the new world order is determined by the rivalry between the United States and China.[91]

---

88 Jisi, 2011.
89 Rolland, 2020: 51.
90 Götz-Merlen, 2019: 148.
91 Bekkevold (2023) argues that the international order is bipolar and, fond notions among the European opinion-forming elite notwithstanding, by no means multipolar, (though, contrary to the opinions of certain Americans, no longer unipolar either). There are currently two pole-forming superpowers: the USA and China. Thus, for example, though much-discussed India does indeed have the third largest defense spending budget in the world, it remains barely a quarter of second-place China's. Japan's economy is the world's third largest, but only a quarter the size of China's.

Based on the theory of a new cold war, two different worldviews, ideologies, and state organization models clash under the leadership of Washington and Beijing.[92] Some analysts—basing their conclusions on historical parallels—see a confrontation of this sort between the two superpowers as virtually inevitable.[93] In essence, this would create two main blocs and alliance systems. It would entail a tectonic rupture if the hitherto more or less globalized economy were replaced by two different systems of trade rules, two dominant currencies, two world networks, and two geopolitical strategies.[94] Given the complex interconnections

---

If we look at the EU, it could just be a pole-forming great power from an economic point of view, but in military terms it is negligible. In total, the two superpowers are responsible for half of the world's defense spending, and their economies are as large as those of the 33 next-largest countries combined. Multipolarity therefore does not describe the real state of the international order and is mostly a political notion. It can serve Western interests, in that if they manage to convince the non-Western world of the existence of multipolarity, it may be possible to bring emerging countries to the negotiating table—under Western conditions, of course—thus preserving Western dominance. In an Eastern reading, by contrast, the narrative of multipolarity may help China persuade the countries of the global South to condone its geopolitical ambitions, instead of alarming them with the image of a dominant great power. Overall, the narrative about multipolarity is just the panicked reaction of American, European, and allied Eastern leaders to the fact that, after three decades of unipolar peace, a bipolar—and therefore confrontational—period looms on the international political horizon.

92   Bradford, 2022.

93   In addition to Bradford, Kupchan (2022), Bekkevold (2022), Mearsheimer (2003, 2021), Ben-Ari (2013), and Brands-Gaddis (2021) also argue that the world order is currently bipolar. Zakaria (2019) does not clearly identify a challenger or challengers, and nor does he see the influence and power of the American position disappearing. For this reason, Washington must still be considered a decisive and dominant actor. Still, in his view, the United States no longer possesses the degree of unilateral power it held during the era of unipolarity.

94   The basic tool of foreign policy planning and decision-making is the examination of historical analogies. Winokur (2023) points out, however, that in recent decades, US foreign policy decision-makers have relied exclusively on the Cold War period as a frame of reference. Conflicts are read through the lens of the Cold War, meaning that everything in international relations is black and white, and every actor is either a friend or an enemy. The same schematic method is also characteristic of diplomatic negotiations. Episodes such as the negotiated *détente* with the Soviets or Nixon's US-China rapprochement are an integral part of every other country's daily diplomatic operations, but for the Americans, every deal is existential, and

of today's globalized economy and long supply chains, the vast majority of experts agree that closed economic blocs of this sort cannot form in the twenty-first century in the same way they did during the Cold War.[95] This type of closure and complete separation is presumably only possible for strategically important technologies (e.g., artificial intelligence, defense innovation, space research, telecommunications, and microchip production). In such a situation, the rest of the world's countries fall into one or other of the blocs (actively or tacitly) or, similar to the "movement of non-aligned countries" during the Cold War, attempt to chart their own course. In a rigid, bipolar system, economic, political, and cultural transfers are directed through the leading states of the blocs, which would mean a competitive disadvantage for the smaller states.

4. *Multipolarity.* In the fourth scenario, no single superpower (or pair of superpowers) has sufficient power to dominate the international system.[96] In a multipolar world order, in addition to

---

an agreement can only be excellent or catastrophically bad from the point of view of American interests. Accordingly, the Americans understand how historical analogies work, but they refuse to deal with pre-1945 history, which leads them to misleading assessments of situations. (On the topic of bloc formation as a politically imposed solution, see also Georgieva, 2022.)

95 According to Ferguson (2023), our best hope now is the return of a bipolar world order. But at the same time, he takes it for granted that Cold War-style blocs will ultimately form. According to the British historian, the economic costs of this will be high, because the global world economy is falling apart. However, the advantage of such an outcome is the reduced chance of great-power conflict. The operational logic of the Cold War showed that large-scale armed conflicts and major wars can in principle be avoided. The Cold War situation is a more favorable scenario for humanity, in terms of overall human cost, than a multipolar world order, where the chances of a third world war breaking out are much higher.

96 An alternative to multipolarity is outlined by Prakash (2023) and Shearing (2023). They both accept that economic bloc formation as a consequence of political decisions is a real possibility, and most indications point to this becoming the new model of the world economy. On the other hand, it is possible that a group of countries may form that are linked to one bloc by the bonds of a political alliance, but for geopolitical reasons continue to import, for example, elements of their production chains from the opposing bloc. According to Shearing's (2023) calculations, in a bloc-based world

the great powers (the United States and China), middle powers and regional powers also play an important role.[97] In such a scenario, globalization becomes regionalized and regional spheres of influence may emerge.[98] However, this may lead to a sharpening of geopolitical fault lines and an increase in the number of regional military conflicts.[99] It is important to note that the definition of multipolarity itself is also culturally dependent; for instance, the concept appears in a radically different form in Russian and Chinese discourse.[100] The literature suggests that, besides the United States and China, the European Union, Russia, Brazil, or India could form their own poles. In addition, Japan, Iran, the Republic of South Africa, and Turkey are typically listed as important middle powers.[101] However, there are currently many question marks (independent army, strategic autonomy) around the EU's ability to function as an independent major power.[102]

---

economy, up to 17 percent of trade in goods and services may be conducted through such "fully uncommitted" countries.

97 Zakaria, 2019.

98 Haass-Kupchan (2021), Posen (2012), Virmani (2005), and Layne (1993) also argue in favor of the development of a multipolar world order, and indeed argue that the multipolar world order actually came into being in the 2010s.

99 Dodds, 2023

100 Culbreath, 2023.

101 Stuenkel, 2016.

102 The European Union faces a number of problems that clearly reduce its international weight and influence. One such problem is that it is increasingly falling behind in international economic competition. In 1990, it accounted for 23 percent of global economic output, but in 2022 it made up only 15 percent. And to all this it should be added that, during this period, the world economy almost tripled, while the EU economy did not even double. Meanwhile, the EU is an increasingly uncompetitive player in global production chains (for more on this, see García-Herrero-Turégano, 2020). The EU is also suffering from a leadership crisis. The history of European integration is essentially about the delicate balance between federalist-institutional and nation-state leadership (for more on this, see Moravcsik, 2012; Lindseth, 2014; Von Bogdandy-Schill, 2010). Instead, the EU institutions want to conduct politics according to bureaucratic logic, while political leadership can be carried out by the nation-states (see more about this in Van Middelaar, 2014; Cliquennois, 2020). Overall, Europe's biggest problem is a lack of independent strategic thinking. This

5. *Chaos in the international order.* In the fifth and last main scenario, the international order is headed toward chaos.[103] The chance of this is relatively small: such a situation does not favor any state or institution, so all have an interest in avoiding it. In this Hobbesian scenario, there is no single state (or alliance of states) capable of bringing order to the international arena and imposing its will. Multilateral forums (such as the UN) would be unable to fill the void left by strong states. This would make global politics vastly more unpredictable.[104]

---

is what French President Emmanuel Macron was referring to when he spoke of "European sovereignty" in his Sorbonne speech (Macron, 2017), while German Chancellor Angela Merkel spoke of "strategic sovereignty" (Merkel, 2020). The German and French concepts are of course different: the former points more towards European federalization (for more on this, see the material of the German Institute of Foreign Affairs: Lippert et al., 2019), while the latter relies more on member states, and more precisely on the French-German axis (see the analysis of the French Institute of International Relations: Gomart-Hecker, 2023). Strategic sovereignty, formulated as a goal, seems to be moving further and further away from Europe. According to Tierney (2023), Europe has plenty of political ammunition to use against both Washington and Beijing in order to carry out a program of strategic sovereignty. Washington's fundamental interest is the stabilization of the current international order. Europe basically strives for an economic partnership with China, which moderates the geopolitical ambitions of the Chinese side precisely because economic interests coincide. The United States can achieve an important goal, in that it will have to spend much less on European defense, since the development of European countries' armed forces would give NATO sufficient military presence in Europe. However, Washington must continue to ensure that it remains a close ally of Europe, meaning, as in the case of Beijing, that it must align its geopolitical goals with Europe, which in turn would mean a less confrontational American foreign policy. European strategic sovereignty is therefore key to stabilizing the international order.

103 According to Zeihan (2022), we are currently living in a period of global order, which will be replaced by one of global disorder. In this new order, the United States will voluntarily relinquish its hegemonic role. In the last ten years, it has achieved total energy security, partly through its own domestic sources and partly through reliable Canadian imports. What is more, it is in a much more favorable position from a demographic point of view than any of its prospective great-power rivals. Thus, it will use its military, economic, and diplomatic power not to maintain the broader global order, but only to protect its own interests. From an economic point of view, the consequence of this will be that the growth potential of the world economy will decrease significantly, and, from a geopolitical point of view, we must prepare for an era of self-help.

104 Haass, 2017: 8.

Figure 6: From Caspar David Friedrich's painting *Wanderer above the Sea of Fog.*
According to the commonly accepted interpretation of the picture, it represents
the programmatic vision of romanticism, while at the same time reminding us
that the rational and predictable world requires transcendence
over the irrational and unpredictable chaos, though the irrational element
can rise up and engulf us again at any time.
Source: Getty Images, photo: DeAgostini

So we have five scenarios. In addition to necessity, contingency also plays an important role in determining which one ultimately comes to pass. According to the multiverse theory, which has recently become widespread in pop culture, there is not merely a single universe, but rather an infinite number of universes. All potentialities happen somewhere, as the number of universes is infinite. In one universe it is Peter Parker who pulls on the Spiderman mask, in another it is Miles Morales. Fortunately, our task is easier. We do not have to evaluate an infinite number of universes, only these five scenarios, to determine what kind of world order we can expect. Whether the future will be a well-oiled, predictable machine, or prey to random contingencies, is the question the next chapter seeks the answer.

1.3. It Seems the West is Set on a Bloc-Based World

We have already discussed at length the decisive, hegemonic role of the most important actor in the post-1990 world order—i.e., the United States. We did so in terms of the free trade ideal it espoused, the conception of the human condition underlying its philosophy, its attempt to westernize the world on this basis, and finally the rules and institutions by which it sought to shape the framework of international cooperation in accordance with its own interests, or at least its long-term goals. A change in the global order is likely to be seen in these elements, and so if we wish to say something about the possible future direction of the global order, then those elements must be examined.

The survival of the current hegemon, in our sense of the term, is a condition of the first scenario only. If the United States can maintain its current role, then there is the greatest chance that the world order of the coming decades will be very similar to the post-1990 world, since in such a world the leadership of the United States is likely to conclude that the status quo still basically serves its interests. But even in this scenario, it cannot be ruled out that perceptions of free trade, and thus the operation of free trade regimes, will change. The latter may occur if the USA decides that, even with its continuing hegemonic role, it wishes to exercise greater control over the world's commercial and political relations, primarily to prevent challengers from continuing to strengthen to the extent that we have seen in the last thirty years.

The situation is very different if the role of hegemon passes to another power. As we have seen, China is the most likely aspirant to the role of new hegemon. In such a scenario, however, it is difficult to imagine that any desire to adopt Western models will remain, for the simple reason that China is not a Western state. The question is whether the institutions will remain, or whether alternative institutions will be built—something not beyond the bounds of possibility, as we will see. Another question is whether free trade will remain. We noted that China has an idiosyncratic attitude toward free trade systems: it gladly exploits their advantages, while frequently counterbalancing their disadvantages with state subsidies. If it continues this practice as hegemon, then those parts of the world that see the newly hegemonic China as a rival will respond with market protection mechanisms.

The scenario again changes dramatically if instead we see the emergence of a bipolar world, in which no power center clearly dominates its rival. In such a world, as during the Cold War, both power centers can be expected to compete. Were this to occur, the global spread of Western values would logically be out of the question, as would the form of free trade we have known to date. It is much more likely that both power centers would gather their allies around themselves, exercising close control over their commercial and political relations—as we saw in the second half of the twentieth century. In terms of institutions, this scenario has the greatest chance of developing parallel institutional structures, so existing institutions with Western roots can be expected to decline in importance.

The two most unpredictable scenarios are self-evidently the multipolar world order and the state of chaos. In both circumstances, it is conceivable that the institutions and rules would remain, together with a framework enabling the interaction of many actors, but without either a single clear hegemon or multiple competing centers of power. In the same way, one could easily imagine free trade remaining, as well as the links between different nodes of power. At the same time, these scenarios could also result in an even more complete rupture.

What emerges clearly from these analyses is that the most important issues for the future world order concern whether the interoperability of the globalized world, free trade, and Western-inspired institutions remain intact, or alternative forums of contact are formed, or whether a new ideological iron curtain will fall, meaning that each country will be forced to choose its partners according to its political system. If separate institutional systems are formed, together with a new ideological iron curtain, and free trade is restricted on ideological lines, then the international order of the future will be characterized by geopolitical blocs. In the year 2023, however, it is still unclear whether this is in fact the future in store for us. All the same, it is already apparent that the above scenarios all contain, at the very least, some degree of clustering. In the following, we will argue that there are already signs that the process of bloc formation has begun.[105]

As an introduction, it is worth clarifying what we mean by blocs. The logic of the bloc-based world order is in many respects similar to that seen during the Cold War.[106] The blocs are held

---

105 The World Trade Organization also writes about geopolitical blocformation in its latest report. The trade indicators also show that intra-bloc trade has picked up, while inter-bloc trade growth has stalled. There is currently no risk of deglobalization, it is more a matter of clustering. All this is a consequence of the fact that both the right and the left pursue values-based politics instead of interest-based ones, to which corporate actors are now also adapting when making their investment decisions (Reinsch, 2023).

106 There is also an idea according to which, if the world does indeed go down a path toward bloc formation, it is worth preparing for the possibility that it will be quite different from what was experienced during the Cold War. Sohrab Ahmari draws attention to the fact that, although Western liberalism and Soviet Communism were opposing ideologies, there was an element of similarity between them. Both ideologies saw themselves—and wished others to see them—as the guarantors of expanded human liberty, given that both ideologies were fed by Western roots

together by an—accepted or imposed—ideological binding force, and all relevant economic, political, and cultural relations can exist only with the approval of the great power leading the bloc. In its latest risk analysis, the expressly globalist World Economic Forum (WEF) names the consolidation of geopolitical blocs as the biggest geopolitical threat.[107]

There is one more concept related to bloc formation that is worth clarifying for the analysis in this subsection. This is the concept of decoupling or, more recently, de-risking. Decoupling describes the efforts of leading Western actors to offset the negative effects of the current world order. As we will see, decoupling or de-risking are also the most significant steps in the direction of bloc formation.[108] Decoupling, or separation, begins with strategic technological sectors, then other segments of the global economy, and finally results in the most complete possible severing of political and cultural relations. US Secretary of the Treasury Janet Yellen is describing the same phenomenon when she talks about "friend-

---

(Ahmari, 2021). In the case of a possible future bipolar rivalry, we cannot speak of such common ground.

107 WEF, 2023: 40. However, opinions are already divided as to how many such blocs the world will be divided into, as shown by the individual scenario analyses. According to Friedberg (2023), the world will split into two large blocs: the "coalition of democracies" led by the United States will face the "authoritarian axis" led by China. And when it comes to influence over the global South and the Middle East, the struggle will be reminiscent of that seen during the Cold War. Prakash (2022), on the other hand, believes that only one true bloc can emerge, namely between the United States and its European and Asian allies, though several great powers or alliances may be able to stand against this bloc, or, alternatively, cooperate with it. According to Leonard (2023), bloc logic is a more salient feature of American foreign policy thinking. The Chinese, by contrast, believe that the world is not a new international order but is moving towards disorder, but that there is a possibility of establishing a loose alliance system against the West.

108 Jon Bateman points out that the term "decoupling" only appeared in the political dictionary of Western states, including the United States, a few years ago. The term denotes the political desire to separate what had been closely connected economic actors through the increased application of technological restrictions—such as increased control of exports, state control of sales, denial of permits, visa bans, sanctions, and protective tariffs. Bateman notes that this process is the polar opposite of the previous political impulse to build connections (Bateman, 2022).

shoring"—i.e., the breaking up of the global production chains in strategic sectors and their relocation to countries allied with the USA.[109] At the May 2023 Hiroshima summit of the G7 countries—for the first time in the organization's history—a separate statement on world economic security was adopted, the essence of which is that the production chains of strategic industries must be connected with "reliable partner countries."[110]

In light of all this, we can already say in advance that bloc formation is a new model of globalization, which is supposed to remedy the anomalies of the old model based on American hegemony, free trade, and Western institutions. In this model, the flow of goods and information is controlled to a much greater extent, as it is informed by bloc logic, and the interconnectedness of the world remains, but the "right" to build relationships belongs only to the largest actors, namely the bloc leaders and most influential states within blocs.[111]

---

109 Yellen, 2022.

110 G7, 2023. The same logic is followed by the World Bank (Okonjo-Iweala, 2023) and the IMF (Georgieva, 2023; Aiyar et al., 2023) when they publish analyses of the growing threat of so-called geo-economic fragmentation. The former organization puts the economic loss resulting from geo-economic fragmentation at 10 percent, the latter at 7 percent. Ngozi Okonjo-Iweala (2023), secretary general of the WTO, argues against the fragmentation of the world economy for geopolitical purposes. According to him, it would, from the start, entail a significant loss: according to WTO calculations, economic output would decrease by 5–13 percent annually. Moreover, it does not solve geopolitical problems either. From the American side, friend-shoring, i.e., the relocation of production chains to friendly countries, has been given a security policy interpretation. Okonjo-Iweala, on the other hand, argues that the US is taking on new geopolitical costs, since it has to maintain friendly countries as friendly countries for decades—either by granting them preferential treatment or by force. According to the secretary general, fragmentation also reduces the possibility of diversifying production, since there are significantly fewer target countries to choose from. O'Neil (2022) claims that the logic of the USA's industrial and trade policy over the last forty years has always been that it has maintained much more intensive economic relations with its political allies. In other words, the American strategy has always pointed in the direction of decoupling.

111 Mark Leonard identifies three such blocs: the United States, the European Union, and China (Leonard, 2021). In his view, the connectivity superpowers, despite their very different starting points, are becoming more and more alike, because their

Of course, the above description is only a sketchy hypothesis. What matters here is to describe the process of bloc formation in a way relevant to Hungary's strategy. It is not yet "proof" that this process has started, though there are already examples of its beginnings. We identified five such pieces of evidence:

1. The erstwhile champions of globalism speak no longer of connection but of separation, and the West's leading power, the United States, has taken several concrete steps since the middle of the last decade to keep its allies under closer control—i.e., to make them subordinates within a US-led bloc. The concrete steps themselves provide further evidence.
2. Economic policy and diplomatic efforts to persuade US allies to reduce the extent of their economic relations with third parties, primarily with China.
3. A reinterpretation of the international role of the United States, whereby the USA no longer identifies itself as a global hegemonic superstate but as the leader of the democratic bloc fighting against autocracies (democracies versus autocracies).
4. In this context, the development, application, and control of sanction regimes.
5. And lastly, the fact that the integration of Western military alliance systems has begun.

In the following section, we will examine this evidence.

---

successful strategic trajectories are the same. The similarity is particularly striking in the case of the United States and China, while due to the different nature of the European Union and its subordination of security to politics, it is not yet able to follow the optimal strategy.

An Increasingly Unfashionable Idea: Maximum Possible Global Interconnectedness

One of the strongest arguments that bloc formation is a real possibility is that Western theoreticians and politicians have begun to take a different view of the earlier model of globalization, which made the most of the connectivity, and they now see it as a risk. One of the reasons for the change in mood can be found in the failure to spread the Western model. The argument that the Western political system and form of government can be spread with the help of economic connectivity is becoming less and less tenable. Indeed, the reverse seems true. As we have already pointed out, non-Western states were able to connect to the free trade system established by Western institutions while leaving their own political systems intact, which allowed them to gain a competitive advantage.

Another reason for the change in narrative is that the permanent conflicts generated by globalization and the system of mutual international dependencies have now become undeniable even for the most committed supporters of globalization.[112] Thus, interdependent relations are seen no longer as a win-win situation but as a threat.[113] Alongside China, the United States has now also arrived at the strategic decision that the management of conflicts

---

112 By organizing the international system into blocs, American foreign policy is also attempting to eliminate mutual dependencies. Members of the Biden administration, such as National Security Advisor Jake Sullivan, Treasury Secretary Janet Yellen, or Senior Presidential Advisor Brian Deese, repeatedly talk about the need to reduce mutual dependencies. For example, Sullivan (2023) writes about the "strategic competition" prevailing in the age of interdependencies and, among other things, about how exposure and vulnerability in supply chains can be mitigated by building relationships with partners and allies instead of turning to unpredictable (for example, Chinese) markets. While asymmetric dependencies can destabilize the international system in some cases, experience tells us that mutual dependencies stabilize it. A good example of this is the energy cooperation between Europe and Russia, which has now largely been liquidated. This system of interdependence, known in the literature as the natural gas bridge, had a stabilizing effect on the European security order (for more on this, see Gustafson, 2020).

113 Martín, 2022.

makes it necessary to reduce interdependencies between the poles—in other words, the biggest winner of globalization to date has become interested in limiting the process of globalization in certain areas, cutting back as much as possible. This attempt to cut back can be seen in action in several areas.

The first such area is the economy. Sanctions, consumer boycotts, subsidies that put foreign competitors at a disadvantage, exchange rate manipulation, and even state interventions in the capital market may be considered here as means of cutting back.[114] These are all signs that the state's role has been strengthened, in contrast to the previous era, during which the role of the state was kept to a minimum.[115] States seem to be renouncing the benefits of interdependence, as the risks are considered greater.[116]

The second area of separation can be seen in the assessment of international institutions. This means that open, multilateral, global organizations will lose their dominance, and will face new challengers in the form of institutions characterized by a

---

114 For a scientific evaluation of the effectiveness of sanctions over a long period of time, we may turn to Hufbauer et al. (1990). By examining more than a hundred instances of economic sanctions between 1914 and 1990, the authors concluded that the punitive economic measures imposed were clearly successful in 34 percent of cases, i.e., they fully fulfilled the stated political goal. Re-examining the data, Pape (1997) came to the conclusion that only 5 percent of the sanctions were truly successful. The primary reason for this discrepancy was that, in many cases, the sanctions regimes, though initially considered a success did not achieve the desired effect independently, but did so in combination with some other threat, such as of military force. The study points out that for sanctions to succeed, it is vital that practically all countries in the world accept and fully comply with them. In addition, countries have proven to be much more resistant to their effects than was once supposed, and the tightening or extension of sanctions does not significantly increase their effectiveness. The most extensive research on the success of punitive measures was conducted by Felbermayr et al. (2020). They examined 729 sanctions regimes between 1950 and 2016, of which roughly 30 percent were found to be effective. The research also pointed out that the number of instances in which sanctions were imposed has increased significantly since 1995, but their effectiveness has not improved.
115 Leonard, 2016.
116 Henderson, 2023.

closed, club-like operation.[117] These "minilateral" groups, such as the BRICS, the Shanghai Cooperation Organization (SCO), the Trans-Pacific Partnership (TPP), and the Transatlantic Trade and Investment Partnership (TTIP), can be described in terms of "gated globalization."[118] The transformation of institutions also encompasses the changed role of international law: previously the international legal framework sought to de-escalate conflicts, but today it is precisely on the basis of that framework that conflicts can be generated.

The third area is infrastructure, as some actors in the international system no longer see it primarily in terms of connectivity, but rather in terms of the extent to which a state can project power: that is, how an actor can preserve and expand its influence in a given area through infrastructure.[119] In this context, we see that all the large economies are striving to reduce dependencies and rewrite the old rules. Thus, for example, the US wants to reduce its energy exposure,[120] China wants to shift the economic growth emphasis to strong internal consumption,[121] and Russia wants to build pipelines deep into Asia in order to diversify its energy exports.[122] All this is precisely the opposite of what we were told about the direction of globalization and the "opening of economies" after 1990. Still, this change of narrative does not in itself mean that the individual actors are acting differently—though there are signs of this too.

The Tools of "Soft" Economic Diplomacy in the Service of Bloc Formation

Alongside this ideological reorientation, certain concrete measures taken in the Western world in recent years indicate that it has chosen

---

117 Telò, 2020: 25.
118 Sinha-Saran, 2020.
119 For more on this, see Allison, 2020; Martin, 2021; DiCarlo-Schneider, 2022.
120 Yergin, 2023: 71–85.
121 Riordan, 2023.
122 Von Essen, 2023.

Figure 7: The EU's TTIP chief negotiator, Ignacio García Bercero,
and his American counterpart, Dan Mullaney, at a press conference
at the European Commission headquarters in Brussels on 26 February 2016,
after the completion of the twelfth round of negotiations
of the Transatlantic Trade and Investment Partnership.
Source: Getty Images, photo: Dursun Aydemir

the path of bloc formation. Many elements in the American foreign policy of the last eight to ten years indicate that the USA wants to keep its allies on a much shorter leash, so to speak, within a bloc organized under its own leadership.

The softest method is diplomatic pressure. Through diplomatic channels, the United States encourages its allies to reduce their economic relations with China and instead increase their trade with the United States. The USA regularly tries to exert diplomatic pressure on its allies in multilateral forums such as the G7 or the Quadrilateral Security Dialogue (the Quad), with more success in the former and less in the latter.[123] The use of economic incentives can also be classified among these soft methods. The US offers its allies economic incentives—renegotiation of trade agreements, the

---

123 Gan et al., 2021; Menon, 2021.

Change in share of China's overseas
investment from 2018 to first half of 2023

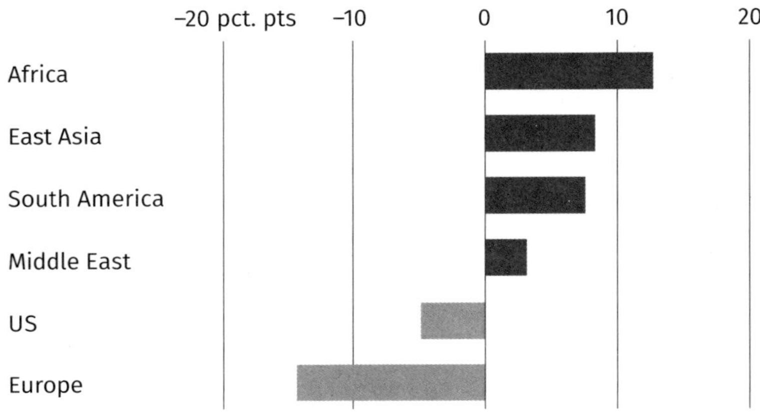

Note: Europe excludes Russia.

Figure 8: China reacts immediately, changing the prioritization
of investment target areas—and the biggest loser is Europe.
Source: The Wall Street Journal, 2023

creation of economic blocs—to encourage them to reduce their trade with China. After America's withdrawal from the Trans-Pacific Partnership (TPP), which was created to counter China's economic influence in the East Asian region, the Indo-Pacific Economic Framework for Prosperity (IPEF) is the latest institutional effort to curb Chinese influence.[124] The Transatlantic Trade and Investment Partnership (TTIP) also played a similar role, shifting the economic relations of America's European allies from China toward the United States. However, due to a number of controversial issues, the negotiations on the agreement were interrupted in 2016.[125] Since 2021, the United States has joined the Trade and Technology Council

---

124 Schöttli, 2023
125 Patnaik-Kunhardt, 2022.

established jointly with the EU (Trade and Technology Council, TTC) and is trying to increase the pressure on its European allies to join anti-Chinese export controls.[126]

"Hard" Tools: Sanctions Regimes

However, the shift away from soft tools shows that the USA is also willing to use sanctions as well as incentives to "encourage its reluctant allies to reconsider."[127] The secondary sanctions imposed by Washington present market participants outside the United States with a choice: they can trade either with sanctioned entities or with the United States, but not with both. By applying secondary sanctions, the USA is trying to make trade with rivals such as Iran or China unprofitable for America's allies. In the case of Iran, for example, European companies abandoned economic relations, fearing the consequences of secondary sanctions. In the case of China, it is more difficult for Washington to extend secondary sanctions, given that country's economic weight and potential retaliatory measures. When it comes to moving against actors who violate secondary sanctions against non-Chinese targets, China is

---

126 Gehrke-Ringhof, 2023.

127 According to Sabatini (2023), the international sanctions imposed by the West and especially the United States work against Western interests. Based on 2021 data, the countries affected by American sanctions already account for one-fifth of the world economy. They are working more and more intensively to create alternative financial systems, thus removing themselves from the scope of the sanctions. According to the leading researcher of Chatham House, the systemic challenge is the fact that countries not affected by the sanctions, such as Brazil and India, which otherwise maintain good relations with the Americans, also supported the initiative. In other words, the West is constantly losing its partners because of the sanctions, who switch to the side of the challengers in the multipolar order. Moreover, even though the anti-sanctions world economy only exists on the negotiating table, the West is already losing ground. A good example of this is that due to secondary sanctions, countries cannot sell their distressed debt in the Western-dominated financial system. This is how it happened that Venezuela sold its government bonds to various actors in the East and South instead of the West. Since such government bonds are backed by Venezuela's significant mineral reserves and extensive state energy market ownership, the West's influence over energy sources has decreased, while that of challengers has increased.

already hardest hit by American measures.[128] In addition, in the long term, Washington may subject more and more Chinese companies to secondary sanctions, which will not only seriously harm key market players in the US but will also put allied states in a difficult situation. China is trying to block these measures by developing its own sanctions regime. In this context, it can launch legal proceedings against companies and persons who act in accordance with the sanction measures introduced by the United States, if they violate Chinese interests. These processes increasingly limit global trade.[129] Finally, the US has particularly powerful tools when it wishes to forbid its allies from trading with rival countries, especially China and Russia, on national security grounds. Citing security concerns, the United States often puts pressure on its allies to reduce trade and economic relations with China.[130] This happened in the case of Huawei, when, as a result of Washington's pressure, the vast majority of its allies avoided the Chinese giant's technology in their own telecommunications networks.[131] What is more, American allies that hold key positions in the value chain of microchip production, such as Taiwan and the Netherlands, have complied with Washington's hardline policy and denied Huawei their products and services, encouraging the Chinese giant, which is trying to avoid these restrictive measures, to pursue a policy of in-house development when it comes not only to design but also to the field of high-tech chip production.[132] In the autumn of 2022, the United States also introduced export controls on the export to China of microchips, and it is currently trying to persuade key allies that play an important role in the global semiconductor industry—above all Taiwan, the Netherlands, Japan, and South Korea—to

---

128 Bartlett-Bae, 2021.
129 Chu, 2022.
130 Bateman, 2022.
131 Cerulus-Wheaton, 2022.
132 Deng-Pan-Perez, 2023.

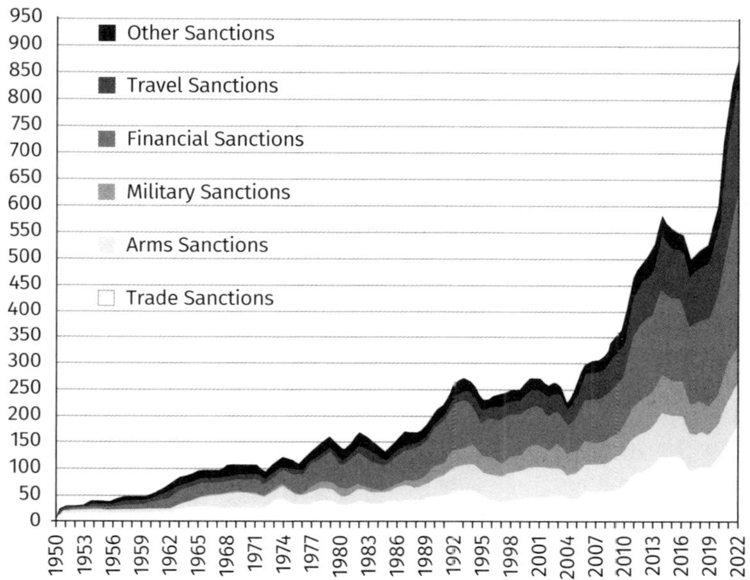

Figure 9: Change in the number of sanctions imposed between 1950 and 2022.
Source: Syropoulos et al., 2022

follow suit. However, because it would be extremely detrimental to these countries to lose China, which is the world's largest microchip purchasing market, they are reluctant for the time being to give in to Washington's pressure. In the meantime, all this encourages China to develop its own chip supply chain in the long term, further weakening global trade.[133]

But it is not only with regard to alliances that the USA's bloc-forming efforts can be seen in action. The US Inflation Reduction Act (IRA) is considered a protectionist measure by both opponents and allies, as it supports American companies and green investments in the United States to a degree that distorts competition, in contravention of WTO rules. As such, the IRA can encourage

---

133 *Global Times*, 2023.

companies worldwide to relocate their investments to the United States—an extremely sensitive matter for Washington's allies in Europe and East Asia. The IRA can be interpreted in the broader context of the strategic confrontation between the United States and China, in which the United States wants to become self-sufficient in a number of key industries by rebuilding its own production capacities. In this confrontation, the interests of the United States take precedence over the interests of its allies.[134]

Changing Narratives: Global Democracy is out, Democracy Versus Autocracy is in

In addition to these methods of economic diplomacy, the narrative of the Western world, and especially the United States, is changing in terms of how it speaks about the most important challenges facing us in the world today. A striking sign of this change is Francis Fukuyama's oft-quoted article published in *The Atlantic* at the end of 2022, which on the one hand defends the "end of history" thesis he formulated thirty years earlier, while re-evaluating it at the same time.[135] He continues to insist that the world is gravitating toward liberal democracy, proof of which he sees in Russia's failures during its war in Ukraine, and in the shortcomings of China's handling of the COVID pandemic. He is convinced that these phenomena illustrate the systemic problems of autocracies, in that these systems are incapable of correcting bad decisions. At the same time, in contrast to the optimism that ended the Cold War, Fukuyama also argues that it is first necessary for Western powers to defeat these autocratic regimes for the unquestionable primacy of the liberal democratic model to become evident. Thus, before we reach the end of history—

---

134 Fazi, 2023.
135 Fukuyama, 2022.

which, of course, is within arm's reach—one more big push from the West is needed.[136]

The greatest challenge in the decade(s) ahead will therefore be the competition between democracies and autocracies.[137]

All this remains theoretical. But of course, theory usually precedes action, and principles accumulated over the years tend ultimately to appear in practice. Nowadays, however, we see that theory and practice genuinely go hand-in-hand, and Fukuyama's theorizing is becoming official political doctrine. In March 2020, future US President Joe Biden published an article in *Foreign Affairs* magazine.[138] This, by definition, was a campaign article, since the election campaign was in full swing. In it, he presented his political ideas, interspersed with criticism of the Trump administration. Biden blamed Trump for eroding the institutions of democracy at home along with the trust people had in them, and also for cooperating in his foreign policy with autocratic regimes rather than with the democracies that are traditionally considered America's allies.[139]

---

136 That is why Fukuyama's comments have a certain discreet charm, since the countries of the former Soviet sphere of influence are very familiar with arguments structured in this way: "One more great effort is needed to achieve the world proletarian revolution and full communism."

137 Fukuyama's article—as well as his book, *Liberalism and Its Discontents*, also published in 2022—sparked intense debate. According to Ahmari (2022), Fukuyama is wrong when he claims that neoliberalism was merely a misstep, a faulty implementation of liberalism. Neoliberalism was, in fact, the perfect realization of liberalism and, as such, it precisely shows the many flaws that liberalism suffers from. Thus, we should not seek to return to some kind of proto-liberalism but instead desire an alternative to liberalism. According to Deneen (2023), who, incidentally, is referred to in the book, the distinction between liberal democracies and autocracies is nothing more than an attempt to artificially create the conditions necessary for the survival of liberalism. We can accept that the Cold War was the golden age of liberalism, but at the time, given the existential threat represented by the Soviet Union, no one dared to question liberalism and its flaws. The logic of the present is therefore that all alternatives to liberalism are simply to be labeled autocracy, thereby filling the antagonistic void left by Communism.

138 Biden, 2020.

139 It is worth noting that, in at least two instances, the Biden administration represents a continuation of President Trump's policies. Firstly, both governments assess the geopolitical situation similarly: China poses the greatest threat to the Western-led

Biden promised to correct these mistakes: he would restore trust in democracy at home and rebuild relations with democratic countries, so that together, united and coordinated, they could take up the fight against external challenges to democracy. Here already, we can see the narrative of democracy versus autocracy.

As president-elect, Joe Biden stuck to his ideas. In a speech before the UN General Assembly in September 2021, he spoke about the competition between democracies and autocracies.[140] He declared that, although the age of democracies is over, democracy is in fact always found where people struggle against authoritarian regimes, and that, in the end, democracy will win.[141] Interestingly, his argument is similar to Fukuyama's: according to Biden, democracy is the political system that spurs individuals to achieve their best, and this quality also results in higher performance at a systemic level. Then, after the outbreak of the Russian-Ukrainian war, Biden's rhetoric about the struggle between democracies and autocracies intensified. In his speeches in Warsaw and Kyiv, the American president argued in that vein as he urged the continuation of the ongoing war and the most extensive possible support for Ukraine.[142]

---

international order, while Russia, Iran, and other middle powers also pose a threat. The USA must act proactively to counterbalance these countries, and the preferred means of doing so is to strengthen existing alliance systems. On the other hand, there is a marked difference in that the Trump administration paid little heed to ideological considerations. In other words, in contrast to the Biden administration, it did not set ideological expectations, and left significantly more room for policies that fit the national self-image (for more on this, see Grygiel-Mitchell, 2017).

140 The White House, 2021.

141 The fact that the juxtaposition of democracies and autocracies emerged as an essential new element of American foreign policy doctrine in recent years is perhaps not unrelated to the fact that the post-World War II world order has, as the US president himself admits, run out of steam, and a new world order is needed (cf. The White House, 2023c). In other words, one interpretation of the narrative put forward by the current Democratic Party leadership is that it forms a scaffolding for a new world order and specifies its main fault line and arena of conflict.

142 Kyiv Speech: The White House (2023b); Warsaw speech: The White House (2023a). And we should note that this framing has appeared with even more pronounced

And this is not just rhetoric. President Biden is—it seems—sticking to his idea of working more closely with democratic allies, and he is trying to encourage moderate or extensive democratic reform in allied states that are considered less democratic, or that even have different positions on public policy issues. However, this pressure does not stop at the enforcement of general democratic principles; the US government formulates detailed expectations.[143] In the summer of 2022, US Secretary of State Antony Blinken, for example, explained that he expects America's Middle Eastern ally, Saudi Arabia, to take more decisive steps regarding the protection of LGBTQ rights.[144]

Strength in Unity: A Coalescing Western Military Bloc

Over the past eighty years or so, the United States has concluded many multilateral defense cooperation agreements, of which NATO is the most far-reaching.[145] Most of these defense cooperation agreements were concluded during the Cold War, in regions of strategic importance to the USA, meaning, in the spirit of the Monroe

---

contours in response to the Hamas attack on Israel. According to Kahana (2023), following the terrorist attacks, shortly after returning from Israel, the American president presented a map dividing the world between the good side and the bad side: Israel, Ukraine, and other democracies in the former, and Russia, Iran, Gaza, and North Korea in the latter. According to Biden, one thing Russia and Hamas have in common is the desire to completely destroy a neighboring democracy (The White House, 2023d).

143　It is surely no surprise that this attitude causes displeasure among allies of the US that do not share the principles of the incumbent Democratic Party. Yoram Hazony points out that one of the most important goals of a country's government is to preserve its sovereignty. The right of citizens to freely and democratically decide upon the values by which they organize their state is hardly the least of these sovereign freedoms (Hazony, 2022).

144　Heath, 2022.

145　One example of this is the ANZUS military cooperation agreement concluded with Australia in 1951. New Zealand was also a party to this, but in the 1980s Wellington was not convinced that renewing the pact would serve its national interests. In 1986, the USA suspended application of the treaty with respect to New Zealand.

Figure 10: Instead of a peaceful panda, China is now a dragon,
while America is represented by an increasingly menacing bald eagle
and a belligerent Statue of Liberty—the change in the international mood
can also be seen in the illustrations of the mainstream press.
*Sources (clockwise): Financial Times, Ingram Pinn; The Manila Times; iStock;
The Washington Post, Daren Lin; The Economist, Edmon de Haro; Clipart Library;
South China Morning Post, Craig Stephens*

Doctrine, with the countries of Latin America and, of course, also in Southeast Asia.[146]

Militarily, the United States is also trying to shift the operation of the international system toward an American-centered bloc, and the Biden administration clearly wants to tighten regional alliance systems. Like almost every new administration, Biden's issued a new national security strategy, and the relationship with China shows continuity with Trump's policies. Biden's official report, issued in October 2022 and entitled National Security Strategy (NSS), views China as the USA's biggest rival and indeed as a systemic rival.[147]

---

146 In addition to large multilateral agreements, the USA often concludes bilateral agreements on specific areas of defense cooperation. An example of this is the 1958 US-UK Mutual Defence Agreement on nuclear cooperation. There is also a bilateral defense agreement between the United States and Hungary. See Department of State, Defense One, 2023.

147 The White House, 2022b: 8.

Adhering to doctrinal hierarchy, the 2022 US Southeast Asian strategy report entitled Indo-Pacific Strategy (IPS) is based upon the NSS, and it puts this position even more bluntly: the United States wants to strengthen its military presence and expects its allies to participate in this in accordance with US strategic interests.[148] It wants to strengthen formal military cooperation, both from a political and military operational standpoint.[149]

In September 2021, the American president, together with the British and Australian prime ministers, formulated the basic outlines of the AUKUS defense pact.[150] The primary declared goal of this American-Australian-British collaboration is the joint development and commissioning of AUKUS-class submarines.[151] About a year later, we learned significantly more. The real underlying goal is to modernize and significantly increase the capabilities of the Australian fleet, but it goes well beyond that—and the devil is in the details.

AUKUS is clearly the result of American geopolitical thinking and fits well into the process dictated by US strategic doctrines, whereby America should strengthen its alliances and follow bloc-based logic.[152] Given the costs and implications of the projects included in the arrangement, and the doctrinal alignment they entail, Australia will depend on the US defense industrial complex in the long term, which of course also narrows its political room for

---

148 The White House, 2022a: 5.

149 The White House, 2022a: 12.

150 Of course, Western countries have not been alone in concluding defense agreements. One example of this is the Collective Security Treaty Organization (CSTO), established in 1994 between Russia, Belarus, Kazakhstan, Armenia, and Kyrgyzstan. CSTO member countries, such as NATO, also undertake to guarantee collective security. In January 2022, Russian peacekeepers were sent to Kazakhstan under CSTO auspices to quell unrest in the country. However, unlike NATO, the CSTO does not take part in operations, and therefore did not participate in the Russian wars in Georgia or Ukraine.

151 At one point, this caused a significant diplomatic storm (also highlighting American strategic interests), because Australia had originally planned to develop its fleet in collaboration with France.

152 Jennings, 2023: 23; Shoebridge, 2021; O'Sullivan-Orbán, 2021.

maneuvering and makes it a more committed ally.[153] The magnitude of this strategic shift is clearly demonstrated by the fact that in 2015 Australia concluded a free trade agreement with China.[154]

Another development that should be noted in the context of this change in Western military alignment is the new strategic document adopted in Madrid in 2022, which replaces NATO's twelve-year-old strategic concept. According to the document, the North Atlantic region is not at peace, and the possibility of an attack on the sovereignty and territorial integrity of a NATO member cannot be ruled out. This assessment marks a sharp change from the Lisbon strategy of 2010.[155] Another important new element is that Russia featured in the previous document as a possible partner, whereas according to the assessment of the new strategic concept, Moscow poses the greatest and most immediate threat to the security of NATO members.[156] In addition, NATO's long-term strategic material mentions for the first time that China is a country that poses a challenge to the alliance. (It is worth comparing this with the aforementioned 2022 US report entitled National Security Strategy (NSS), especially as, according to the NATO document, processes in the Pacific region can affect Euro-Atlantic security).[157] This fundamental change is also clearly visible in NATO's deterrence and defense posture, in view of the old axiom that "the alliance does not regard any country as its enemy."[158] In contrast to this, the document declares the organization's readiness and ability to use nuclear weapons, and indeed it highlights the role of nuclear deterrence.[159]

---

153 Townshend, 2023.
154 *The Economist*, 2021.
155 Kuo, 2022.
156 Brzozowski, 2022.
157 Swicord, 2022.
158 Szenes, 2022: 13.
159 Ibid.

1.4. Bloc Formation is Not Really in the West's Interest, and It Increases the Risk of a Major War

"But fickle indeed are the fortunes of war."
(Géza Gárdonyi)

The five scenarios detailed above clearly show that the Western world is increasingly committed to pursuing a bloc-based strategy. This is not changed by the fact that in recent years, instead of decoupling, the strategy is increasingly referred to as "de-risking," in recognition of the risks associated with connectivity. But this is nothing more than a bit of clever semantic sleight-of-hand, as in Western thinking de-risking means the liquidation of connections—i.e., decoupling.[160] The real question is whether this five-part bloc-formation policy can fulfill the hopes invested in it. Do those five scenarios improve the position of Western civilization, are they neutral from this point of view, or do they achieve the opposite effect to their intentions? Certainly, we cannot have the rose without the thorn. In other words, every step has consequences, intended and unintended, positive and negative. The question is whether one has correctly assessed the possible consequences, and whether the negative consequences are worth the perceived positive consequences. Below we focus on

---

160 The term "de-risking" simply sounds more diplomatic than "decoupling," cf. Cave (2023). Similarly, Miller (2023) concludes that de-risking is preferred over separation because, with this softer rhetoric, America is attempting to persuade its allies to take its side in the competition with China. Regarding the overlaps between the two concepts, it can be said that precisely because of the vague and uncertain meaning of de-risking, it may follow that de-risking with reference to national security—as the United States does, for example—is essentially identical to separation, cf. Gewirtz (2023). In a study, the Bruegel Institute also points to similar parallels in meaning, by which it draws attention to the fact that de-risking can even be a means of deglobalization, cf. Demertzis (2023).

the factors that show why separating the Western and non-Western worlds does not seem like a great idea.

Economic Separation: To Successfully Flaunt Power, You Must Have a Preponderance of It

The tools of soft diplomatic power and the ever more frequently employed sanctions are fundamentally based on economic logic. One of the important goals of soft diplomatic tools is to keep money in-house, meaning that Western countries primarily trade with each other. The application of sanctions also has an economic impact, namely that it cuts off rival non-Western countries from "life-sustaining" Western resources and technologies.[161] But this

---

161 To understand the objectives of modern-day sanctions, it may be worth going back to the early twentieth-century understanding of these tools. Based on the ideas of US President Woodrow Wilson, it was argued that political goals could be achieved through economic restrictions, without the deaths entailed by warfare, and at far more limited expense than deploying an army. However, research has refuted these assumptions: sanctions can endanger, and even kill, and it is very difficult to accurately measure the consequences directly linked to sanctions. Thus, it sometimes appears that the primary purpose of sanctions is to be a symbolic tool, which the government of the imposing country can use to try to increase its own popularity, cf. Barber (1979) and Lindsay (1986). This may be the most important objective if only because, as experience shows, sanctions have rarely effected political changes in the targeted country, cf. Adler-Karlsson (1979), Doxey (1971), and Wallensteen (1968). In the twentieth century, sanctions against Italy during the Abyssinian War, North Korea during the Korean War, North Vietnam during the Vietnam War, and Iraq during the Gulf War were all unsuccessful. In terms of the "hit rate" of punitive measures, it is also worth noting that the list of the most sanctioned countries is for the most part led by deeply entrenched political systems. The Iranian regime currently laboring under the second most comprehensive array of sanctions has been in power since 1979, and it has been subject to sanctions for almost as long. The third most sanctioned nation is Syria, where Hafez al-Assad was in power between 1971 and 2000, and his son, Bashar al-Assad, has ruled since then. The fourth most sanctioned country is North Korea, where the current political system has existed since 1948, and the first sanctions were imposed in 1950. Sanction pressure therefore often only strengthens political regimes. This supports the view that the political effectiveness of sanctions is doubtful at best. Furthermore, the soft tools of influence (brands, products, communication panels) intended to spread the success of the Western model do not reach the society in question, or at least are much reduced in influence, further lessening the chances of regime change.

entire logic works only if the sanctioned party is economically much weaker than the sanctioning party.[162] From this point of view, the preponderance of economic strength that the West had thirty years ago no longer exists. Thus, this approach no longer makes sense. Moreover, it looks very much as though this sanction-based process of bloc formation is causing the whole world to lose out.[163]

In the following graphs, we present variables that clearly show the current place of East and West in the world economy and their positions relative to each other. In this way, we examine their shares of economic output and change over time, the amount of added value in some national economies, the amount of raw material and energy resources available, and finally the population indicators that serve as a proxy for the size of the potential domestic consumer market.

The first graph shows the proportion of the economy occupied by the ten largest economies, based on GDP measured at purchasing power parity. In 1990, shortly after the collapse of the Eastern Bloc,

---

162 The economic effectiveness of sanctions is impacted by the way the self-sufficiency of the sanctioned country often increases, while its dependence on the global economy decreases. A good example of this process is Russia, which announced its policy of import substitution as early as 2014 and has endeavored to the greatest possible extent to develop or prepare Russian systems, methods, and products independently of the West. Although Russia became the second most sanctioned country in the world after 2014, this did not stop it from starting the war in Ukraine. This is because it succeeded in developing alternative production and trade mechanisms. In other countries, sanctions also contributed to the independent development of certain sectors. Both the Iranian and North Korean nuclear programs are the result of efforts to isolate these countries. Cuba eased its isolation through the construction of its healthcare system, which it used to provide medical assistance and medical training programs to developing countries. In exchange for assisting the local healthcare system, Cuba has thus been able in recent decades to acquire cheap crude oil from Venezuela.

163 In its biannual Global Financial Stability Report, the IMF devoted a separate chapter to the negative effects of bloc formation on financial affairs (IMF, 2023a). In addition to the flow of FDI, the formation of economic blocs has also had a substantial impact on cost accounting, transactions, the pricing of banking assets, and the lending potential of banks. The report highlights, for example, that the United States and China have reduced cross-border portfolio and bank allocation by 15 percent since 2016 (IMF, 2023a: 81). In the document, IMF experts put the economic losses resulting from financial bloc formation at 3 percent of GDP (IMF, 2023a: 90).

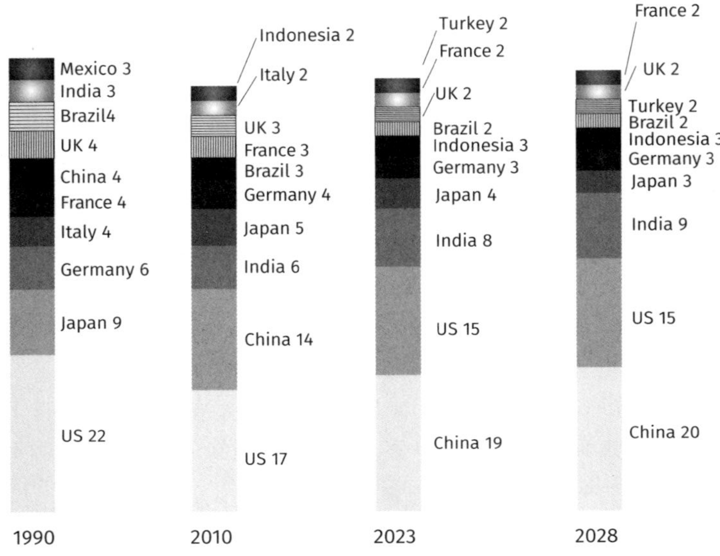

Figure 11: The ten largest global economies
based on their share of world economic output (GDP PPP, %).
Source: IMF, 2023b

six of the world's ten largest economies were Western. Moreover, the first six places were held by the G7 countries, excepting only Canada. At that time, these six Western countries were responsible for 48 percent of global economic output. Two decades later, the global economy was still characterized by Western dominance, because although only five Western countries made it into the top ten, they still accounted for nearly half the global economy. However, change was already indicated by the fact that China's share of output had tripled, making it the world's second largest economy, while India occupied third place. In the subsequent thirteen years, the centers of gravity of the global economy have fundamentally changed. In 2023, measured in terms of purchasing power parity, China became the world's largest economy, overtaking the United States. This year, although five Western countries were still represented among the world's ten largest economies, their share of global economic output fell to approximately 27 percent, while that of non-Western countries increased to 33 percent from around 25 percent previously. On a global level, we can see that in 2010, developed and developing or emerging countries produced economic output at a ratio of 60:40.[164] By 2023, this ratio had been almost completely reversed.[165] This shift in the center of gravity will be even more noticeable by 2030. A few years before the pandemic and the war in Ukraine, forecasts of which countries would be make up the world's ten largest economies in 2030 were extrapolated from IMF data. According to the bank Standard Chartered, there will be only three Western countries on the list, and India will push the United States into third place.[166] According to PricewaterhouseCoopers (PwC), in 2030 there will be four Western countries among the ten largest economies, and the USA will still retain second place. In their view, India could become the second largest economy by 2050, by which time only three Western countries will be in the top ten club.[167] It is worth looking at this year's IMF forecast for 2028. According to the currency fund, in 2028 there will still be five Western countries in the top ten list, but their share of the global economy will decrease to 24 percent, while that of non-Western countries will increase to 35 percent. China will maintain its leading position, and the gap between India and the US will continue to narrow.

The center of gravity for world economic manufacturing capacity is now clearly in the East (earlier we discussed in more detail the reasons for this and the consequences of neoliberal economic policy).

In the mid-1990s, the West produced more than 40 percent of the world's industrial added value, while in 2019, China alone

---

164 The International Monetary Fund defines the term "developed countries" as covering the Western world and the USA's closest Asian allies, such as Japan, while developing and emerging countries represent the non-Western world.

165 IMF, 2023b.

166 Martin, 2019.

167 PwC, 2017.

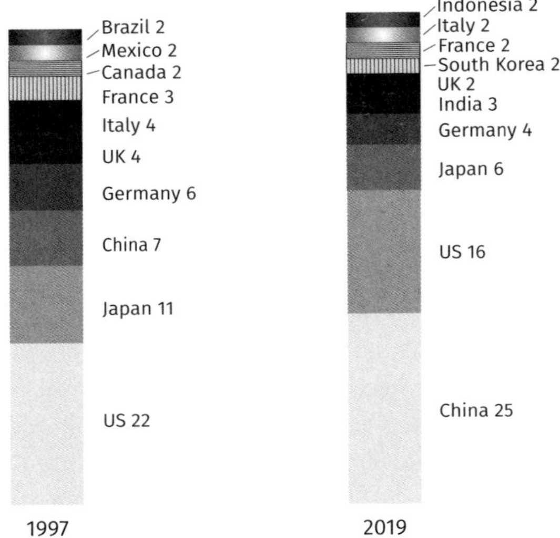

Figure 12: The top ten national economies in terms
of generating industrial added value.
Source: own calculation based on World Bank (2022a) data

accounted for a quarter, the United States' share fell to 16 percent, and India, South Korea, and Indonesia became significant players. In addition, the absolute technological advantage of the West is also disappearing.[168] As the following figure shows, the high-tech content of the exports from Eastern countries is already extremely high.

---

168 One important area is chip production. Undoubtedly, American companies remain the most important in terms of chip technology development, but manufacturing capacity is concentrated in the East. More than 80 percent of the most modern microchips are manufactured by a single Taiwanese company, and the rest are made by South Korean companies (García-Herrero, 2022). Chinese chip development and production also contribute to this. Although large Chinese tech companies such as Huawei or Lenovo generate roughly half their revenue abroad, China produces less than 20 percent of the required number of chips, so it is currently a net importer of technology (Lewis, 2019: 1). At the same time, Chinese chip production capacities are currently expanding at the most rapid pace (Tseng, 2019). Another important area is renewable energy technology. At the beginning of the last decade, China dominated half of the production steps in the manufacture of solar panels, while this ratio has now risen to over 80 percent (IEA, 2022: 7).

2019

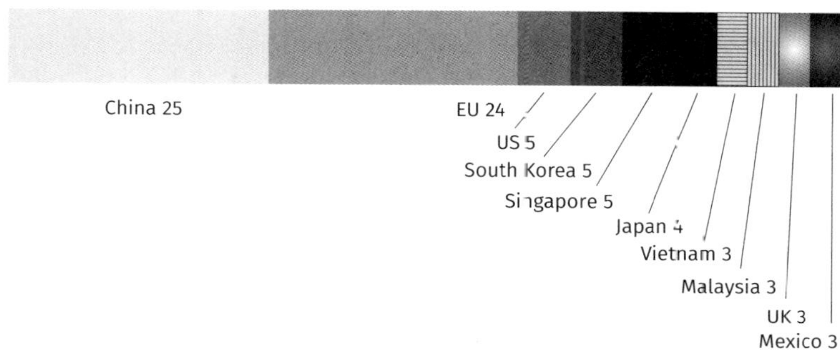

Figure 13: The ten national economies
with the largest high-tech export value (%).
Source: own calculation based on World Bank (2023) data

Another key question is who has control over the energy carriers and mineral resources that drive the world economy. As a first step, it is important to state clearly that crude oil and natural gas will remain decisive in terms of the operation of the world economy for decades to come.[169] In the case of the two most important energy carriers—if we take production as a basis—the dominant role of the East since the Second World War will be maintained. From the figure below showing the top three countries, although the United States has clearly become a dominant player[170] in the crude oil and natural gas markets, the Gulf monarchies, together with Russia

---

169 According to forecasts by the US Energy Information Administration (EIA), the world's energy consumption will increase by about 50 percent by 2050 (EIA, 2021). According to the EIA (2021), the most important source of energy in the future will continue to be petroleum products, and the use of natural gas will not decrease significantly (renewable energy sources and nuclear energy will account for most of the increase).

170 Due to the shale oil and shale natural gas revolution that took place in the second half of the 2010s, the United States became a net crude oil exporter (though US crude oil exports only marginally exceed its imports) and emerged as an important player on the natural gas market. For more on the shale revolution and its economic and geopolitical implications, see Yergin (2023).

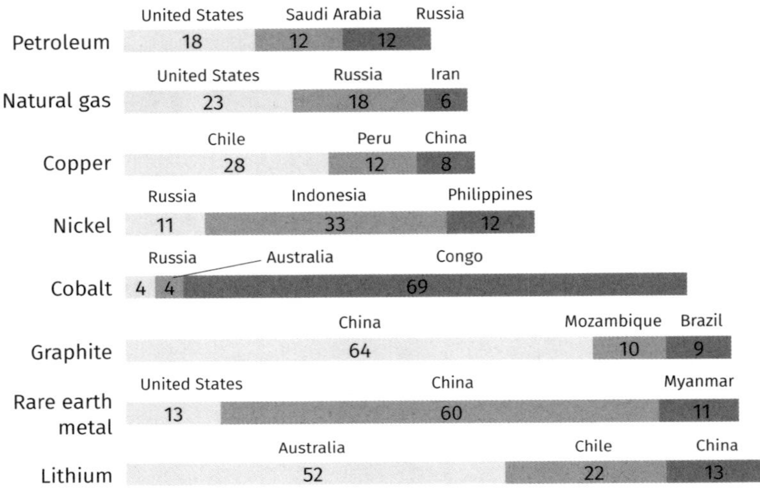

Figure 14: The three most important producers
of individual mineral resources and energy carriers.
Source: own calculation based on IEA (2023) data

and Iran, remain the most important producers.[171] Meanwhile, the non-Western world also has access to the largest supply of mineral resources used for the development and production of modern technologies. Forty percent of copper comes from South America, more than half of nickel comes from Russia and Southeast Asia, and more than 60 percent of graphite and rare earth metals is produced in China.[172] The dominance of the East in terms of population has been clear for many decades. From a Western perspective,

---

171 Decisive elements include not only volume of extraction, but also the export and import position of individual countries. Eastern countries account for more than half of crude oil exports, and China and India alone are responsible for 31 percent of the world's crude oil import volume (OEC, 2023). The East is also dominant in the export of liquefied natural gas, as these countries provided nearly 60 percent of total export volume, while the top three importers—China, South Korea, and Japan—accounted for more than half of import volume (*Groupe international des importateurs de gaz naturel liquéfié*, GIIGNL, 2022).

172 Cobalt is also a key mineral resource in modern technologies, and China has taken decisive steps to secure control over its supply. Almost 70 percent of cobalt is mined

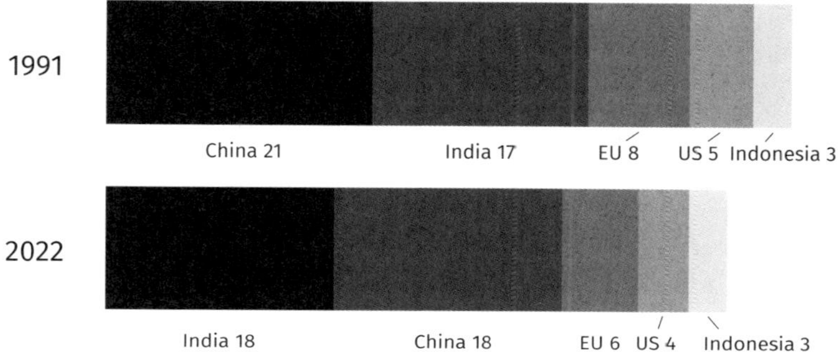

Figure 15: Population ratio (%) of the most important regions.
Source: own calculation based on World Bank (2023h) data

it is undeniably disconcerting that the East, despite its current demographic problems, is clearly dominant in population terms.

Summarizing the above, we can see that economic separation—and the soft diplomatic tools and sanctions policies driving it—is a strategy entailing significant risk.[173] Indeed, the risks of decoupling to the functioning of the Western economy appear greater than the risks arising from interconnectedness.[174]

---

in the Congo. Today, 15 of 19 mines are operated by Chinese companies, and 80 percent of the cobalt extracted in this way is shipped to China (Ahlijian, 2022).

173 The managing director of the IMF, Kristalina Georgieva, points out that trade fragmentation can reduce world economic output by 7 percent in the long term, equivalent to the combined economies of Germany and France. If combined with technological decoupling, this could rise to as high as 16 percent. According to Georgieva, economic fragmentation almost never stops at this point, and would likely lead to a complete geopolitical separation, i.e., the formation of rival blocs.

174 Proponents of free trade remind us that state subsidies and market-restrictive measures are bad in themselves: they artificially make goods produced in one country cheaper and reduce economic efficiency. An example of this is the package of anti-inflation laws adopted by the United States, the content of which was discussed in detail in the previous subsection. The IRA is particularly objectionable, in that beneficiaries must meet local content thresholds (for example, products must be assembled in North America, or a certain percentage of components must come from this region). The world can do little against the protectionism of the United States: WTO rules unequivocally prohibit the threshold values used in the IRA, but it was precisely Washington that ensured the WTO would be unable to effectively enforce these rules. The other option would be the imposition of tariffs on American

First, the economic output of the Western world is markedly inferior to that of the non-Western world. And if that were not enough, the ability to produce added value is also greater in the East than in the West. In terms of raw materials and energy carriers, the Western world also lags behind. The United States is doing relatively well, while Europe is a major underperformer in this regard. The situation is similar in demographic terms: the Western world accounts for only one-eighth of the world's population, meaning that it has a much smaller population than the non-Western part of the world.[175] In addition, the last three factors—access to cheap raw materials, a secure energy supply, and a large population serving as a domestic consumer market—are three of the most important conditions for economic growth. Relatedly, as a fourth factor, the decline in the dominance of the dollar, which currently plays the role of a global currency, is often raised as an additional argument.[176]

---

products that benefit from IRA-provided or other subsidy support (Amaro, 2023). However, this would cause significant damage to world trade. US allies and challengers alike are thus forced to fight money with money, increasing their own government subsidies to counter Washington's policies. If this results in global subsidy competition—signs of which can already be seen following the response measures of the EU, Japan, and South Korea—it could lead to fragmentation of the international trade system, higher costs for consumers, increased barriers to innovation, and reduced willingness to cooperate politically (*The Economist*, 2023).

175 It is worth looking at Carnegie's analysis from more than a decade ago, which discussed the biggest changes the world would face in the period to 2050 (Dadush-Stancil, 2010). At the time, experts predicted that the non-Western world would supplant the West as the largest proportion of the world economy, primarily because of its demographic advantages and the narrowing technological gap. As a result of this, Western countries would become increasingly protectionist, which would lead to a decrease in economic output and thus of living standards (though standards of living would still be higher in relative terms). Geo-economic changes would lead to significant geopolitical changes. And the last big change—or rather, absence of change—was that the relative income gap between the Western and non-Western world would remain. In Africa, there would still be many people below the absolute poverty line, which would have a major impact on global migration.

176 One consequence of the United States' former hegemonic role and great power status is the US dollar's role as global reserve currency. It is no coincidence that the non-Western world is responding to the war in Ukraine and the geopolitical changes catalyzed by the conflict with de-dollarization. In other words, an alternative monetary system, driven primarily by cooperation among BRICS countries, is

Thus, by separating or distancing itself from the non-Western part of the world, the West will not weaken the sanctioned party but only itself, because it will be cutting itself off from those markets with the greatest growth potential and most promising opportunities.

The "Democracies Versus Autocracies" Framing Alienates the West's Allies

One of the striking signs of global decoupling—that is, of the separation of the non-Western and Western worlds—is the strengthening of a new element in the foreign policy of the United States, namely the narrative of "democracies versus autocracies," described in detail in the previous subsection. In general, it can be said that democratic expectations are part of the political agenda of the progressive wing of the US Democratic Party and are the subject of debate in the United States as well.[177] The phenomenon raises many problems.

---

taking shape. Several ideas about the system have emerged. Some speak of a digital currency, which could be backed by precious metals and other raw materials (Krikke, 2022). Another alternative—as suggested by the BRICS development bank—would be to conduct at least half of foreign trade between the five countries in local currencies (Chenoy, 2022). Experts agree that the dollar will decline strongly as a reserve currency—the only question is whether this will happen over a few years (Fazi, 2022) or a few decades (Ferguson, 2023b).

177 Zemánek (2023: 96–97) views Western geopolitical thinking and ideas about the transforming world order as being shaped primarily by domestic politics. In recent years, the West has entered the post-liberal era, in which liberal political forces are increasingly trying to maintain their power by means of an authoritarian "us versus them" logic. This logic has also been transferred to foreign policy, and thus the ideological struggle of "liberal democracies versus autocracies" arose. What is more, just as liberalism's loss of ground in domestic politics led to a new logic of power, the relative loss of the West's position in international relations has also led to a new geopolitical ideology. However, the non-Western world is able to resist the will of the West precisely because of its relative strength, and so we find ourselves at the beginning of the Second Cold War. The neoconservative wing of the Republican Party sympathizes with the foreign policy direction of the Democratic mainstream. American foreign policy thinking, however, is broader and more discordant than this, and several have spoken out against the "new Washington Consensus." Richard Haass (2022), Colin Powell's chief of staff and then director of the Council on Foreign Relations for two decades, is one such voice. In his view, the USA no longer possesses the full range of capabilities that would allow it to once again become a hegemon in the international space. For this very reason, it is

On the one hand, it is now accepted that the number of democracies is decreasing. This is primarily shown by the way an increasing number of countries that had previously been considered full democracies have slipped into the status of "partial democracies" according to the democracy indicators of various institutes. Though more than one such country is considered a firm ally of the United States, among the traditional allies of the United States we also find a number of entirely undemocratic countries, primarily in the Middle East.[178] It is thus a logical consequence that the United States finds itself faced with a strategic dilemma.[179] If it wants to unite countries committed to democracy—and if, moreover, by "committed to democracy" it specifically means the type of democracy and value commitments shared by the progressive wing of the Democratic Party—then the number of countries with which it can expect smooth cooperation will be greatly reduced.[180] This also highlights the problem that the existence or non-existence of democracy is difficult to determine, and its measurement or quantification is next

---

in America's interest to maintain intensive dialogue with emerging powers, and to eschew a policy of bloc formation.

178 Funnell, 2021.

179 Ferguson (2023a) criticizes the Biden administration for again using a simplistic ideology that reduces the world to a struggle between liberal democracies and autocracies. According to the British historian, it is inherently problematic to classify democracies, and especially to identify them with American-style liberal democracy. There are also no objective indicators for where to identify the borderline at which a democracy turns into an autocracy. In addition, the USA itself is struggling with many serious challenges, including the over-expansion of certain branches of power, which it would be quite legitimate to view as democratic backsliding.

180 Such expectations can force even the USA's closest allies to change course. According to French President Macron, if a multipolar world order truly does come about, Europe must become an independent pole in terms of economic, military, and technological strength (Cercas, 2023). To do so, however, contrary to the current Euro-Atlantic narrative, it must maintain strategic relations with Russia as well. Incidentally, some Republican-affiliated experts have come to the same conclusion. For example, DerSimonian (2022), analyzing the German-Russian relations, points out that in the future Europe cannot restrict itself wholly to the economic aspect of the Russian relationship. Instead, what is needed is a complex approach that takes into account the European security system as a whole, in addition to economic and energy requirements.

to impossible.[181] Because the concept of democracy espoused by the democratic leadership in Washington is subject to fierce political debates at home in the United States, to demand its wholehearted adoption elsewhere is, at the very least, presumptuous. The fact that the USA expects its allies to comply with the rules and norms of its institutional framework even though it has broken those rules on numerous occasions is a further cause for complaint. It is no surprise that many non-Western countries, such as India, despite accepting American arguments regarding the inviolability of Ukraine's territorial integrity, continued—for reasons of *realpolitik*—to be significant importers of Russian energy.

This unpleasant situation creates further problems. Requiring existing and potential allies to endorse strictly codified moral strictures, even when they are the subject of fierce debate at home, can easily cause the opposite effect from what was intended. The range of allied countries thus narrows, and even former partners may decide to pursue their foreign policy by other routes, bypassing the expectations of the USA.[182] This, in turn, creates an opportunity for the USA's challengers to strengthen their own role in the international system. A good example of this process is the rapprochement between Saudi Arabia and Iran, which was

---

181 Funnell, 2021.
182 According to Mead (2023), the transformation of the world order is also being helped by the rebellion of the global South. In his view, the West continues to operate based on the legacy of Wilsonian principles. According to American President Wilson's liberal internationalist approach, a peaceful world order can be ensured by technocratic global institutions and regimes, which will self-evidently follow Western principles. The South has remained part of this order until now, because it has gained significant advantages through liberalized international trade. However, the war in Ukraine rang the alarm bells for the global South. The West has become more and more protectionist, while sanctions against Russia have caused significant damage outside the Western world as well—and the South is well aware of the danger of bloc formation. In addition, the West also gave an ideological reason for its measures against Russia: those who side with the West are good, those who do not are bad. Such a reformulation of the world order will have negative consequences for the South, and it now has the ability to do something about it.

primarily brought about by China.[183] This unique case also draws attention to a more systemic risk. If a sufficient number of former US allies or countries oriented toward the United States decide not to accept the new conditions—i.e., the obligation to implement progressive ideologies at home—this could create an opportunity for Washington's challengers to set up alternative institutions outside the current institutional framework. In a curious way, the foreign policy doctrine of "democracies versus autocracies" actually helps China portray itself an advocate and leader of the non-Western world.[184] In practice, this means that states on the periphery of the Western world could eventually separate completely from the West, leaving the core states to fend for themselves, and in such a situation they would inevitably lose the competition between democracies and perceived or real autocracies.[185]

Where Confrontation Could Work:
Militarily the West Still Has the Upper Hand

The dominance of the West in terms of military power remains—for the time being—unquestionable. At the end of the Cold War, the United States was the largest spender on defense, accounting for 41 percent of all global defense spending. In this period, the top ten countries in terms of defense expenditure were all Western, and together with the United States they made up nearly 60 percent of

---

183 Walt, 2023.

184 Guyer, 2022.

185 According to Levine (2023), the growing tension between the United States and China is not really rooted in technological, military, or trade issues, but rather in deep ideological differences. The real cause of the conflict is that the two great powers have completely different understandings of competition. For Washington, "directed strategic competition" resembles a sports match, where the better competitor wins, but the loser can prepare for the next matchup, when it will again have a chance to win. For Beijing, by contrast, drawing from its Maoist historical past, competition means a life-and-death struggle. So long as the United States does not recognize this difference and learn to reduce pressure, the tension between them will remain unresolved (on this subject, see also Stiglitz, 2022).

defense spending. By 2022, the picture had changed to the extent that there were only four Western states among the ten largest defense budgets. Nonetheless, the US and Western nations still account for nearly half of global defense spending. China is now second in terms of absolute spending, but its defense budget is still only about a third of what the USA spends.[186]

In addition to expenditure, we can see from individual armament categories that, thanks to the clear dominance of the United States, the Western allies retain land, sea, and air superiority. According to the ranking of Global Firepower Index, which examines military power, roughly half of all aircraft carriers belong to the USA, and when it comes to naval power (warships), three of the five most powerful countries are Western.[187] The same is true of armored combat vehicles. And in terms of air power, the United States has almost twice the combined potential of Russia and China, which follow it in the ranking.

From the data above, the Western world clearly has a real advantage—primarily thanks to the United States—exclusively in terms of military power. Of course, such an advantage is, in a certain sense, reassuring. Since our accession to NATO, we Hungarians are also proud members of what is currently the strongest military alliance in the world. We take seriously the obligations that the treaty places upon us, and we perform them to the best of our abilities. This is of fundamental importance for Hungary's security. However, it must not be forgotten that this organization defines itself as a defensive alliance, based on the principle of collective defense.

Examining this question contextually, we find that there is still cause for concern. A central figure in Isaac Asimov's famous *Foundation* series is psychohistorian Hari Seldon, who, using a

---

186 SIPRI, 2023.
187 Global Fire Power, 2023. The leading position of the West is clearly demonstrated by this ranking, in which six of the ten most militarily powerful countries are part of the Western alliance system.

comprehensive mathematical model, predicts the collapse of the Galactic Empire. It can be argued, with a little exaggeration, that Asimov's putative field of psychohistory has emerged as a genuine science in the form of so-called cliodynamics. The essence of this discipline is that, just as with Asimov, we can make predictions about future events by conducting a careful mathematical and statistical examination of historical events, and drawing conclusions based on the recurring patterns that emerge. As in the famous science fiction novel, so the real research concluded that during their existence, empires and hegemonic powers go through many cycles, some spanning centuries, in which eras that are balanced and peaceful are followed by periods of social imbalance, and vice versa. What is more, it transpires that a weakened, declining hegemon goes to war with increasing frequency, while the peaceful, socially balanced periods between times of conflict and instability gradually become shorter.[188] These patterns show a frightening similarity to the world political processes taking place today.[189] And we have plenty of reason to worry, if we add to this that, if the only advantage it possesses is in military power, it is quite possible that the declining hegemon, the

---

188 Turchin, 2007: 229.

189 Other signs also point in the direction of a possible military conflict. According to Beckley (2023), the USA and China are so-called enduring rivals. The literature of international relations shows that such enduring rival pairs are formed when the basic interests of two countries are radically opposed, when their declared spheres of interest overlap, and especially when the economies of the two countries are closely linked and they have intensive commercial relations. An important feature of enduring rivals is that the peaceful periods in their relations serve only as an opportunity for the two antagonists to gather strength for the next bout. All these elements characterize Chinese-American relations. Such eternal rivalries are also very difficult to resolve. Colaresi et al. (2008), for example, pointed out that since the Napoleonic Wars, twenty-seven eternal rivals have clashed with each other, and each such period lasted, on average, half a century. There were three possible ways in which these rivalries could be resolved. The first is obvious: one side defeats the other in war. The second is when an external, common enemy appears (this is how the First World War dissolved the rivalry between Britain and France). The Cold War is the only example of the third way, when the Soviet Communist system simply capitulated to its rival.

United States, will eventually seek to maintain its position by force, because this is where it has the best chance of success.[190]

Takeaways from a Long Chapter

It is still impossible to say whether the model of the world order that we have known until now will remain. But there are already signs that the leaders of the Western world, and especially of the United States, have decided that bloc formation offers their best chances of success. However, the politics of fragmentation and rival blocs is a double-edged sword. It works only when you are holding good cards. And now follow the takeaways from a long chapter:

- Economic withdrawal could easily lead to the West falling behind.
  - The East accounts for a larger share of the world's economic output than the West.
  - In terms of useful raw materials, the East is much richer.
  - The same is true for energy carriers.
  - Only one-eighth of the world's population lives in the Western world, making it a much smaller market than those of its challengers.
  - This equation predicts that the West will be shut out of markets that have the greatest potential for development over the coming decades.
- The formation of political blocs alienates the West's non-Western allies.
  - Defining the struggle as one between democracies and autocracies places an obligation on America's allies to march in ideological lockstep.

---

190 Allison (2017) very plausibly outlines such a possibility. He argues that the United States and China have fallen into a recurring historical situation known as the Thucydides trap. In his book, Allison suggests that if a declining hegemon is challenged by another rising power, war between them becomes almost inevitable. Reviewing five hundred years of history, he found sixteen such cases, and in twelve of them it led to war. Layne (2020) also deals with this.

- The United States has many non-democratic allies.
  - These countries, if they are put under excessive political pressure, will turn away from the US as an ally.
- The West still possesses an overwhelming military advantage.
  - This is the only area in which the West can still be shown to possess an absolute advantage.

However, if it is in the military sphere that the advantages of the current hegemon are most apparent, this also makes it the most logical domain in which to take on potential challengers. That is, by war. And in an age of weapons of mass destruction, this is in no one's interests. In other aspects—i.e., politically and economically—the West may stand to lose rather more than it gains by retreating into a bloc. Therefore, the clear conclusion of this chapter is that the policy of bloc formation does not serve the interests of the United States specifically or the West more broadly.

Of course, we Hungarians have little say about the path the world follows, or about what the great powers decide. This subchapter evaluating the tendency toward blocs was also born out of a concern for the fate of Western civilization. It is a warning that, from our standpoint here in the middle of Central Europe, things look like they are going in the wrong direction. But we can do little to shape them, so we must adapt to them instead.

As such, the next chapter will be about how bloc formation affects Hungary, and what principles and considerations Hungary should follow to navigate in a bloc-based world.

2 FIRST STEPS—WHO ARE THE HUNGARIANS, WHERE HAVE THEY COME FROM, WHERE ARE THEY GOING, WHAT ARE THE POTENTIAL STUMBLING BLOCS?

"They are repulsive in appearance; they have deep-set eyes, they are short in stature, and in their morals and speech they are so barbarous and wild that one may justly condemn the caprice of Fortune, or rather wonder at the patience of God, for leaving so beautiful a land as this as spoils for these monsters of humankind." Startling language, and downright insulting when we learn that Bishop Otto Freising wrote them about us Hungarians. The wars of the twelfth century are, of course, at the root of this uncharitable character study. In those days, as in our own, it was not the fashion to lavish an opponent with praise.

Still, the situation is far from hopeless, and there is always something positive to cling to. Even the blinkered bishop could not deny that our country is beautiful. Moreover, he did not stop at an aesthetic description. In his writings, he notes Hungary's excellent geographical location, its spectacular natural wealth, and its extremely favorable topography. In the end, he concludes, "you may now be persuaded that this is the very Paradise of God, or the majestic Egypt."

Almost nine hundred years have passed since then. Some things have not changed. Hungary still has an advantageous location, an excellent climate, and is rich in natural beauty. We might almost imagine it to be paradise on earth. However, the world around us has changed. Major geographical discoveries rendered Central Europe increasingly insignificant, and Hungary was condemned to a subordinate role in both economic and political terms, first by the invasion of the Ottoman Turks, and then by compulsory absorption into a wider imperial project. We were dragged into all international conflagrations, lost two-thirds of our territory, and endured forty years of Communism.

They say that to have come back from all that is already a win. But that is no reason to lower our sights. We have regained our sovereignty, and in today's world the main global trade routes are not necessarily trans-Atlantic or trans-Pacific. Just as in the distant past, our geographical circumstances are outstanding. It is up to us how we make use of the advantages we enjoy.

But how should we characterize these Hungarians, so blessed in their circumstances? To begin with, let us consider some surprising but revealing data. Most people, when they think of Hungary, picture it as a tiny, almost imperceptible dot on the world map. After all, it covers just 93,000 square kilometers, making it the 108th largest country in the world.[191] Moreover, with a population of just under ten million, it is only the 94th most populous in the world.[192] In a ranking of 145 countries examined, it boasts the 54th strongest military force.[193] Presented with statistical data of this sort, it would be easy to conclude that one's first impression was correct—Hungary is not a particularly significant place.

But nothing could be further from the truth! After all, it is not raw area or population data that makes our country significant, but the Hungarian people themselves. Consider, for instance, the number of Nobel laureates. In absolute terms, Hungary ranks fifteenth in this listing, and eleventh when adjusted for population size.[194] But Hungarians do not excel merely in intellectual pursuits: Hungary

---

191 UN, 2021; Hungary's ranking among 195 countries, in a list based on the country codes published by the International Organization for Standardization (ISO) in 1974.

192 CIA, 2023.

193 *Global Fire Power*, 2023.

194 When it comes to lists of Nobel laureates, the list featured on the Wikipedia web page is most frequently cited. The Nobel Peace Prize laureates are not included in the list, but laureates for the Nobel Prize in Economics are.

has also become famous as one of the fifteen safest countries in the world.[195] We also punch above our weight when it comes to sporting endeavors. Hungarian athletes have won the thirteenth most Olympic medals, counting all gold, silver, and bronze medals. We are also forging ahead in economic terms. We try to use our talents and hard work for our own benefit. Hungary now has the world's twelfth most open economy,[196] and based on nominal export volume, we are the world's thirty-fifth largest exporter.[197] What is valuable to us is valuable globally, and we put it out there, all ten million of us on our 93,000 square kilometers.

As such, you might say that we have at least got something to work with here. However, a strategy based solely on these well-known strengths would be lopsided. In the following, we undertake to present the difficulties Hungary formerly confronted, how these were managed, and, in this context, the continuing impact of the solutions found on our present circumstances. We examine Hungary's economic and social structure, and then, based on our findings, evaluate the extent to which a bloc-based world order serves our country's interests, whether in geographic, cultural, or economic terms.

---

195 The ranking was made by weighting data from the Global Organized Crime Index and the *Global Law and Order Report* prepared by Gallup. See also Zaidi, 2023.
196 World Bank, 2023b.
197 World Bank, 2022.

2.1. A Dependent Hungary was Never a Successful Hungary—The Economic Distortions of Dependent Relationships

Let us imagine an everyday situation: For instance, perhaps we are visiting a lifestyle consultant. We would like this person to put together a long-term diet for us so that we can live a healthier, happier, more balanced life. We know that this is, broadly speaking, what motivates people to turn to a lifestyle consultant. In the worst-case scenario, the consultant has a single dietary template to offer to all clients. One does not have to be a dietitian to see that this probably will not work. We are different, and in consequence our ideal diets will be different too. The situation is one degree better if the consultant has, say, five off-the-peg diets and chooses which to recommend after placing us in one or another group according to certain characteristics. Thus, the diet recommended to a woman in her forties who exercises regularly would differ from that recommended to a retired man who lives a relatively inactive life. But let us face it, there is still a good chance that the diet recommended is less than optimal for our specific circumstances. The best-case scenario, then, is if our chosen specialist asks a detailed series of questions, becomes familiar with our habits, life history, and the changes we have gone through to that point, as well as the goals we want to achieve. Some lab tests may also be appropriate. Based on all this, the consultant can provide us with much more personalized advice. This story is the essence of all situational ethical teaching. General principles must be applied to the requirements of the situation, and this requires what the Ancient Greeks called *phronesis*, i.e., practical wisdom. This is exactly the task before us.

We need to find a strategy for Hungary that best fits the situation in which this more than one-millennium-old Central European country finds itself in the first years of the third decade of the third millennium AD. That is why we must first familiarize ourselves with the country's current situation and history, so that later we can use this knowledge to shape our goals.

In the language of the technocrats, we are looking for ways of helping Hungary to catch up. "Catching up" has some unpleasant connotations, suggesting as it does that a country that has not yet done so is somehow less sophisticated, or even, pardon the phrase, more uncultured than the states it is catching up with. This is most certainly not the case. Thus, the first thing that must be stated is that catching up does not mean mindless imitation, the abandonment of one's own identity, or an all-pervading inferiority complex. In fact, it means just one thing: namely that the given country, in our case Hungary, should be able to provide its citizens with the same or at least a similar level of prosperity as that ensured by countries that are currently better off.

There are far-reaching reasons why it is not currently able to do so, and why catching up is necessary at all. Since at least the Age of Discovery, the Eastern half of Europe has been economically inferior to the Western half.[198] But for our purposes, it seems sensible to limit our focus to the events of the modern, postwar world.[199] In the period after 1945, Hungary was forced to join the

---

198 Acemoğlu-Johnson-Robinson, 2005: 546.

199 Hungary suffered heavy losses because of the Treaty of Trianon. It lost—if we consider all the territories formerly under the Holy Crown—71 percent of its territory and 64 percent of its population. The crude oil and natural gas fields discovered up to 1920—together with the refineries completed to that point—all lay outside the new borders. Although more than 70 percent of the black coal remained within the borders of post-Trianon Hungary, the country retained control of just over 17 percent of the iron ore after the treaty, and only half of the metallurgical industrial capacity remained. A total of 80 percent of machinery manufacturing capacity lay outside the new borders, and half of the chemical and food industries went to the successor states (KSH, 1938).

Eastern Bloc. The Hungarians did not choose this fate, but the great powers agreed to divide Europe in this way. It also became clear relatively quickly, in 1956 at the latest, that Hungary had no wish to be a member of the Eastern Bloc, but the iron laws of geopolitical interests were stronger. Belonging to the Soviet sphere of interest meant the mandatory adoption of a Soviet-style economic model. By the end of the 1970s at the latest, in no small part thanks to the 1973 oil crisis, it had become clear that the Soviet socialist model was not competitive against Western capitalism.[200] In addition, due to the peculiarities of Hungarian foreign trade, even the profits of those products that could be sold on the global market did not return to the Hungarian economy. Thus, the necessary developments were not made, and the states of Eastern Europe fell behind in terms of productivity and energy efficiency. What is more, given that rising living standards were the most important source of legitimacy for Hungarian Communists, the state took out huge loans to maintain the unsustainable economic structure.[201] This is how we arrived at

---

200 The economic history of the Soviet Union most clearly illustrates the causes of the crisis that ultimately afflicted the Soviet-type economic model. From the end of the 1920s, the Soviet Union rapidly became integrated into the functioning of the global economy. During this era, state-controlled heavy industry was able to produce competitively and for export, creating jobs with higher added value compared to the Tsarist period. The decline of the 1970s was primarily caused by the fact that the system was too inflexible and could not adapt to new divisions of labor in the world economy in the same way capitalist countries could, for example, by changing technology (see Allen, 2001 for more information). The Soviet economic model therefore remained stuck in a mass-production dead-end, and unlike Western countries, it was unable to transform vast expenditure on military industrial developments into civilian technology (for more on this, see Harrison, 2017).

201 The economic policy of the Kádár era was fundamentally flawed, and not only because of the socialist-style model of a planned economy. Some of the products of socialist Hungary—such as the output of the Videoton factory, the pharmaceutical and chemical industries, or the agri-food industrial complex—could be sold on Western markets for the convertible currency that was so vital to the Hungarian economy. However, instead of investing these profits into the technological modernization of the national economy, the Kádár government partly channeled these profits into unviable companies and partly used them to help prop up Western Communist parties (Borvendég, 2017: 163). All this was incumbent upon Soviet satellite states, hence Hungary's significant borrowing from the 1970s on. This borrowing was

the wave of democratization that swept Central and Eastern Europe in 1989–1990, at the same time as the Communist economic balloon burst. The Hungarian economy had no competitive products, and the state was deeply in debt. In these circumstances, one of the most important promises of the new democratic regime was that it would raise living standards closer to those of the West.

Be that as it may, after 1990, for the first time in many decades, or indeed centuries, there was an opportunity for Hungary to take its destiny into its own hands. However, this proved far more difficult than might have been imagined. Several problems had to be confronted simultaneously. The political system had to be transformed into a Western-style democracy. Since this was primarily a matter of passing laws and establishing institutions, it was perhaps the easiest task, though still by no means easy. It is no coincidence that the political science trend of studying transitions—and in particular examining the possibilities of democratization—was most popular in Hungary in the early 1990s.[202] But the transformation

---

fundamentally rational. The operation of COMECON was transformed, and the previously "hard" products of Hungarian industrial export became "soft," which led to a reversal of the foreign trade balance, while the oil price explosion and resulting increase in import prices only added to the country's problems (Szalai, 2022: 4). The logical response was to increase exports to the West, which required investments and the purchase of technology, which consequently required credit. These loans were taken out in currencies that appreciated in value significantly (Szabó, 2016: 6), and thus debt servicing began to divert funds from investment. On the other hand— and most importantly—only a small part of the taken loans, barely 7 or 8 percent, was invested in export industries (Cseszka, 2008: 101). It is therefore unsurprising that, despite this huge borrowing (Kaser-Nötel, 1986: 230–40), the share of CIS countries, including Hungary, in Western markets fell significantly, and relative GDP began to decline year-on-year (Germuska, 2014: 285).

202 The science of transitology was built on investigations into the Latin American political and constitutional systems of the 1970s. It is therefore no surprise that the works examining the transitions in Eastern and Central Europe of 1989– 1990 were based on scientific papers from twenty years earlier. This is well exemplified by the fact that one of the professional reviewers of a fundamental work of transitology (Huntington, 1993) was Dankwart Rustow, whose democratic transition model (Rustow, 1970) was used as an analogy by most representatives of transitology. Rustow's logical system also had a fundamental influence on Huntington's Hungarian contemporaries, for example Ágh (1995). However,

of the economic structure proved an even greater challenge. The shortcomings of the uncompetitive socialist economy came to light as soon as it was tasked with operating on a market-economy footing, and a severe lack of capital meant that there was no way to make improvements.[203] This catch-22 situation seemed to offer few avenues of escape. In the following, we will attempt to show how and by what means we managed to get out of this vicious circle. To do so, we compare the data from the early 2000s with the data from 2010 and then from 2023 to get an idea of the areas in which Hungary has made significant progress. The direction of this improvement also indicates where we should look for future prosperity.

Results of Regained Independence

At this point, then, the task is similar to that of the dietitian we spoke about at the beginning of the chapter. The situation must be assessed, goals must be identified, and a diet recommended to help achieve the desired result. As such, the first step must be to assess the situation and propose a plan of action. How far have we progressed, and to what extent has Hungary succeeded in catching up?

Situational Assessment: the Hungarian Economy is Complex

The so-called Economic Complexity Index (ECI) is an indicator that ranks countries based on three criteria:[204] the extent to which the

---

trenchant criticism of transitology began to emerge barely a decade after the rise of the discipline. The principal thrust of these criticisms was that it leaves too narrow a space for interpretation, is excessively teleological, and is insensitive to national characteristics. As one of the most important critics of the discipline, Carothers (2002), put it, transitology presents countries undergoing system change with a list of tasks, and if the country is unable to tick off any particular item on the list, then its democratic transition must be classified as a failure. The currently fashionable model of "democratic decline," which originates from the same roots as transitology, is subject to similar criticisms: see Cianetti-Hanley (2020) for more on this. For Hungarian critiques of transitology, see also Csizmadia (2019) or Körösényi-Illés-Gyulai (2020), who takes a Weberian approach.

203 Botos, 2003: 3; Schweitzer, 2002: 17; Bélyácz, 1993: 115; Ligeti, 2010: 72.
204 The Atlas of Economic Complexity, 2023.

country is able to diversify its export structure, how many countries export the same product (product ubiquity), and the technological sophistication of the products it exports. In 2000, Hungary was 23rd in the ECI ranking, but significant progress has been made since then, and by 2021 it had risen to eleventh place. This shows that the country's export structure has become much more diverse over the years, and it is able to export an increasing number and quantity of high-tech products to international markets. Hungary is also in a good position compared to its regional neighbors. The Czech Republic is sixth in the ECI rankings, Poland twenty-fifth, and Slovakia twelfth. In other words, increasing economic complexity is a regional trend, and the countries of the region uniformly expect a more complex economy to strengthen their own position. As such, it is hardly surprising that Hungary's economy has overtaken countries such as Greece or Spain in terms of complexity. Indeed, Hungary has overtaken or is about to overtake these countries in terms of overall development as compared to the EU average, so Hungary's export-oriented economic strategy and the technological level of its exports have resulted in significant progress by the standards of the international competition. The Economic Complexity Index is an extremely important tool for analyzing economic development and understanding international competitiveness. A diversified export structure with a large proportion of high-tech products contributes to growth and economic stability. It is vital to maintain and develop this trend, especially in the midst of global economic challenges of the sort we have experienced recently.

Situational Assessment:
The Hungarian Economy is Export-Oriented
To understand our situation, it is important to bear in mind the resources at our disposal. Though there were times in history when this was not the case, today Hungary is relatively poor in natural resources. Nor does the country possess outstanding advantages

in terms of land area or population: both are below the European average, and many European countries possess significantly more of each. Thus, in order to prosper, we must rely on our wits and on the cleverness, originality, and diligence of Hungarians. Translated into economic language, this means we must have an open economy to import the raw materials needed for the goods produced here and to export the goods that can be sold abroad with higher added value (this is where the diligence and ingenuity of Hungarians comes in). This explains why the emphasis of the Hungarian economy shifted in this direction after the first decade of the twenty-first century.

Leaving aside tax havens and microstates, Hungary currently has one of the most open economies in the world.[205] This is judged by the percentage of exports as a proportion of GDP, which in the case of Hungary amounts to 90 percent. Over the past twenty years, Hungary has gradually switched to an export-oriented economic model.[206] The ratio of exports to GDP in 2000 was only 67 percent. This export-oriented trend clearly affects GDP growth as well, as shown by the contribution of individual factors from the consumption side. According to the data, in 2022, exports made the largest contribution to GDP growth.[207]

All this indicates that Hungary's economic development and growth is closely linked to export activity. This export-oriented strategy creates an opportunity for Hungarian businesses to sell their products and services on wider international markets, thereby increasing the performance of the economy. At the same time, such dependence can also entail risks, since an economy that relies on exports may find itself more sensitive to changes in foreign markets and fluctuations in the world economy. The best antidote to sudden market shifts and fluctuations is an export-oriented economy that stands on multiple legs—meaning that a complex economy, of the

---

205 World Bank, 2023b.
206 Ibid.
207 CSO, 2023j.

sort that characterizes Hungary's economic structure, is the most effective countermeasure against these risks.

Situational Assessment: FDI is Continually Increasing

Hungary's economic model—open, complex, and driven by export and investment—was largely decided during the post-1990 period. In all the countries of the region, the ratio of exports and FDI to GDP is higher than the EU average,[208] but there are significant differences between their respective economic models. The Czech Republic, for example, is often referred to as the seventeenth German *Bundesland*—though strictly in terms of economic geography. At first glance, this somewhat pejorative statement seems to be supported by the macroeconomic data: the Czech economy—predominantly machine manufacturing and the automotive industry—is much more highly integrated into German value chains.[209] In addition, the Czech industrial complex is historically much stronger than Hungary's.[210] In the case of Poland, meanwhile, a domestic market of 38 million people represents a significant propulsive force, accounting as it does for nearly 60 percent of the GDP—more than 10 percentage points higher than the same figures in Hungary and the Czech Republic.[211] The Slovak model is perhaps the closest to the Hungarian one, but our northern neighbor may perhaps be considered to have shown the least economic dynamism among the Visegrád states in recent years.

Taking all these particularities into account, in a regional comparison, Hungary today has the second largest FDI as a percentage of GDP after the Czech Republic, with a total value

---

208 OECD, 2023.

209 Although Germany is the most important trade partner for all countries in the region, the Czech Republic trades a much larger share of exports and imports with the German market (for detailed data, see OECD, 2022).

210 Czech industry accounted for nearly 45 percent of the industrial production of the Austro-Hungarian Monarchy (Klein-Schulze-Vonyó, 2017: 72), and this industrial complex remained largely intact at the end of the Second World War.

211 Eurostat, 2023a.

amounting to 59 percent of GDP. In the region, only the Czech Republic, where this ratio is 70 percent, has a higher pool of working capital.[212] In addition, last year, despite all the economic difficulties, Hungary received the highest level of FDI in the region, amounting to 4.8 percent of GDP, which incidentally also exceeded the EU average.[213]

Situational Assessment: The Hungarian Economy is Innovative
It makes sense that the pursuit of an increasingly complex economy must go hand in hand with an increased capacity for innovation. After all, it is necessary not only to have a variety of exported products, but also that Hungary should be able to manufacture products that can be obtained from few other places worldwide. This requires an outstanding ability to innovate.

In terms of innovation capacity, over the last ten years Hungary has fought its way up from the bottom third of the EU rankings to the middle of the field. In terms of research and development expenditure as a proportion of GDP, Hungary has now overtaken a number of Western European countries, including Italy, Greece, and Spain.[214] Examining the number of registered patents, we can see that over the last twelve years this figure has grown more than two and a half times, so that by the end of 2021 the number of valid patents had reached almost 35,000.[215] All this despite the fact that there was hardly any significant increase in the 2000–2010 period, with the number of valid patents increasing only from 11,000 to about 13,000 or 14,000 across the decade.[216] Hungary's conception of universities and colleges as a strategic innovation sector also contributed greatly to the successes of the past thirteen years: in 2022, the country

---

212 OECD, 2023b.
213 OECD, 2023c.
214 Eurostat, 2023k.
215 CSO, 2023g.
216 Ibid.

spent nearly 2 percent of GDP on higher education.[217] Since 1990, the average number of years spent in education has never been as high as it is today. This is reflected in the fact that, in 2021, Hungary was the tenth best-performing EU country in terms of the proportion of the population with greater than primary education, while the number of those obtaining university degrees has increased by nearly 40 percent in the past dozen years or so.[218]

These positive developments are also reflected in the performance of Hungarian economic actors. The performance of Hungarian-owned companies has clearly improved over the past decade. Compared to 2010, Hungarian-owned companies and enterprises are already responsible for more than half of the gross investment value, and the same is true for companies' sales revenues. In 2010, foreign-owned companies accounted for the majority of investment and sales revenue.[219]

Special attention should be paid to small and medium-sized enterprises. The vast majority of these are owned by Hungarians, and as the Austrian example shows, they can be the "secret champions" of the future, demonstrating pioneering performance in niche markets at the European level.[220] Over the last decade, SMEs have significantly developed their regional and EU outlook.[221] Today, the Hungarian SME sector is the largest employer, with 70 percent of the workforce employed in such businesses. This is approximately 6 percentage points higher than the EU average, and only Slovakia has a higher overall percentage. As in our northern neighbor, the Hungarian SME sector contributes more than half of business added value—a figure nearly 5 percentage points higher than the EU average. Over the past ten years, Hungarian small and medium-

---

217 Kormány.hu, 2022.
218 Eurostat, 2023d; Eurostat, 2023e.
219 CSO, 2020.
220 For more on this, see Hausmann, 2020.
221 European Commission, 2023b.

sized enterprises have been able to increase their investment share, which now exceeds 37 percent.[222]

*Results: The Performance of the Hungarian Economy Has
Never Been So Good, and Catching Up is a Realistic Goal*
The complex, export-based, innovation-enhancing economic model works. And we have the data to prove it. Hungarian GDP at nominal value was HUF 27,000 billion in 2010, HUF 66,000 billion in 2022, and, based on 2023 trends, it is not impossible that it will soon reach HUF 80,000 billion. In other words, the size of the Hungarian economy has tripled in less than a decade and a half. But this raises the question of whether we have managed to achieve the goal set during the period of democratization: have we caught up with the developed countries?

In order to assess the growth potential of the Hungarian economy, we need to take a closer look at another metric, namely the growth of GDP per capita measured at purchasing power parity, in our primary international economic area, i.e., compared to the average development level of the European Union. In 2010, Hungarian GDP per capita, measured at purchasing power parity, was 66 percent of the EU average. This had risen to 77 percent by 2022.[223] Thus, in just over a decade Hungary came eleven percentage points closer to the average level of development of the European Union, which is one of the highest rates in the region. Moreover, in doing so, Hungary overtook Greece, an EU member since 1981, and Portugal, a member since 1986, in terms of GDP per capita measured at purchasing power parity. Examining this economic convergence in historical terms makes it clear that its extent is not independent of the government's performance. From a macroeconomic perspective, Hungary appears to have followed a similar growth path as the other countries in

---

222 CSO, 2021.
223 Eurostat, 2023h.

the region, since the average growth rate of the Czech Republic, Poland, and Slovakia was likewise around 10 percent.[224] Romania is the only one that, having started from a much lower base, had a faster pace of catch-up—though the assessment of its development is nevertheless quite controversial.[225] However, the distribution of Hungarian growth over time has been far from steady, and after the first Orbán government's term of office (1998–2002), under socialist

---

224 Own calculation based on data from Eurostat, 2022a.

225 On the one hand, it is worth noting, as a circumstance of economic history, that Romania—at least in the immediate post-1990 period—chose a different economic model from other post-Communist countries. At first, it did not implement full market opening and liberalization, but took its economic model in an autarkic direction. In many sectors, for example heavy industry, the mammoth state companies set up during socialism remained, and these could only be maintained through direct budget support (thus massively increasing external debt), amounting at one point to 13 percent of GDP. In later years, the Romanian government instead chose to follow the same neoliberal economic policy that Hungarian governments adopted in the post-2002 period. For more on the characteristics of Romania's economic transition, see Roşu, 2020. On the other hand, in recent years the success of the Romanian economy in terms of catching up has been truly remarkable: last year, GDP per capita, measured in terms of purchasing power parity, reached 77 percent of the EU average, which puts Romania on the same level as Hungary and Portugal. One may reasonably ask, in analytical terms, whether it is truly worthwhile to compare Hungary's economic performance with that of a country possessing double its population, access to the sea, and significantly greater mineral resources. Indisputably, per-capita GDP in Romania and Hungary are virtually the same, but key macroeconomic data—especially from concerning sustainable growth—indicate a Hungarian advantage. Although, for reasons of economic history, Romania inherited a lower public debt-to-GDP level from the Communist era, in the last ten years its debt has risen by almost 10 percentage points, while that of Hungary has fallen by almost 4 percentage points (Eurostat, 2023i). Hungary's economy is the 11th most complex in the world, while Romania's is only 19th (*Atlas of Economic Complexity*, 2023), and this is well reflected in the fact that 16 percent of Hungarian manufacturing exports are high-tech products with high added value, while this is true of only 11 percent of Romanian manufacturing exports. In addition, according to the EU's regional competitiveness index, all NUTS 2 regions in Romania, apart from the region that incorporates the capital, lag behind those in Hungary (European Commission, 2023). It is also worth looking more closely at welfare issues. Net average earnings are higher in Hungary, especially if we take families as the base unit. Childless Hungarians earn on average 5 percent more than their Romanian counterparts, while those raising at least two children earn an average of 8 percent more, measured in terms of purchasing power parity (Eurostat, 2023). In all, 18 percent of Hungarian residents are at risk of falling into poverty, while in Romania every fourth person is at risk (Eurostat, 2023b).

governments, it lagged significantly behind its regional peers. The growth potential experienced during the period of the first Orbán government returned only under the third Orbán government, i.e., after 2014, when it even exceeded the first. After the eight wasted years under socialist governments, four additional years were needed to put the economy in order, i.e., for Hungary to return to parity with its regional peers.[226]

Results: Tax Reduction, Improved Social Indicators

All very well, we may say. But does Hungary's economic growth look like this only in a sea of Excel tables, or does it have a noticeable effect on the country's everyday life as well? That is, have things changed in Hungary as a result of improved performance, a more complex economy, and higher levels of innovation? We are convinced that they have several different instances. One such instance is that the tax system has become simpler and more efficient, and even more importantly, the tax burden has decreased.

---

226 An important element in the drive to regain economic maneuvering room was the reduction in the national debt. Incidentally, since the adoption of Hungary's Constitution, the Fundamental Law, the so-called state debt rule has also incorporated this as a constitutional requirement. This amendment states that Parliament cannot adopt a budget that would result in the national debt rising above 50 percent of GDP, and so long as the national debt is above this level, budgets may only be adopted if they reduce the national debt relative to GDP (cf. Article 36 of the Fundamental Law). In accordance with this framework, the state debt level of 80 percent in 2010 was reduced to 65 percent by 2019, before the onset of the economic crisis that accompanied the COVID pandemic. As a result of the fiscal stimulus that mitigated the economic consequences of the pandemic—in line with the EU model and based on the temporary suspension of the Maastricht criteria—the level of public debt increased, but this one-off phenomenon did not cause a trend reversal: the public debt ratio has been on a downward trajectory since 2021 (Eurostat, 2023i). From the point of view of economic and financial sovereignty, what matters is not just the size of the debt, but also its internal structure. In 2010, almost half of the national debt was in foreign currencies, but in 2023, only a quarter was in a foreign currency (ÁKK, 2023). This has a bearing on the extent to which the population owns the national debt. Within the EU, Hungary has the largest proportion of government securities in public hands (21 percent), which reduces financial dependence on foreign institutional players, improves the income situation of households through the interest paid to the public, and thus circulates financial resources back into the economy (Eurostat, 2023j).

In recent years, significant positive changes have taken place in the so-called tax wedge and tax burden distribution. The tax wedge shows what percentage of the total labor costs (that is, gross wages and employer costs) is deducted by the state in the form of taxes and contributions. In 2000, the tax wedge significantly exceeded 54 percent, but by 2022 it had fallen to 41 percent.[227] The single-rate personal income-tax system introduced in 2013 applied a uniform rate of 16 percent, which was further reduced to 15 percent in 2016, while the level of contributions also decreased. This shifted the tax burden from work to consumption.[228]

The tax system was successfully transformed. In 2008, the share of indirect taxes as a proportion of revenue was still around 16 percent, but by 2020 it had increased to 18 percent. At the same time, direct taxes burdening labor, such as income tax, were reduced from 10 percent to below 7 percent.[229] Transforming the tax system made it possible to validate the principle that taxes should not be increased but collected. Hungary has performed exceptionally well in this regard, as the VAT margin, i.e., the difference between collectible and collected VAT, is barely 5 percent, making it one of the ten best-performing EU countries.[230] In Hungary, family support plays a prominent role in the tax system. Various discounts and exemptions have been introduced for several tax brackets. Young people under the age of twenty-five are uniformly exempted from paying social security, thus helping them find employment and work. Women under the age of thirty who have children receive an additional income-tax discount, thus encouraging childbearing and starting a family. And after the birth of children, there is an additional tax discount.

---

227 OECD, 2023e.
228 European Commission, 2022a: 134.
229 Ibid.
230 European Commission, 2022a: 32; European Commission 2023a.

The transformation of the tax system and the introduction of discounts have a positive effect on the economy and society. The reduction in the tax wedge helps economic growth, while the realignment of the tax burden from work to consumption has improved competitiveness and reduced the tax burden on particular social strata. Supporting families contributes to improving the demographic situation and easing families' financial burdens.

Of course, the meaning of all these measures and their outcomes cannot be sought in themselves. Their goal is to create an (economic) regulatory environment conducive to better living conditions for the Hungarian people as a whole. This is the measure of whether it made sense to transform the tax system and encourage people to start families. By now, it has become clear that the answer is an unambiguous "yes," while the development of a larger middle class has accelerated. In this context, another important societal indicator is the number of people at risk of falling into poverty. In terms of forestalling this, Hungary ranks among the top ten EU countries.[231] Crime levels are also telling in this regard, since they simultaneously indicate the efficiency of state institutions and indirectly reflect the financial situation of the Hungarian people. Moreover, by definition, a low crime rate and high levels of public safety are essential for a secure, predictable life. Given all this, it is gratifying that only 5 percent of the population in Hungary fell victim to crime of any

---

231 Eurostat, 2023b. The official fixing of energy prices and the reduction in utility bills played a key role in improving the living standards of the population, especially those in the lower, lower-middle, and middle-income groups. Annual per capita spending on housing maintenance and household energy was 25 percent of total spending in 2010, whereas, based on the available data, this rate dropped to 18.5 percent in 2020. Although all income groups were affected by the decrease in the cost of utilities, the several-percentage-point reduction in this type of expenditure was most significant for the fourth through the seventh and the second income deciles. This suggests that the social policy program of introducing fixed residential energy prices primarily benefited the middle class and had the largest effect on the financial situation of lower-income groups (KSH, 2023h). It should also be added that, despite the energy crisis, prices in Hungary for both electricity and natural gas are among the lowest (Hungarian Energy and Utilities Regulatory Office, MEKH, 2023).

sort, half the rate a decade ago. This makes Hungary the fifth safest country in the EU.[232]

The improving economic, social, and public safety indicators are only one side of the coin. In Hungary, the amount of time devoted to all kinds of relaxation, cultural enrichment, and recreation has perhaps not been as high as it is today since the era of the Austro-Hungarian Monarchy. Within a decade, Hungary has almost tripled the sums spent on culture and increased spending on sport more than tenfold.[233] From an EU perspective, as a proportion of GDP, Hungary spends the most on culture and on sporting opportunities available to the general public.[234] Spending on education has increased by about 35 percent over the last decade.[235] The number of young people with a higher education degree has likewise increased significantly in recent decades. In 2000, fewer than 15 percent of 25- to 34-year-olds had a degree, but by 2022 this proportion had

---

232 Zaidi, 2023. In the changed security environment, the ability to guarantee public safety, protect borders, and organize the performance of military defense tasks is emerging as a fundamental, even vital, state capability. Since 2015, Hungary has been one of the frontline countries in terms of migration pressure on Europe. According to data from the European Border and Coast Guard Agency (Frontex), in 2022, nearly half of all illegal border crossings in Europe were registered along the Western Balkan corridor on which our country is also located; the 145,000 illegal entries detected last year marked the highest level since 2015 (Frontex, 2023). It was precisely because of the security risks and the dangers inherent in uncontrolled mass illegal migration that Hungary strengthered its border protection system by creating a technical and legal border lock. The government has spent HUF 650 billion on this so far. Another key element in the changed security environment is the Russian-Ukrainian war currently being fought in our immediate vicinity. It was of vital importance for our country that we began to develop the armed forces years before the war began: the development of modern Hungarian armed forces began with the Zrínyi 2026 program announced in 2017. Between 2010 and 2022, defense spending increased nearly fourfold, and this year Hungary is meeting NATO's requirement that defense spending should come to 2 percent of GDP (including our country, only nine NATO member states will reach that level this year). At the same time, the production and development capacities of the Hungarian military industrial complex are becoming increasingly large scale.
233 CSO, 2023a; CSO, 2022.
234 Eurostat, 2021.
235 CSO, 2023c.

increased to almost 32 percent.[236] Between 2010 and 2022, turnover in the Hungarian hospitality sector—including spending by both domestic and foreign tourists—rose by 63 percent.[237] Worldwide, one of the biggest losers of the COVID pandemic was the tourism sector. Hungarians also traveled abroad less. If we look at the last "year of peace," i.e., 2019, the number of days Hungarians spent abroad had increased by around 50 percent compared to 2010.[238] The Hungarian film industry, meanwhile, has grown into a 650-million-dollar business.[239]

Results: Decreasing Unemployment, Improving Demographic Indicators

The demographic and employment statistics of Hungary in recent years show positive developments stemming from improved economic performance and changes in the tax system. The labor market situation has undergone significant development, with the unemployment rate falling to 3.4 percent in 2022, its lowest level in the last two decades for the 15–74 age group.[240] Youth unemployment also showed exceptionally good results, since the rate of approximately 10 percent was also the lowest in more than two decades. The employment rate also developed extremely favorably, reaching 74 percent, which is the highest result in the last two decades.[241] This indicates that more and more people are able to find a job in the labor market, which has a positive effect on the country's economic performance and social stability.[242]

---

236 CSO, 2023i.
237 CSO, 2023c.
238 CSO, 2023e.
239 Vourlias, 2022.
240 International Labour Organization (ILO), 2023a.
241 ILO, 2023.
242 In 2010, Hungary's employment rate was still 10 percentage points lower than that of Germany, but the difference between the two countries had fallen to 2 percentage points by 2022. In a global comparison, data are only available going back to 2013, but they too speak for themselves: During the early period, Hungary was in a club

The level of willingness to have children is another indicator by which the positive or negative direction of deep-seated social processes has traditionally been inferred. It is a telling fact that, starting in the 1960s, the fertility rate began a long, steady decline, but a turning point was reached in 2014, and since then the figures have improved somewhat. By 2021, the relevant figure had increased to 1.59, indicating the average number of children women give birth to over a lifetime.[243] The number of marriages also began a steady decline in the 1870s, but the turning point was reached in 2013.[244] Such trends reflect a change in recent years in attitudes toward social values and the idea of starting a family. The decrease in the number of divorces is another positive development: in 2001, approximately 24,000 divorces were registered, but by 2022, this number had fallen below 18,000.

What are the Consequences of All This,
and What Realistic Goals Can Hungary Set Itself?

So, it seems that the client of our imaginary dietitian instinctively followed a healthy diet and has better health than twenty years ago. As a result, the way is open for a genuine change of lifestyle—meaning, in Hungary's case, a realistic prospect of catching up. But we should not nurse any fond illusions that any of this will happen by itself. Before any big change, extra effort is needed. But it is all the more necessary to see where we have succeeded, what could

---

with countries even less fortunate in their historical development, such as Bosnia and Herzegovina, the Dominican Republic, and Moldova, but today it is already performing better than the EU average (ILO, 2023). In terms of numbers, the growth of employment is clearly indicated by the fact that in 2010 there were only 3.8 million people employed in Hungary, whereas by 2022 that figure had increased to 4.7 million, meaning that nearly one million new jobs were created during this period (KSH, 2023). Given the tight labor market and almost full employment, the real challenge for our country today is not unemployment, but a labor shortage.

243 CSO, 2023b.

244 Since 2010, the number of marriages in Hungary has doubled, meaning that 70 percent of children are born inside marriage, as opposed to 59 percent in 2010.

have been done better, what has so far only been done half-heartedly, and what needs to be improved. Fortunately, the above data and the processes behind them indicate the direction to some extent.

In any event, one thing that is clear from the above is that the export-oriented, open economic model works for Hungary. If managed competently, the Hungarian economy is capable of growth and innovation, produces its own added value, and the whole population benefits from these surplus goods. This is good news. As a result, it seems that we have already escaped the middle-income trap, as defined by the World Bank, which is also good. But it would be a mistake to pretend that this favorable situation is set in stone, or that we can now afford to rest on our laurels.

When the Hungarian people and the Hungarian political system began the process of democratization, the future they envisioned was not the world we now see before us. Nonetheless, we can now truthfully say we have come closer to the idea imagined at the time. The range and quality of goods and services now available in Hungary is essentially the same as in Western countries. We can travel freely, there is no censorship, information is freely accessible, there are jobs, wages are rising, and a Hungarian student is free to enroll in any high school or university in the world. All the same, we all instinctively feel that we are not yet where we want to be. This is not yet the level of development we dreamed of.

Two indicators support this sense of dissatisfaction. First, Hungary's level of economic development is currently at around 77 percent of the EU average, while Austria's stands at 125 percent. Average earnings lag behind the average earnings of countries that are still ahead of us in terms of development, or that joined the EU earlier. We now stand, like a character in a fairy tale, at a three-way fork in the road. Either we can forge ahead, or we can maintain our current position, or—God forbid—we can slide backward. It is this thought that gives Hungarians committed to the future of their country no peace of mind.

What is more, the data on development lend some weight to our disquiet, because as we will see, there is such a thing as a country dropping out of the ranks of developed countries and falling back into what the World Bank calls the "middle-income trap." There are also other questions regarding the international rankings: What if the scale is insufficiently nuanced? What if there are in fact degrees between moderately developed and developed countries, and Hungary is in this intermediate state?

These are serious concerns. That is why the task of the years ahead will be to get Hungary out of this category, which does not exist on the World Bank scale, but lies somewhere between moderately developed and developed. In other words, let us choose the path at this three-way fork in the road that leads upward, so as to avoid stagnation or backsliding.

2.2. Paths of Progress: How Can the Development of a Country be Measured, and What Do Development Indices Tell Us?

Most international development rankings class Hungary among the developed countries, whether in terms of income levels or economic performance. However, these rankings are not necessarily divided proportionally. There can be huge differences between developed countries, whereas countries classed as low-income and middle-income may in fact be quite close to each other in terms of overall development. There are grounds for suspecting that the "developed country" category could be further subdivided.

Alongside the consideration that further subdivisions may be useful, there are worrying signs that it is particularly difficult to get from the lower bracket of high-income countries to the true top tier. It is as if this invisible category also conceals a trap analogous to the middle-income trap. In light of this, in the following we will examine Hungary's development indicators, present the difficulties that moderately developed countries have to overcome, and outline how this might be done. We will then apply these formulas to the level of development Hungary currently finds itself at.

The Development of Hungary

The level of development of a given country, in our case Hungary, can be examined in terms of several key indicators.[245] One important

---

245 In this regard, we should also note that inconsistent definitions mean that the same country may be placed in a different category by each international organization. Of course, the G7 countries have a permanent place among the developed, high-income countries, but the categorization of, for instance, Hungary changes regularly.

indicator, at least in our case, is the level of development compared to the EU average, typically calculated on the basis of GDP. The World Bank—which provides the most widely used and referenced division—simply uses gross national income (GNI) per capita as a basis, immediately sorting countries into four large categories.[246] Countries with per capita income above $13,205 are categorized as high-income countries. Moving down the scale, countries with per capita incomes of between $4,256 and $13,205 are classed as upper-middle-income countries, whereas lower-middle-income countries have per capita incomes of between $1,086 and $4,256. Per capita income of less than $1,086 puts a country in the low-income category. On this basis, Hungary, with per capita annual income of $19,000, clearly belongs in the high-income category.[247] Hungary reached $13,000 in 2008, the year the global economic crisis began, and that Europe-engulfing crisis had naturally eroded some of that wealth by 2010. However, between 2010 and 2021, national per capita income in Hungary increased by about 25 percent. In regional terms, the increase was 24 percent in Poland, 21 percent in the Czech Republic, which had been considered a kind of economic model for Hungary, and 15 percent in Slovakia.[248]

---

246 Hamadeh-Van Rompaey-Metreau, 2023.

247 World Bank, 2023f.

248 Growth of per capita income measured at purchasing power parity before 2010 was of course higher than in the ten years that followed. Explosive development was a widespread phenomenon in Eastern and Central Europe at that time and can be explained by the transition from a planned to a market economy, the extremely low base the country was starting from (Fischer et al., 1996), and the appearance of EU development funds after 2004. The impact of these structural change to the economic system was so pronounced that economic growth in our region exceeded that of the "Little Tigers" of Southeast Asia, which burst onto the world economic stage during that period, and even of the Baltic states (Leigh-Fabrizio-Mody, 2009: 4). To all this, we must also add that the countries of our region embarked on the economic transition from different economic starting situations, which in turn forced them to take different economic and political paths. For more on this, see Réti, 1995.

Another prestigious organization, the International Monetary Fund, has developed three categories: developed economies; emerging middle-income economies, and developing low-income economies. However, when it talks about income categories, in addition to GNI per capita, the IMF also takes into account a number of other economic variables such as budgetary position, foreign trade, and public debt.[249] The UN also predominantly uses World Bank data, but in addition to GNI per capita, it also takes into account whether the country in question is a net energy exporter or importer, as well as GDP growth rates.[250] The IMF places Hungary in its second category, meaning that it is placed among the group of emerging middle-income countries, whereas the UN lists it as a developed country.

Everything Seems Fine at First Glance, But We are Still Far Behind the Truly Developed States: We Need More Finely Calibrated Measurements

Looking only at the above categories and data, the reader might be forgiven for thinking that there is no real challenge facing us. All existing scales categorize Hungary as a high-income developed country. But on closer examination, we can see that this is because the scales themselves are biased. Think about it this way: the lowest category includes countries where per capita income is below $1,000. Any state with per capita earnings above $13,000 is categorized as high-income. But countries with the highest values, such as Luxembourg, which admittedly is considered extreme, have GNI per capita levels of $120,000 dollars. But if we were to set the scale between the real top and bottom, so say from $0 to $130,000, then the bottom 10 percent would make up the lowest three categories and the upper 90 percent would form a single

---

249 IMF, 2022: 38.
250 UN, 2022: 153–59.

category. But in order not to deal with extremes only, let us take a look at countries a little more typical than Luxembourg: The average GNI per capita of the G7 is $55,000. This is approximately $35,000 above the level in Hungary, whereas the upper limit of the lowest income category is approximately $18,000 dollars below the level in Hungary. With such disproportionalities, it is easy to see that even the most frequently cited and widely used scale cannot show the differences that exist between our country and the G7 countries.[251]

Of course, we have no intention in these pages of seeking to develop a new methodology for the World Bank that would more precisely represent the differences between individual countries. But if we were to attempt to roughly partition the higher end of the scale, i.e., between the lower boundary of officially high-income countries ($13,000) and the G7 average ($55,000), we might choose $40,000 per capita GNI measured at purchasing power parity as a reasonable cutoff point demarcating what could be called the elite club of high-income countries.[252]

The suspicion that the scales have been unevenly divided is reinforced by the fact that there have been instances of countries slipping back from high to medium levels of development. Just as a country can break free from the trap of medium development through improved performance, so it can also return to that state. Between 1960 and 2022, there were several such examples, including

---

251 Nielsen (2013) and Vázquez-Sumner (2013) also point out that the World Bank's classification is more of a wide-angle perspective on the relative development of countries. Thus, some general relationships can indeed be formulated, such as that the greater part of the world's poorest are concentrated in countries belonging to lower income categories. However, the classification does not consider other aspects of development, and thus only gives a rough picture. A good example of this is India, which according to the World Bank belongs to the lower-middle income group, but has a significant, independent space program. What is more, as the aforementioned studies also show, the fact that a country has been placed in a higher income category does not mean that it has also made substantial structural developments.

252 It is worth noting that this value roughly coincides with what Prime Minister Viktor Orbán designated as the 2030 goal for Hungary in his 2023 Tusnádfürdő speech.

Argentina, Brazil, and Venezuela. In the first half of the 2010s, all three were considered high-income countries based on GNI per capita but, in the second half of the decade, they were pushed out of this group.[253] By contrast, we are not aware of any countries above the $40,000 level slipping back into a lower category.

In other words, it seems that such an intermediate category does indeed exist, but those in this intermediate category are at greater risk of backsliding, stagnation, or of slipping into a trap from which they will struggle to extricate themselves. Hungary must therefore strive to avoid this. The good news is avoiding such traps is indeed possible. After all, countries in the $4,000–13,000 category also face a trap, known as the middle-income trap. In contrast to the potential trap that Hungary may face as a high-income country, much research has already been conducted on the middle-income trap, and the findings on how to avoid it also serve as a good starting point even for countries with a GNI per capita of $19,000.

What is the Middle-Income Trap?

The situation is complicated by the fact that, as so often, definitions of the middle-income trap are not always consistent. The possible definitions can be divided into at least three categories,[254] in that the question can be approached from a political, functional, or economic perspective. From a political point of view, the trap consists of an inability or unwillingness on the part of a country's leadership to transform its institutional and economic structure, in which low-wage sectors have tended to predominate.[255] Looked at from a functional

---

253 It is important to note that the World Bank recalculated the threshold values for each group in 2021, and stated at the time that this recalculation would be repeated annually on the basis of inflation. In addition, the per capita gross national income of the three mentioned countries only just exceeded the threshold even in the short period when they were officially categorized among the developed countries.

254 Glawe-Wagner, 2016: 511–12.

255 The examination of political systems is a comparative discipline, and its purpose is to place a given political system somewhere on a spectrum between democracy and dictatorship. Political science has identified countless ideal types between the two

point of view, meanwhile, the trap is a self-perpetuating condition that can be described in terms roughly analogous to the poverty trap.[256] Pierre-Richard Agénor similarly argues that the trap is a pernicious, suboptimal but stable equilibrium (bad equilibrium).[257] The definition taken from an economic perspective is perhaps the most accurate of all. The essence of this is that a country's GDP per capita, measured at purchasing power parity, plateaus at a certain level.

---

endpoints, so we can talk about Western, liberal, pluralist, substantive (maximalist), procedural (minimalist), controlled, illiberal, quasi, or incomplete democracies, as well as hybrid regimes, authoritarian states, and totalitarian dictatorships. This framework can be usefully applied if we take into account the individual characteristics of a country's political system. However, many of the variables cause major interpretative difficulties, even if autocracies and dictatorships can be confidently identified (see, for example, Geddes-Wright-Frantz, 2018). We have already spoken about the methodological problems of transitology. In the last two or three decades, however, political science has become more blinkered than ever. A good example of this is that one sector of the discipline has attempted to measure the adoption of a well-defined system of values and norms in institutional and societal terms (see Linz, 1996: 16–22; Mayre-Geißel, 2018), while another has attempted to categorize "hybrid regimes" by dividing the concept into more than a dozen new categories, so that even the slightest deviation from the ideal, specified form of democracy immediately lands a state in the "hybrid" category (see Bozóki-Hegedűs, 2017: 8–17; Friedman, 2011: 48–49; Diamond, 2002: 23). Deviation from the ideal type can occur for many reasons: it may be on account of the political elite (Zakaria, 2007), due to local characteristics or historical antecedents (Levitsky-Way, 2002), or because the process of democratization has stalled (Cassani, 2014). This logic also fits, for example, the evaluation of good governance as a prerequisite for democracy. Most of the literature considers it desirable to reduce the role of the state (for more on this, see Ewalt-Jennings, 2004; Nekola, 2006). However, after reading through it, we have come to the conclusion that from the perspective of the political science literature, the categorization of states as democracies or hybrid regimes (and various subvariants thereof) is fundamentally based on the level of a country's compliance with the worldview of liberal democracy.

256 The fundamental elements of this were summarized by Hajnalka Katona: "The essence of the poverty trap is that someone who was born poor needs a certain level of (human or monetary) capital to rise to a higher social status, which—precisely on account of having been born poor—cannot be obtained" (Katona, 2021). The theory of learned helplessness can also serve as an analogy. This theory is well-known in psychology and describes a state in which individuals becomes so passive as a result of successive negative stimuli that they do not even try to change their situation. The phenomenon can be observed both in the animal world and in human societies (Seligman, 1972: 407–12).

257 Agénor, 2017: 772.

Approaching the question from a different angle, it is possible to use all these definitions to spot the warning signs of an imminent trap situation. These can be briefly summarized as follows: slowdown or grow stagnant following a period of continuously rising GDP per capita. That is, a country is able to increase its GDP for a while, but then loses this ability, at which point stagnation sets in. This is not a rare phenomenon. Indeed, it seems to be more the rule than the exception. Of course, comparing individual countries in this way is inherently problematic, given their differing economic and geographical circumstances, but the problem is well illustrated by the fact that, according to several analyses, since 1960, just thirteen out of sixty countries in the middle-income category managed to escape it and join the elite club of developed countries.[258]

This low proportion is shocking and perhaps even worrying. The low number of successful countries indicates that it is easier to fall into the trap than to escape it. This should in turn warn us that the middle-income trap is a real problem that needs to be tackled. Fortunately, theories have also been developed concerning the reasons for its persistence. Just as its definitions are multifaceted, so its causes can also be described from multiple perspectives.

How Can the Middle-Income Trap be Avoided?

Briefly, in economic terms, we can define the middle-income trap as a process by which moderately developed countries lose the

---

258 According to Glawe-Wagner (2016), Equatorial Guinea, Greece, Hong Kong, Israel, Japan, Mauritius, Portugal, Puerto Rico, South Korea, Singapore, Spain, and Taiwan are the countries that have successfully escaped the middle-income trap in recent decades. Doner-Schneider (2016) argues that we can also include Ireland and Finland. Although the studies are based on a solid methodological foundation, certain difficulties relating to the analysis of the middle-income trap are still perceptible. The global classification, which is considered the starting point for most analyses of this sort, already classifies Hungary as a high-income country—even though Equatorial Guinea and Mauritius remain in the upper-middle income category, while in the list of raw GNI per capita, in addition to these two countries, Puerto Rico also ranks below Hungary.

competitive advantage of cheap and abundant labor compared to less developed countries but remain unable to move up in global value chains. There can be many reasons for this situation, such as:[259]

- low productivity
- decreasing yields from existing production methods
- inadequately or improperly trained human capital
- insufficient infrastructural development, or poorly maintained infrastructure
- poor access to credit and financial services in general
- low levels of innovation
- an unfavorable business environment
- high income inequality[260]
- weak political institutions
- poor access to public services[261]

If we look through the economic reasons, it may appear that we are still only dealing with symptoms. Even if we identify these symptoms, the real question is what kind of antidote we can provide for their causes. From this, it directly follows that the political and institutional elements of the medium development trap must also be dealt with. In other words, we must ask what the leadership of a country can do to avoid the above symptoms and successfully break through the glass ceiling that looms above moderately developed countries. This question strikes us as obvious because it is easy to see that the political reasons for becoming mired in the middle-income trap may be that the political leadership is unable to transform the

---

259 The aspects indicated here were compiled on the basis of the combined criteria used by several articles dealing with the middle-income trap and its causes (for more information, see Agénor, 2017: 778–82; Doner-Schneider, 2016: 612–27; Glawe-Wagner, 2012: 25–26).
260 Inequality is classically measured according to the so-called Gini coefficient, which has also proved relevant in evaluating Hungary's current situation.
261 See more about this in Calderón-Servén, 2004; Kharas-Kohli, 2011: 288.

institutional and economic structure of the country in such a way that ongoing development is stimulated.

What should the political leadership do? The state can best help break out of the trap if it takes an active role in rethinking cooperation between the private and public sectors and assumes a coordinating role.[262] This entails both vertical and horizontal coordination. Horizontal coordination means that the government invests adequate energy in goal-oriented cooperation between its own organizations, and at the same time develops the ability to effectively coordinate with market players. Additionally, market players have to be convinced that close cooperation with the state is necessary. Vertical coordination means that the state must enforce new protocols of institutional transformation at all levels of the public sector.

In addition, education, including the transformation of higher education so that it better fits the needs of market players, is extremely important. This is most important in the field of research and development because it creates an opportunity for the country's economy to move up in global production chains. In addition, the country's leadership must attempt to ensure that the increase in economic performance does not entail drastic disparities in income, so that destabilizing wealth and income inequality can be avoided. That is why it is important not to deindustrialize too early.[263] But effective cooperation between the government and the private sector is not sufficient to avoid the middle-income trap. Broad social

---

262 Doner-Schneider, 2016: 612–15.

263 Harvard economist Dani Rodrik also points out (2016: 2) that the decision-making pressure of transitioning toward a service economy and downsizing industry is actually a false dichotomy for countries that want to level up economically. Underlying this assumption is the apparent fact that services play a prominent role in the economic structure of developed countries, so it seems logical to direct all resources toward the service sector, and scale down industrial capacities. However, instead of deindustrialization, what is needed is the parallel development of both the service sector and industry. Like Doner and Schneider, he considers income differences due to deindustrialization as a starting point.

support is also necessary, as economic growth requires a structural change across the public and private sectors, and the lack of broad social support breeds resistance, making it impossible to achieve the stated goals.[264]

So, in addition to these elements, it is also worth mentioning the two criteria of Homi Kharas and Harinder Kohli, who are among the most eminent scholars of the middle-income trap.[265] In their view, to be successful it is not necessary for a country to excel in every element outlined above. It must, however, specialize in some area of the economy, designating key strategic breakthrough sectors. Moreover, in spite of what may be strong impulses to intervene, state coordination must stop at the designation of goals and frameworks and leave the realization of these goals to the private sector.[266]

Real-World Examples of Success

Having looked at these theoretical aspects, it may be worth examining some real-world examples. South Korea, Finland, and Ireland are textbook examples of successfully escaping the middle-income trap. These countries show not only that it is possible to enter the group of developed countries, but also that there is not just one way of doing

---

264 Doner-Schneider, 2016: 618.

265 Kharas-Kohli, 2011: 286.

266 Modern development economics primarily examines how structural changes in economies, and the accompanying technological change, can serve economic convergence (see Lewis, 1954; Chenery, 1979; McMillan-Rodrik, 2011; Thirlwall, 2011). For many years, the key claim of this branch of economics was that as part of economic development resulting from structural change, countries would sooner or later de-industrialize, and their economy would ultimately come to be driven more or less exclusively by the service sector (for more, see Fisher, 1939; Colin, 1940). In addition to Rodrik (2016) cited above, Dasgupta-Singh (2007) and Jaef (2023) have also examined this theory and the supposed necessity of deindustrialization. In the context of technological change, the literature of development economics has identified a series of independent variables that are necessary for successful development. These include competitive economic institutions (Hall-Jones, 1999), a state that creates such institutions, but also plays an active role in its own right (Acemoğlu-Robinson, 2013; Glaeser et al., 2004), infrastructural connectivity (Radelet-Sachs, 1998), and social and cultural traditions (Tabellini, 2010).

so. Quite the reverse: these three economic development models are based on different strategies and rely on separate elements of the global economy.

In addition to the development of an export and investment-oriented economic structure, one of the main pillars of South Korea's effort to catch up was an industrial policy and form of industrial development that assumed an active state role. The Korean miracle that took place between 1960 and 1980, the great economic leap, led to the world of today, in which South Korean companies such as Samsung are at the forefront of global technology. However, it is important to note that Korea's national champion companies—contrary to the popular business myth—did not start as garage enterprises. Companies like Samsung were built on foreign working capital from both East and West, including Japanese and American investment, as well as the further development of purchased licenses.[267] In other words, before South Korean companies were capable of developing on their own, their success was based on outside capital and licensed technology transfer. The South Korean model emphasized structural change, and instead of traditional sectors, new technologically successful industries such as electronics and IT became important. The result of this strategy was the attraction of foreign capital, as well as the retention of the highly qualified domestic workforce and the ability to innovate.

Finland's economic growth was based on two key elements: one was its invaluable policy of active neutrality during the Cold War, and the other was economic restructuring. In the 1950s, the Finnish economy was driven by manufacturing—chiefly shipbuilding, timber, and the chemical industry—that was especially energy intensive during this period. The oil crises of the 1970s therefore had a major impact on Finnish economic growth. The risk of even more serious ramifications was mitigated by the country's geopolitical

---

267 Chung, 2011: 336.

position. Extensive trade links with the Soviet Union meant not only a market for its manufactured goods, but also energy imports at a price significantly below the global market rate.[268]

Alongside the spectacular economic performance of South Korea and Finland, the economic leap of the "Celtic Tiger" may also be of interest. During the period of the Irish miracle, Ireland's economic growth far exceeded not only the EU average, but also the growth rate of the large European economies, i.e., the United Kingdom, France, Germany, and Italy.[269] During this period, Ireland caught up with the EU average very quickly,[270] and escaped the middle-income trap.[271] The Irish model was based on radical tax reductions and the stimulation of foreign investment.[272] Starting in the mid-1990s, Irish governments continuously reduced corporate tax, while at the same time the ratio of inflowing FDI to GDP increased from 1.5 percent in 1994 to 16.1 percent by 2021.[273] The Irish economic strategy

---

268 Hjerppe, 1989.

269 The period of the Irish economic miracle is typically seen as running from about 1995 to 2007. At that time, Ireland's average annual economic growth rate was roughly three times that of the EU and the major European economies. Ireland's peak economic growth rate was reached in 1997, when the output of the economy increased by more than 11 percent in one year, while in the following years this figure remained between 8 and 10 percent (World Bank, 2023d).

270 Ireland reached the EU average of GDP per capita, measured at purchasing power parity, in 1995, and by 2020 it could already boast double the EU's average level of development. Last year, its GDP per capita, measured at purchasing power parity, was 234 percent of the EU average (Eurostat, 2022a).

271 The Celtic Tiger also exited the group of middle-income countries in the first half of the 1990s. Based on the World Bank's classification, Ireland is today a high-income country, and its GNI per capita value is nearly six times the entry threshold of $13,205 set for high-income countries (World Bank, 2023g).

272 The assumption of the Irish government was that a radical reduction in the corporate tax rate would significantly increase the volume of FDI coming into the country. Today, the economic literature agrees that this connection exists. This strategy works particularly well if the country in question can create a competitive interest rate environment in the region by reducing corporate tax rates. For more, see Benassy-Quere et al., 2001; Ghinamo et al., 2007; Gropp-Kostial, 2001.

273 In 1994, the Irish corporate tax rate still stood at 40 percent. The radical tax reductions were carried out by the Ahern government, which cut the corporate tax rate from 32 to 12.5 percent in 2003. Ireland's corporate tax rate is one of the lowest among OECD countries (OECD, 2023d).

bases growth on external factors, thus primarily on multinational companies, most of which operate in the service sector.[274] These genuinely represent high added value, and in many cases companies do not merely open subsidiaries in Ireland, but choose to locate their European headquarters there. However, the hyperglobalized nature of the modern Irish economy means that it is very exposed to external shocks.[275]

Conclusions? It is Impossible to Get Ahead Without FDI, Coordination Between State and Market Processes, And Good Economic and Cultural Relations

These challenges, based on the lessons learned from countries that have escaped the middle-income trap, prompt us to reflect on Hungary. The most important lesson, in terms of escaping this trap, is that the operation of the state needs to be thoroughly reformed, and close cooperation with market players is needed. Coordination between market players should not be taken lightly, as it is essential for successful performance in the international arena. Strategic areas must be identified where we expect competitive national champions to emerge on international markets, thereby stimulating investment. However, the state cannot stop there—it must ensure that high-intensity working capital continuously flows into the country. To date, we know of no examples of a real increase in income without significant working capital.

In addition to the above, the state has a central role to play in supporting domestic innovation. Facilitating cooperation between higher education institutions and market participants is not merely desirable; it is vital. Equally important is the active participation of the state in ensuring that money-market and banking services are

---

274　O'Leary, 2011: 81.

275　The significant role of FDI also entails vulnerability. FDI accounts for nearly 15 percent of Irish employment, and 70 percent of foreign operating capital comes from the United States (CSO, 2017). See also O'Rourke, 2017: 41.

easily available to everyone, and that citizens have easy access to public services. While the latter help to stimulate economic growth and raising income levels, it is important also to remain attentive to the potential emergence of excessive disparities in income levels. We must likewise remain mindful of the role of industry, which provides a stable source of income for society and paves the way for a broader economic rise. By ignoring the importance of industrial production, we risk the futures of broad sections of society. As we will see later, all these stipulations fit neatly into a strategy aimed at exploiting the opportunities inherent in connectivity.

2.3. Hungary's Prospects: Bloc Formation Does Not Serve Hungarian Interests, and a Strategy is Needed to Reverse the Prevailing Logic

"It is in our long-term interest that the nations of the Danube Basin should learn to understand one another, become better acquainted, and discover the prerequisites for peaceful coexistence…"
(Count Gyula Andrássy Jr.)

After examining trajectory for catching up, the primary remaining question concerns the degree to which it can be sustained in the future. Does the world presented in the previous chapter, seemingly headed as it is toward the formation of rival blocs, benefit Hungary? As the West increasingly downgrades its relations with the rest of the world, can Hungary succeed in climbing to a higher level and permanently joining the ranks of truly developed states? By this point, the reader may well have surmised the answer: blocs are not in Hungary's interest. The reasons for this can be summarized in at least three ways. It is disadvantageous on cultural, geographical, and—perhaps most importantly of all—economic grounds.

The cultural element is the "softest" of the three: Hungary is a Western state but one that remains proud of its Eastern cultural roots. We understand and speak the language of the West, having been a part of it for a thousand years thanks to Western Christianity. But Hungary was always most successful when it was able to balance between Western and Eastern empires. It was able to do this by communicating not only with Western allies, but also with Eastern partners. This was the case when Hungary was independent, during the first half millennium or so of its history, and also when it could exist only as part of some larger empire or federal system. Failure was always assured whenever either a Western power or an Eastern empire decided to change us, attempting to alter our culture and shape us in their own image. A bloc-based world and an international order viewed as a struggle between democracies and autocracies threatens us once again with the imposition of cultural models, the denial of our own historical experiences, and the abandonment of our values, all of which are barriers to our success.

The geographical reason is somewhat "harder." Hungary is not only culturally open to both West and East, but also geographically, as it is positioned on a geopolitical fault line. This can present dangers but also opportunities, and the task of Hungarian geopolitical thinking is always precisely to minimize the dangers and make the most of the opportunities. Today, the biggest opportunities are found in the fact that East-West trade routes almost without exception pass through Hungary. Therefore, it is in Hungary's express interest to develop East-West and North-South trade, as well as transport and energy infrastructure. But in an increasingly bloc-based world, where infrastructural relations are seen as a liability and an increased risk of hostile intrusion, the developments necessary for economic progress are rejected, and our country cannot rise.

Finally, the strongest and most measurable reasons are economic. Hungary is poor in both natural resources and energy carriers. In a world order based on rival blocs, Hungary would be unable to acquire the cheap raw materials and energy necessary for economic growth. The same is true regarding the inflow of FDI and foreign capital. According to all current calculations, global economic growth in the coming decades is expected not primarily within the Western world but outside it. As we have seen, no country can become truly developed without a significant influx of foreign operating capital. As such, Hungary cannot afford the luxury of renouncing non-Western sources of FDI in the future. In addition, it is important to bear in mind that Hungary is a complex, export-oriented economy, so smooth international trade and good connections to trade channels are of fundamental importance. Bloc formation and the erection of trade barriers favors neither. And finally, in recent decades, the technological differences between the West and the East have also disappeared. This means that now equally advanced technology can reach Hungary from both directions, and we can participate in related innovation and research and development. A world order based on blocs, by contrast, would preclude all this. In the following, we will examine these points in more detail.

Cultural Reasons

Culturally, Hungary is situated in a very special part of Europe. The Hungarian language is unique and difficult to learn, but its culture has free valences in all directions. It can be considered an essentially Western state, but its historical and cultural heritage preserves links to the Eastern world, since the Hungarian tribes came from the East a thousand years ago, and the Hungarian people still maintain this heritage. Kinship relations are also taken into account in the East, and more than one Central Asian country views us as distant relatives, or at least as old acquaintances.

This double identity determined and shaped the destiny of the nation in the past centuries, both in successful periods and in times of trial. In the first five hundred years, the Hungarians made excellent use of their talents and successfully balanced between two cultural worlds. One of our most prominent relics, the Holy Crown, also demonstrates this: the two parts of the crown, which were made in two different cultural centers, namely Rome and Constantinople, were united and made into a single symbol, perfectly symbolizing this duality.[276]

During the founding of the state, at the beginning of the reign of Saint Stephen around the turn of the first and second millennium, the Hungarian leadership successfully applied a similar strategy to counterbalance the influence of the Byzantine Empire, which was then considered the dominant power, by strengthening relations with the West. But this did not mean the development of unilateral

---

276 For a detailed examination of the origins of the Holy Crown, including its dual structure of *Corona Graeca* and *Corona Latina*, see Barabássy, 2018; Bartoniek, 1987; Péri, 1994; Zétényi, 2002: 40–69.

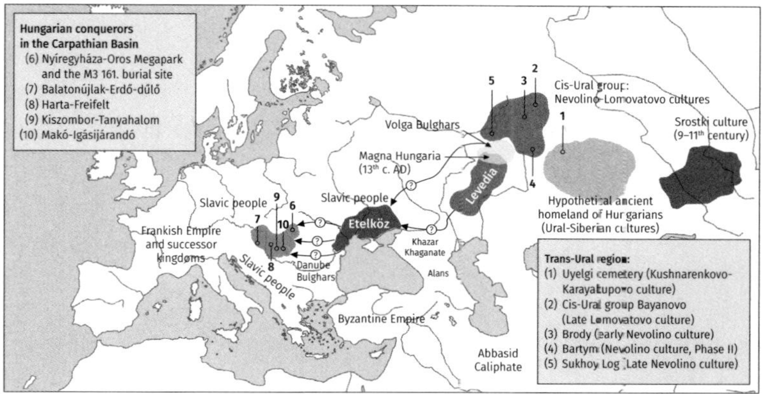

Figure 16: The migration route of the Hungarians from their presumed homeland to the Carpathian Basin. *Source: Csáky et al., 2020*

dependencies. While we asked for a crown from the spiritual leader of the Western world, the Pope, we kept our distance from the mostly German-speaking Holy Roman Empire in order to preserve our independence. The house of Árpád, Hungary's first royal dynasty, established a balance in its relations with the East and the West. This is well reflected in the number of saints among the members of the dynasty, since they gave saints to both the Eastern Orthodox and Western Catholic churches. Historical sources also prove that we were the first to become aware of the Mongol threat, thanks to our excellent relations with those to the East.[277] Before the Battle

---

277 The multiple efforts by Hungarians of the thirteenth century to seek out their ancestral homeland in the east and any of their compatriots who might have remained there played an important role in the perception and recognition of the danger posed by the Mongol Empire. On his first trip, Brother Julianus learned about the Mongols' aims of Westward expansion, and after his return home in 1236, he informed the Pope as soon as he was able. The following year, Julianus set out again, but this time his task was to scout the activities and movements of the invading enemy. Then, he received a letter addressed to King Béla IV of Hungary from the Mongols, in which they made plain their intention to conquer the country. Cf. Fodor, 2012; Szilágyi, 2023: 369–71.

of Muhi in 1241, Hungary spent several years strengthening its defenses and adapting to new challenges.[278]

Then came what the author of the Hungarian national anthem called the "storm-swept centuries of the Hungarian people," when the Turkish conquest split Hungary into three parts, and only the Principality of Transylvania was able to preserve a degree of independence. During the era of Ottoman expansion, Hungary often became a battleground between them and their great-power rival, the Habsburgs. Transylvania's strategy in this situation was to form an alliance with whichever power currently appeared less threatening, in order to counterbalance the influence of the other.[279] Then, when we became part of the Austrian Empire after the expulsion of the Turks, we never completely renounced our independence and our essential otherness: Hungary never became an Austrian hereditary province. We finally came to an agreement with the Austrians in 1867, after many uprisings, two wars of independence, and subsequent periods of oppression, with the fear that the then-dominant Eastern empire, that of the Russians, had played no small role in this.[280]

---

278 Expecting the main attack to come across the Carpathians, as part of his preparations King Béla IV strengthened the fortifications on the Verecke Pass from the Carpathian side and ordered the palatine to defend the pass. In addition, he discussed matters of defense at a national assembly and instructed the gathered dignitaries to prepare their troops. For more on this, see Mika, 1900: 630; Veszprémy, 1994: 28.

279 For a thorough and detailed account of the history of Transylvania, see Köpeczi, 1986.

280 Gerő (2014: 243) draws attention to the "high-level" perspective of the Austro-Hungarian Compromise, i.e., its interpretation at the level of European power politics. According to this view, the Austro-Hungarian Dual Monarchy, which was born in 1867, ultimately created a system of public law that enabled it to solve the challenges arising from its geopolitical situation, meaning it could play a kind of balancing and barrier role by disrupting Russia's presence in the Balkans. This was necessitated by the fact that the Russian Empire—in view of the steady decline of the Ottoman Empire—adopted a policy of vigorous expansion in the Balkans and South-Eastern Europe from the middle of the 19th century (cf. Davies, 2002: 811–13). In other words, the Austrian-Hungarian constitutional settlement, which contemporaries dubbed the Compromise, was underpinned by important geostrategic considerations, and responding to these by reaching such

However, this compromise involved the voluntary surrender of our independent foreign policy, so we had no say on whether or not to participate in the first great global military conflagration of the twentieth century.[281] With the end of the war, Hungary regained its independence but lost its middle power status, and because it had much less room for balancing, it could not resist the growing power of the Third Reich. In the Second World War, Hungary was constrained to become an ally of the Nazis, leading to even greater losses.

During the Communist period, Hungary belonged to the Eastern Bloc, and as a result it lost its connection with the West. After many centuries, this was perhaps the greatest blow of all. It followed from the logic of the bipolar Cold War world that we had to adapt in every way to the model given by the Soviet Union, the bloc leader, whether in terms of political organization, the shaping of social processes, or the development of the country's economic structure.[282] In the absence of active Western relations, we could not counterbalance the influence of the Eastern superpower. And this led us down a dead-end path, with the forced denial of our cultural strengths resulting

---

a compromise—as part of an effort to achieve a balance of power in the Central European region—was largely in line with the centuries-old traditions of Hungarian political thinking.

281 According to Galántai (2006: 35), at the outbreak of the First World War, "the foreign policy of the Monarchy came under the influence of Berlin. And in Berlin, they judged the situation in terms of a *general, continental war*" (emphasis in the original). Prime Minister István Tisza recognized the same thing: although he at first opposed war, he was soon forced to change his position because he saw the inevitability of it—which arose from the structure of the Monarchy and its subordinate position relative to the German Empire (cf. Pritz, 2015: 285). The fact that Tisza played a key role in prioritizing attempts to find a diplomatic solution has been established not only by Hungarian but also by English-language works of historiography. See also Gyarmati, 2015: 201.

282 Glatz (2006). Moreover, after the Second World War, the bipolar world order emerging along the lines of an increasingly antagonistic American-Soviet rivalry accelerated the process of Communist power acquisition and political takeover in the Central and Eastern European region—in other words, the Sovietization of Hungary was a necessary consequence of the bipolar international order. Cf. Bihari, 2005: 62, 83.

in the economic weakening of Hungary.[283] This is also why we have such a gut aversion to bloc formation. It deprives us of the ability to mediate and balance between East and West, which is one of the most important elements of our culture. To date, attempts to force us to adopt culturally alien models have always been unsuccessful, and I see no reason to think it would be any different this time.

Geographical Reasons

Hungary's geographical situation is unique, and it results in the country facing both opportunities and challenges. Being located in the heart of the Carpathian Basin, in the middle of Europe, entails both advantages and disadvantages. Therefore, the task of Hungarian geopolitical thinking has always been to minimize the dangers and make the most of opportunities. Hungary lies along a distinct and well-known geopolitical fault line between East and West, but we should also not forget that the Mediterranean world meets Northern European culture in Hungary. Throughout history, as a result of these fault lines, the country was often at the center of conflicts, and these conflicts sometimes had grievous consequences.[284]

---

283 Tomka (2010) characterizes the economic history of Hungary during the period between 1948/1949 and 1990 as one in which: 1. the real limits on growth were imposed by the political and social system; 2. the stages of the economic development were significantly different from those in Europe's strongest economies; 3. in terms of economic output, Hungary lagged ever further behind Western Europe. Thus, between 1950 and 1965, Hungarian GDP per capita was less than half of the Western European average—a much larger gap than during the previous century. From the late 1970s, Hungary's position relative to Western Europe continued to deteriorate, resulting in the greatest relative decline in Hungarian development compared to the leading economies. The impenetrability and isolation that were the hallmarks of the Communist economic model played a decisive role in this: these factors, among others, hindered technology transfer and import competition, which are indispensable elements of catching up. Again, we see that the logic of blocs, here in specific combination with the Soviet-style state socialist economic model, constituted a major structural barrier to the possibility of successful catch-up and growth.

284 Kalmár (1943: 120–63) defines a geopolitical conflict zone as a place where opposing geopolitical forces (conflicting directions of expansion and objectives) meet. After the Hungarians occupied the Carpathian Basin and established the Hungarian state,

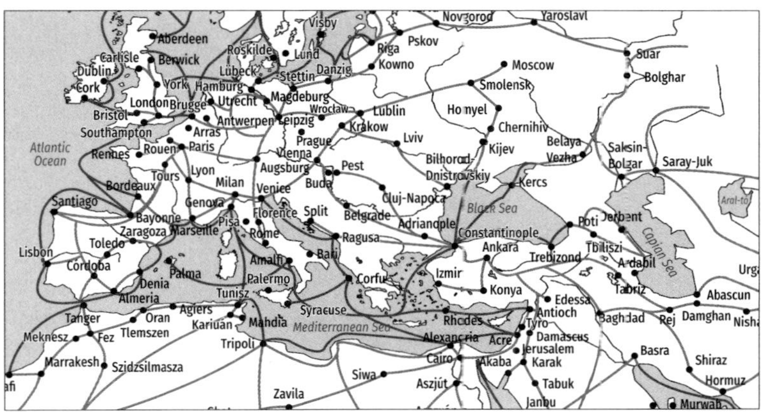

Figure 17: Trade routes at the beginning of the 13th century.
Source: Netchev, 2022

But this geographical location also offers unique opportunities. Hungary's geographical position means that it straddles the crossroads of Eastern and Western trade routes. Over the course of history, this enabled it to become a major trade center through which Asian and European markets could be connected.[285] The traffic of goods coming from the East naturally continues to take

Hungary's primary strategic goal became warding off larger and more powerful neighbors; that is, it can be summed up as an effort to keep conflict areas outside the country's borders. One of the most obvious examples of when this did not succeed is the century and a half of Turkish subjugation and the country's division into three parts. At that time, Hungary, wedged between the Habsburgs and the Ottomans, became a battleground. According to Hóman (1936), the Hungarians have been dealing with essentially the same problem for a thousand years: the balancing of the larger forces of East and West, the maintenance of security between them, and the preservation of an independent national existence.

285 According to Havass (1912: 191), Hungary's favorable geographical location between East and West almost predestines it to conduct significant foreign trade not only with the Balkan Peninsula as its "most natural" market, but also with Asia and Africa as an intermediary. Similar views were held by, among others, Pál Teleki (1934: 156), who said that the Danube is the "continental highway of Europe," and István Széchenyi (1830), who likewise wrote that the Danube is a "natural channel that seems to have been created for Hungary," and which the Hungarians could use to their advantage.

place through Hungary, and the country is an excellent entry point to the territory of the EU.[286]

The geopolitical reality of the Russian-Ukrainian conflict brought both new challenges and opportunities.[287] Some of the East-West trade routes have been closed, which strengthens the strategic importance of Hungary as an alternative route.[288] This new geopolitical reality offers Hungary a chance to play an even more central role in continental trade.

But Hungary is in an advantageous position not only with regard to distant trade partners. Our country has recently participated in many infrastructural development projects connecting it with neighboring countries and the rest of the continent. From new railway connections and motorways to modern logistics centers, these developments further strengthen Hungary's position as

---

286 Serbia concluded a free-trade agreement with China in the autumn of 2023, which shows that our region's geographical location gives it a competitive advantage that Eastern trade partners have also recognized. Given that China can conduct essentially duty-free trade with Serbia as well as Georgia, the transport and trade route between East and West is clearly taking ever more defined shape, a kind of de facto trade area for which Hungary is ideally located to serve as an entry point to the EU (Jevtić, 2023; Starcevic, 2023). For Eastern producers, Hungary is a gateway to Western markets. Precisely for this reason, it would serve Hungary's interests if relations with China were determined by EU institutions not because of de-risking, but rather because of deepening trade relations and searching for new opportunities for cooperation. In this area, the institutional barrier or limitation is the fact that trade policy falls under the exclusive competence of the EU—that is, it is the EU as a whole, rather than individual member states, that enters into agreements with countries outside the Union. However, considering the above geographic framework, the promotion of Hungarian interests within the Union must strive to achieve the connection between distant parts of the world here at the intersection of the Eastern and Western trade routes.

287 For a recently published study dealing with Hungary's geopolitical and foreign policy options, see Magyarics-Mártonffy, 2023.

288 After the outbreak of the Russian-Ukrainian war, traffic in the Northern Corridor, which is one of the main trade routes between China and Europe, fell by an estimated 40 percent, whereas in 2022 the volume of goods transported along the Central Corridor, which also includes Hungary, may have been up to six times the volume of the previous year. Cf. Chang, 2023; Eldem, 2022.

Europe's transport and logistics hub.[289] Thus, although Hungary's geographical location presents us with significant challenges, the country has always been able to find opportunities to achieve development and prosperity. Amidst the challenges of the modern age, Hungary's geographical position must be exploited as a strategic advantage. We are located in a very central position, at the intersection of modern trade routes. However, if these trade routes wither as competing blocs are formed, Hungary will undoubtedly be pushed to the periphery. It will be on a road to nowhere, a dead end at the edge of the Western world. That is why bloc formation is not in our interest geographically either.

Economic Reasons

Beyond these cultural and geographical reasons for opposing the establishment of blocs, the strongest, "hardest," and most numerically quantifiable arguments of all are economic in nature. First, it is worth stressing that Hungary is relatively poor in natural resources, which immediately creates both a challenge and an opportunity. The challenge lies in the fact that we do not have the luxury of relying on our own resources for economic development. We must not forget that natural resources, especially energy, are important not only for their direct economic benefits. The availability and price of these resources directly affects industrial production, transport, residential energy prices, and many other factors.[290]

---

289 Based on available and comparable data, Hungary has the fourth highest density of railway tracks (length of railway per thousand square kilometers) in the EU, and in terms of the motorway network, Hungary has the densest among the Visegrád countries, while also surpassing France, Ireland, and the Scandinavian countries. Cf. Eurostat, 2023n.

290 The importance of this is demonstrated by the situation in the Netherlands. Thanks to the Groningen natural gas field, discovered in 1959, the Netherlands owns approximately 2,800 billion cubic meters of natural gas assets (European Gas Hub, 2023). Such a quantity would be sufficient to cover Hungary's natural gas needs for 280 years. In 2013, the Dutch government decided to phase out domestic natural gas production by 2023. Five years after the decision, production had fallen by

However, lack of resources can also be an opportunity. It encourages a country to be more open toward partner countries[291] with which it can share resources and from which it can obtain them.[292] If we focus too much on the ideological dimension of foreign policy and exclude ourselves from markets that are rich in natural resources, we endanger both our own economic stability and our growth potential.[293]

The same logic leads to another negative effect of bloc formation. Hungary's economy is extremely export-oriented, and it is to this

---

55 percent, while the Netherlands' dependence on imports had risen from 29 to 72 percent, and with further decreases in production, this dependence only grew stronger (IEA, 2020), which naturally means the country is more exposed to the energy price crisis. In the second quarter of 2023, the Netherlands, which previously ranked at the top of the Western European Union countries in terms of GDP growth, entered a recession (Eurostat, 2023c), and industrial production, which was one and a half times the Hungarian level at the time, fell by 8 percent (CBS, 2023).

291 We have already talked about how one of the central elements of the connectivity strategy is to further strengthen the north-south connection, i.e., boosting regional connectivity, thus reducing dependence on the great centers of power in the West and East. However, the strategic situation of Hungary and Central Europe was largely determined by history. For decades, the region was dependent on an East-West energy infrastructure reflecting the logic of the Cold War and then the post-Cold War period. One element of this is that the Soviet Union built the infrastructure for crude oil and natural gas export with a hub-and-spokes design, naturally with the Soviet Union as the hub, thus making regional connectivity impossible. It also helped to keep the Eastern Bloc geopolitically united, especially regarding Central European countries lying on the geopolitical fault line (for more on this, see Marrese-Vanous, 1983). The second historical legacy is that, in the 1960s and 1970s, intensive trade in oil and natural gas began between Western Europe and the Soviet Union, which also enabled the development of East-West infrastructure (see Perović-Krempin, 2014; Zaniewicz, 2019; Franza, 2018: 26). The third legacy is that, in the early 1990s, regional foreign policy, primarily focused on Westward reorientation, was combined with the capital poverty of the Central European countries. It is hardly surprising that only Westward energy interconnectors were built in this period, including the establishment of the HAG (Hungaria-Austria-Gasleitung) gas connection with Austria, while Polish-German and Hungarian-Austrian electricity connections were also established during this period.

292 There are several aspects to energy security, one of which is the strengthening of regional connectivity. For more information on the relationship between regional connectivity and energy security, see Tongsopit et al., 2016; Kanchana-Unesaki, 2014; and Moura et al., 2017.

293 For more on this, see Beyer-Molnar, 2022; Dickel et al., 2014: 12–40.

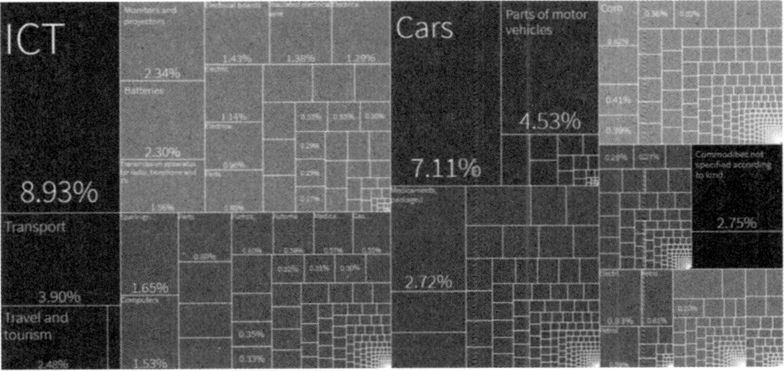

Figure 18: Hungary has the 11th most complex economy in the world.
Source: The Atlas of Economic Complexity, 2023

that we owe most of our growth in recent decades. Diversification of exports and the search for new markets are vitally important. If our export opportunities decrease as a result of the growth of rival blocs, it will seriously hinder our economic growth.

In addition, the importance of the inflow of FDI should not be underestimated, as the development of the economy and industrial modernization often depend on it.[294] As the international economic environment changes, so does the economic importance of non-Western countries. This means that it is essential to diversify sources of working capital and look for new investment opportunities.

What is more, we have already seen that the formation of blocs entails extremely high economic costs even in the most developed countries, as is currently being witnessed in all Western states. Regrettably, these costs affect the lowest income groups to the greatest extent, and as a proportion of their income they pay the greatest price for unfavorable international processes.[295] Increasing

---

294 For more on this, see: Søreide, 2001; Damijan et al., 2003; Gherigi-Voytovych, 2018; Mamingi-Martin, 2018.

295 See: Silva-Leichenko, 2004; Rodrik, 2021; Felbermayr-Mahlkow-Sandkamp, 2022; Gill-Nagle, 2022.

inequality, as we have noticed, harms a country's prospects of attaining a high development level, and it is therefore contrary to our interests.

Last but not least, it is vital to pay particularly close attention to technological development and innovation. Technological innovation is traditionally strong in Western countries, but Eastern countries are also increasingly catching up in this area. If Hungary closes itself off from technological development and innovation in the East, it may miss out on a range of opportunities that could result in further economic growth and development.

As a result, the economic and social political progress we have made in recent years may be in jeopardy. Employment levels may drop and tax incomes decline, threatening the future of the Hungarian family policy and utility-cost reduction. In short, as a result of bloc formation, everything that served the economic and social rise of the past decades may disappear. Consequently, not only may we be unable to continue to develop and grow economically, but there is even a danger of slipping backward.

What Next?

In such circumstances, it is natural to begin asking about how we can move forward. Both the trajectory of Hungary's efforts to catch up, the theories of how this may be achieved, and best practices from other countries, as well as Hungary's cultural, geographical, and economic peculiarities, point in the same direction: a world of rival blocs is not only not in Hungary's interest, but it directly would impede further progress in catching up economically. At the same time, Hungary is too small to influence the direction in which the world is going. If the major powers and superpowers continue to push in the direction of a bloc-based world, then that is what we will have. No matter how loudly ten million of us shout "sorry, but that doesn't work for us," we will not even be among the hundred most influential voices. That is why we must come up with something new. We need a strategy.

We have to come up with a strategy and a corresponding role for ourselves that somehow bypasses the insoluble problem, cuts the Gordian knot, and turns the tide of the battle with a hussar cut. Essentially, we are trying to work out how to best make use of our virtues and talents in a world that is, in all probability, hostile to those virtues and talents. This is the connectivity-based strategy and the *keystone state* concept that can support it, which we will elaborate on in the next chapter.

3 CONNECTIVITY AS THE HUNGARIAN BREAKOUT STRATEGY

"Oh hussar, hussar! You are the light of Hungarian eyes."
(Bertalan Szemere)

Every nation has its mythic heroes, and Hungary is no exception. Some of these legendary figures are shrouded in the mists of the Middle Ages, or even the Asian prehistory of the Hungarians. Nimród, Hunor, and Magor, and even Árpád, who led the Hungarians into the Carpathian Basin, are heroic figures of a long-lost world. In the modern, post-Enlightenment world, new heroes such as Miklós Toldi and János Vitéz were given to us by the poetry of the nineteenth century. Frigyes Karinthy perceptively noted that Toldi and János Vitéz are the Hungarian Herakles and Odysseus. And like all true heroes, they embody something of the people who embraced them as role models.

From our point of view, a particularly interesting Hungarian hero is János Vitéz, or John the Valiant, known at the beginning of his tale as Kukoricza János, or—as translator John Ridland put it—Johnny Grain o' Corn. As in all good Hungarian tales, the orphaned János, forced to leave his home village, sets out, joins the army, travels the world, does battle with natural and supernatural evils, and ultimately receives his just reward: the once penniless peasant boy becomes king of Fairyland.

Of course, it is easy to miss the point when analyzing literary works, because it is almost always impossible to say for sure what the author was thinking. But it is still striking that if we place the countries visited by János Vitéz on a map, we find Tatarstan and India to the east of Hungary and János's village, Poland to the north, Italy to the south, and finally France to the west. Old-fashioned

Figure 19: The original cover of the first edition
of *János Vitéz,* issued on 6 March 1845.
The publisher was Imre Vahot,
while the cover lithograph and other illustrations
were made by Vince Grimm.
Source: Wikimedia Commons

geography helps us understand what is going on here: our hero travels all over the world and gains new experiences everywhere he goes. But there is something else at work: the Hungarian hero's path Westward is not straight, but winding. For him, the way to the West leads through the East.

We cite the story of János Vitéz here because his adventures are strikingly similar to the task facing Hungary in the twenty-first century. We want to become a strong, developed country, decisively and under our own steam, but to get there we must travel the world, and experience what it has to offer.

However, previous chapters have shown all too clearly that recent global developments are not favorable for small countries with open economies, trying to create buoyancy from their economic, political, and cultural relations. This, after all, is precisely what Hungary is: a proud and ancient country with a complex, open economy, located along geopolitical fault lines, with a cultural background that makes it a natural mediator. Given all this, we argue that what will help Hungary become a fully developed country and an important factor in the international order in its own right is a connectivity-based strategy. So, the next step is to review what the international literature says about connectivity to see how these findings can be integrated into our strategic toolbox.

3.1. Connectivity and Resilience: Networking and International Relations

"All of life on the earth's surface is integrated by the thickening of connections between states and continents, and by the fact that every new creation, every economic and political event affects more or less everything, due to the density of these connections."
(*Count Pál Teleki*)

The concept of connectivity originates from research into complex networks, whence it has migrated to the world of political and public policy research. The research on complex networks goes back to the 1950s and has many Hungarian connections.[296] It entered the political lexicon partly as a possible descriptive theoretical model of globalization, and partly as a strategy for economic growth and increasing the overall influence of a given country in a globalized world.[297] Regarding the latter application, a relatively large number of popular, though still definitely academic, works were created. However, for an examination of the former, one must attempt to synthesize a whole series of studies. Most of these studies use the conceptual framework of network theory research.

When it comes to networks, the studies in question generally consider two aspects: one is the growth of networks, when new nodes are continually being added to a system and connected to existing ones, with new connections springing up between them. The other is the "popularity connection," which examines how the

---

296　The social science literature examining connectivity is largely based on the scale-independent network model and, in terms of the results achieved here, Hungary is considered a knowledge superpower. The most important scientific results in this field in recent decades have almost exclusively been linked to Hungarian researchers. One of the most important scientific concepts is the Erdős-Rényi model (Erdős-Rényi, 1959), and another is the Barabási-Albert model (Albert-Barabási, 2002).

297　The best known of these is the Parag Khanna's *Connectography: Mapping the Future of Global Civilization*, published in 2016, which introduced into public discourse the concept of connectivity as a model describing globalization.

probability that a new node will chose to connect to an existing node is proportional to how many connections the existing node already has.

But what does all this have to do with a country's strategy? In essence, if a country is able to interpret its own international and economic relations in terms of connectivity, as explored in network theory, it will be able to use the findings of network theory to its advantage. The task is therefore to meaningfully examine the interpretative possibilities of connectivity in terms of both international relations and global economics. Only then can we develop a concept of connectivity on which to base our Hungarian strategy.

Interpreting Connectivity from an International Relations Theory Perspective

To develop a concept of connectivity relevant to our purposes here, we must first clarify how we interpret the word in relation to international relations. By the late 1960s, the IR discipline had reached a point where scholars began to argue that the international system should be interpreted not only through the prism of political and ideological relations between states but also in terms of cultural, investment, and trade relations. This was born of the realization that states' behavior and possibilities are fundamentally influenced by these relationships, which traditional realist and liberal schools paid insufficient attention to.

The first highly influential experiment came from Robert Keohane and Joseph S. Nye—who would go on to make his name a decade and a half later with his concept of "soft power"—and their theory came to be known as "complex interdependence."[298] According to Keohane and Nye, extremely complex relations have developed between states in the modern world, whether in terms of economic, political,

---

298 Keohane-Nye, 2011.

or cultural relations. These relationships are network-like and—the crux of the theory—create interdependencies. Interdependence determines the operation of the international system in the sense that states strive to establish it, but it also influences their behavior. Interdependence necessarily limits the autonomy of states and is usually asymmetrical. This is where we truly enter the domain of international politics. States try to shape these relationships in such a way that they gain the greatest possible benefit from interdependence and are in the best possible bargaining position. After all, Keohane and Nye argue, states are playing a positive-sum game. Of course, the realists soon had an answer to the theory of complex interdependence. Neorealism was founded by Kenneth Waltz, who, two years after Keohane and Nye, in 1979, outlined his own theory in a work entitled *Theory of International Politics*.[299] This theory is also state-centered, and it views states as the most important among the actors in the international system. He also describes the international system as anarchic, with states fighting for their survival. All states are engaged in the same activities, and the hierarchy among them is determined by the efficiency with which they do so. In contrast to complex interdependence, Waltz draws attention to the utilitarian nature of these relationships. Of course, numerous economic or higher education relations are formed at the initiative of private actors (companies, universities, etc.), but the state always has the deciding word in these relations. After all, in the anarchic international system, states striving for survival and a balance of power exploit these relationships in order to expand their own capabilities.[300] However, if a state were to gain an excessive

---

299 Waltz, 2010.

300 In a work published twenty years later, Waltz clearly clarifies neorealism's attitude towards relationships and interdependencies. From a neorealist perspective, economic relations between states do not meaningfully influence states' decisions. The state maintains or approves these relationships and endorses interdependencies, but if another country takes advantage of them, the state intervenes and breaks them. An example of this can be found in the deterioration of international investment

advantage through these relationships—that is, if it sought to upset the balance of power—the other states would intervene, disrupting the network of relationships.[301] So Waltz acknowledges the existence of relationships and networks, but makes them unambiguously dependent on the political will of the states. Whether we choose to embrace the perspective of the realists or the representatives of the liberal school, there is clearly an opportunity for state management of connectivity, the use of political goals and tools, and for states to take advantage of the resultant opportunities.

Economic Aspects of Connectivity

Another cornerstone of our concept of connectivity is that a state following a strategy based on it will seek to increase the volume of trade, investment, and cultural, educational, and research relations. It also means that by increasing such connections, the state will become more and more open. From an economic perspective, it is worth examining here whether we really ought to axiomatically consider openness a necessity; that is, whether there is a strong correlation between economic growth and openness, which impacts foreign trade, investment, infrastructure, and even academic and R&D relations.

---

relations between Japan and the United States in the 1980s. In this work, Waltz also talks about globalization as being beholden to the same logic. Globalization naturally exists, and is a spontaneous process, but its speed and the quality of its development are determined by states. He points out that there were eras when trade liberalization was replaced by protectionism. The data indicate that, between 1850 and 1914, international trade and capital turnover increased dynamically; however, between the end of the First World War and the late 1960s, it decreased significantly, only to begin increasing again from the 1970s.

301 Just a few years after the end of the Cold War, it was becoming clear that economic relations would replace armed conflict as the main tool of geopolitics. Samuel Huntington took the position that the chance of a military confrontation between the great powers had become insignificant, and that conflicts between countries— thus also the establishment of the hierarchy—would primarily be fought in the economic arena (Huntington, 1993: 72). In a manner reminiscent of Huntington's logic, Edward Luttwak coined the term "geo-economics," which is nothing more than "the logic of war in the language of economics" (Luttwak, 1990: 19).

Sachs and Warner, for example, examined the trade policy of the Soviet successor states and other ex-socialist countries a few years after the breakup of the Soviet Union.[302] In their study, they concluded that the more export-driven and open a country's economic structure is, the higher its growth rate. Moreover, more export-driven, open economies recorded smaller GDP decreases than more autarkic, closed economies.[303] In addition, it was also shown that the more open an economy is in international trade, the faster its rate of productivity increased.[304] The model additionally proved—crucially from a connectivity perspective—that more open economies are able to absorb knowledge and innovation at a much higher rate.[305]

Additional important data relating to connectivity were provided by the research of Frankel and Romer, which, in addition to examining trade openness, also examined geographical factors.[306] Their research unequivocally confirms the connection between openness and economic growth: if the ratio of trade to GDP increases by one percentage point, income per capita will increase by one and a half percentage points—trade openness thus has a multiplying effect. At the same time, the study also indicates that a favorable geographical situation (for example, geographical proximity to a large export market) does not in and of itself increase income. For that, other elements must also be present—for example, the infrastructure necessary for trade.

---

302 This proved to be an especially exciting question because, in another study, they also examined separately the impact on economic growth of the trade policy of countries relying on energy exports and industrial and service exports. They concluded that countries relying on energy exports had a lower growth rate than countries with a more diversified export structure. Exports of energy carriers naturally increased consumption in conjunction with changing global market prices (Sachs-Werner, 1995b).

303 Ibid. 1995: 61.

304 Edwards, 1998.

305 Helpman (2004) also showed a positive correlation between openness and the capacity to absorb new knowledge and innovation.

306 Frankel-Romer, 1999.

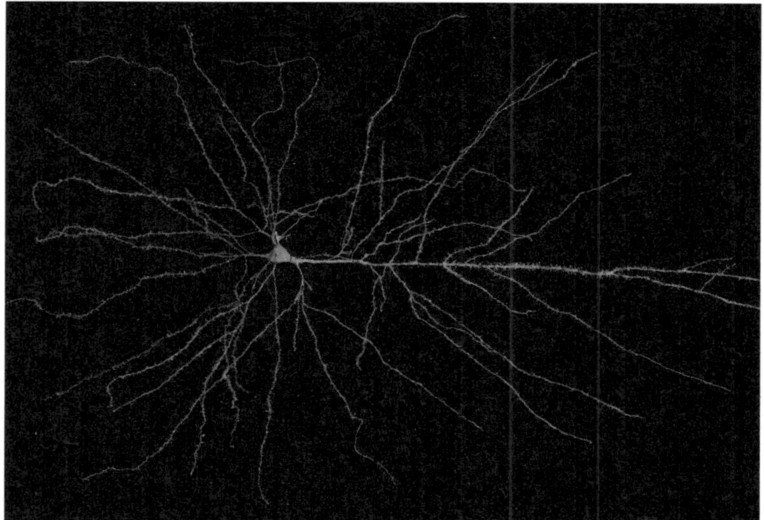

Figure 20: Connection points of a nerve cell—the human nervous system
is one of the most complex networks we know of.
*By Ruth Benavides-Piccione, Isabel Fernaud, Asta Kastenauskaite
and Javier DeFelipe*

Keller's research also focuses on the importance of importing technology.[307] In this regard, he came to the conclusion that the more open a nation's economy is, the more new technology it can acquire. This is known as "technological spillover," which is a positive phenomenon.[308] Of course, international trade—such as when a manufacturing company imports semi-finished products—can also cause technological spillover, which benefits the national economy of the host country, but when it comes to FDI, the chance of this happening is significantly higher. The study also demonstrated that the more similar players from the same industry are present

---

307 Keller, 2009.
308 Technological spillover means that the technology developed by a company becomes available to other actors (states, companies, universities, and research centers) without the intention of the developing company.

in the host country, the greater the possibility of technological spillover, which is also positively correlated with economic growth.[309] This last finding is especially important from the point of view of the interpretation of connectivity. This is especially so because, according to Romer and Helpman's research, in the case of adequately connected national economies, technological spillover sustains growth potential in the long term.[310]

Considering all this, it can be concluded that connectivity is a model describing networks in terms of their connections, and it has certain specific characteristics that arise from this quality. When it comes to economic growth, the most important finding is that when a country is building a network, it should not only focus on developing just a single connection.[311] This is because the entire network has a much greater cumulative effect on economic growth than the sum of the individual connections.[312] If we consider the connectivity strategy of a state, we should not only focus on one type of connection, but develop all connections at the same time,

---

309 On the relationship between FDI, technological spillover and economic growth, see also Alfaro et al., 2004; Keller, 2009: 59.

310 Grossman-Helpman, 1994: 40.

311 The most important institutions of the post-1990 world order, as well as the experts who determine their thinking, interpret connectivity primarily in connection with economic growth and in the context of economic convergence. For example, regarding the implementation of the Millennium Development Goals (MDG), the UN states that world trade is the engine of economic development (De Cordoba-Bouhey, 2008: 16). Jeffrey D. Sachs (2020: 10), who also acted as an advisor to the UN Secretary General, highlights that humanity voted for globalization because the interconnectedness that became increasingly "thick" over the centuries was accompanied by significant economic growth, proving the advantageousness of continuing the program of globalization. According to the IMF, connectivity, "increasing cross-border trade and financial flows, results in strong and lasting economic growth and providing countries with economic benefits such as access to new markets, more favorable financing, and capital inflows" (IMF, 2012). According to the World Bank, "countries that are well integrated into global networks are members of a circle characterized by technological development and economic growth. However, the lack of connectivity is a major bottleneck for future growth and economic development" (Jansen et al., 2014: 1).

312 Gould-Kennett-Panterov, 2019.

thinking in terms of the overall network. Countries following such a strategy are most successful when they can connect to several key network nodes simultaneously, i.e., to countries that have developed economies and a high degree of connectivity. By doing so, they can multiply their own economic growth potential. By a similar logic, the more connected a country's economy becomes, the more likely it is to eventually become a node, increasing its influence on the network both geographically (regionally or globally) and in industrial terms.[313]

Resilience

Based on the above, we can begin to see more clearly how connectivity—i.e., a network formed by interdependencies—can be used to increase a country's economic power and international political weight. However, our description will be incomplete if we

---

313 Regarding the concept of regionally focused connectivity, it is worth noting that the non-Western world is ahead in terms of development. The non-Western world interprets the concept of connectivity somewhat differently, and in this context primarily focuses on increasing regional connectivity and strengthening resilience against the West. Therefore, connectivity primarily means increasing the competitiveness of the non-Western world and creating alternatives to Western institutions. Connecting to global networks is a secondary goal, but it is still a priority in this context. For example, the Asian Development Bank (ADB) puts it this way: "In order for Asia to become more resilient to external shocks, its economies must place greater focus on the elements of the economic development model based on regional demand and trade, and developing regional connectivity is a means of achieving this" (Bhattacharyay, 2010). According to ADB experts, connectivity can also be a means of dealing with the economic threats posed by the geopolitical competition between the USA and China. The essence of this approach is that the countries of the region should diversify their production chains among themselves, thus reducing their dependence on the USA and China (Herrero, 2023: 17). In its strategy for 2022–2026, the New Development Bank (NDB) of the BRICS puts this very clearly: the bank wants to become a new, multilateral financial institution of the world economy, and to play a leading role in the non-Western world (NDB, 2022: 6–7). The Association of Southeast Asian Nations (ASEAN) adopted a so-called connectivity master plan as early as 2010. During its latest review of 2016 for the period up to 2025, the member countries highlighted the need to prepare for a multipolar world order, in which the strengthening of connectivity between member countries will play a significant role (ASEAN, 2016: 6). For Western interpretations of regional and global connectivity, see Bathelt et al., 2004; Giuliani, 2007; Graf-Krüger, 2010.

do not consider the dangers of connectivity, as well as how these dangers can be managed. However, for this we must make a small detour from strategy theory.

In attempting to explore the risks inherent in connectivity, we find ourselves in a delicate situation, since we must simultaneously argue that connectivity—i.e., finding the relative advantages inherent in interdependencies—is definitely in a country's interest. Yet, at the same time, these interdependencies can simultaneously pose a threat to the country in question. This is the key problem that any connectivity-based strategy must address. Naturally, there is a solution, and we refer to it as resilience. There are many definitions of resilience. Yannick Hémond and Benoît Robert quote the UN's definition of resilience in an article on the subject:

> *"Resilience is the ability of individuals, households, communities, cities, institutions, systems and societies to prevent, resist, absorb, adapt, respond and recover positively, efficiently and effectively when faced with a wide range of risks, while maintaining an acceptable level of functioning without compromising long-term prospects for sustainable development, peace and security, human rights and well-being for all."*[314]

Of course, the definition continues, and there are other definitions as well, but the quote adequately captures the essence of it. Hémond also highlights what capabilities the various definitions imply: first, the ability to understand the past, and second, the ability to redesign, and thus to return the given system to normal operation. The concept of resilience can be approached in several ways, depending on what we mean by the ability to learn and return to normal functioning. If we examine the range of possible interpretations, we can see that

---

314 Hémond-Robert, 2012: 97.

the Western world and Eastern countries define resilience on the basis of different principles.

To understand the Western model, here is a simple example from the first film in the *Rambo* series. The protagonist, a Vietnam War veteran, arrives in a small town in the state of Washington. The sheriff does not allow the unkempt-looking man, clearly a military veteran, to enter the town, but when he returns, the sheriff and his officers try to persuade him with brutal punishments to stay away from the town. Resisting the authorities, Rambo flees into the forest, where his continued refusal to surrender leads to the deployment of increasingly substantial police forces, culminating in the deployment of the National Guard. This is not the place to evaluate the film or its characters, but plot of the story clearly shows the logic of Western-style resilience. The inhabitants of the small town perceive the ex-soldier as dangerous, and from then on, following the stipulated regulations and procedures, they try first to keep him away and then to catch him. None of the authorities think to find out who John Rambo is or to ask him to state the purpose of his visit. The system functions, as it were, on autopilot, with all the relevant gears clicking into place.

This example is interesting to us because in the Western world, resilience is primarily interpreted along the lines of processes and procedures that can be standardized, as seen in the film. The starting point for the Western interpretation of resilience is generally agreed to be the study by Crawford Stanley "Buzz" Holling, in which he examines the mechanisms that ensure the resilience of an ecosystem and tries to draw from them conclusions relevant to management theory. These show that resilience requires a framework that can respond to emerging threats and challenges.[315] For this approach, the essential point is the automaticity of the system: the various organizations must build procedures, essentially algorithms, that

---

315 Holling, 1973: 21.

can deal with challenges and dangers when supplied with the relevant information. The central question for research dealing with Western-style resilience is, therefore, the adaptive capacity of procedures: that is, how well standardized systems can adapt to new challenges.[316] The common characteristic of specialized models is that they seek automaticity and algorithmizability. In other words, how can resilience be incorporated into the operation of organizations, institutions and national governments as a procedural mindset?[317]

Take, for example, the world of business strategies: The resilience of the giant Western companies lies in the fact that they can react to challenges faster than their competitors.[318] If the market has recognized a change, the winner will be the business with internal organizational processes that can reallocate resources to new tasks faster. An interesting addition to all of this is that in the United States, for example, there is a special standard for what procedures companies must implement in order to be able to effectively manage market crises, natural disasters, and social upheavals.[319] One of the youngest branches of resilience research is the security policy subfield, which took off in response to the wave of terrorist attacks in America and Europe in the 2000s.[320] These studies chiefly explore ways in which national defense forces, economic actors, and civil society can be organized into a rapid response system with common procedures in order to increase resilience.[321] Given all this, we can begin to appreciate the extent to which the Western concept of resilience, which originated in the study of organization building and corporate management, relies on algorithmizability, operationalization, and rationalized, essentially automatic response capabilities.

---

316 Walker et al., 2004; Folke, 2006.
317 Lentzos-Rose, 2009: 243.
318 Hamel-Välikanga, 2003; Seville et al., 2006.
319 ASIS International, 2009.
320 Bourbeau, 2015.
321 Prior-Hagman, 2013: 295.

However, this approach has its limitations. We started from the premise that in developing a connectivity strategy, we are pursuing two opposing, often even mutually exclusive goals: namely, we want to maximize the benefits inherent in mutual dependence while exposing ourselves as little as possible to the dangers inherent therein. The problem is that the advantages can be exploited by deepening and increasing the number of relationships, and the disadvantages can be eliminated by reducing them. It is almost impossible to manage such contradictory goals by means of automatic procedures. It is no coincidence that the Western actors—be they states (even superpowers) or market companies—which continue to structure their thinking in terms of such procedures, have performed particularly poorly in recent years when it comes to resilience.

Let us see how this unfolds in practice. Using the example of the United States and China, the German researcher Torsten Riecke described this phenomenon as an economic chimera, the two halves of which (the US and China) became dependent on each other to such an extent that their separation would have catastrophic consequences for both parties, yet at the same time their close cooperation—given their conflicting interests—is becoming increasingly unthinkable. Riecke argues that the American side began to become aware of this problem in the mid-2010s, when President Donald Trump, citing national security considerations, banned certain Chinese companies from the American market and imposed a technology embargo on them and everyone who does business with them. Behind Trump's actions lay the realization that the presence of Chinese digital communications products in the United States could create the possibility for these companies to obtain data on American citizens, or even access classified government data. The sanctions prompted the Chinese side to take retaliatory measures, to the extent that the press at the time—naturally exaggerating the scale of the issue— began referring to these mutual restrictions as a trade war. What is important here in terms of our concept of connectivity is the way the high level of connectivity that existed before Trump's actions was first considered desirable to a certain extent by the American side, and then, after the realization of the risks involved, was evaluated as exclusively harmful.[322]

But we need not examine dueling superpowers to understand the nature of the risks inherent in connectivity. The COVID pandemic that began in 2020 laid bare the risks inherent in the interdependencies of the global economy, which is based on connectivity. Entire supply chains were paralyzed, and whole industries had to halt production.[323] The energy crisis afflicting Europe as a result of the Russian-Ukrainian war also exemplifies the dangers of interdependence, since the continent depended on, and still depends on, Russian energy suppliers to such an extent that the price of energy skyrocketed as soon as news broke of possible impediments to trade.[324] The same dependency problem exemplified by the US-Chinese relationship prevailed here as well, as a result of which, after the termination of European-Russian energy cooperation, it was no longer possible to find cheap alternatives to Russian energy imports, meaning that, in this case, breaking the relationship did not result in an increase in resilience, but rather in an increase in the number of uncertainties.

---

322 Riecke, 2020: 3–4.

323 An obvious example of this is Volkswagen. In the late autumn of 2021, the otherwise typically optimistic Herbert Diess stated with a rather gloomy outlook that in that year the VW Group would be compelled to post a loss of 500 million euros. The world's largest car manufacturer had been able to produce and sell far fewer cars, due to a shortage of microchips from Southeast Asia. The German economy lost 47 billion euros in added value—nearly 1.3 percent of GDP—due to the reduced performance of the automotive industry alone (Duthoit-Lemerle, 2022).

324 The European energy crisis had several interrelated causes, one of the most important of which was the operation of the gas market. In Western Europe, the goal was to create a gas market in which natural gas suppliers would compete, determining the price level. The basis of the market model is precisely connectivity: European countries could buy liquefied natural gas not only from the traditional Norwegian and Russian sources but also from, for example, the Middle East or even Australia. Most of Europe renounced Russian natural gas due to the war in Ukraine, so LNG transportation became a matter of life and death for the market.

The problem faced by such closely connected systems as the economy of a country, the energy supply of a continent, or the production chain of a company is, at least in the above examples, that the systems were not sufficiently resistant to newly emerging phenomena that impacted the fundamental principles of their operation. Practices from the field of operations management, which aims to increase resilience, have proven ineffective. It may thus be worth seeking inspiration from other areas of the Western world, and to examine non-Western approaches to the challenge of resilience.

There is also a trend within the Western world that deals specifically with the management of mutually contradictory goals. It is especially fortunate from the perspective of our situation that the solutions have been sought precisely among theories of strategic thinking. John Lewis Gaddis—one of the doyens of the field—likes to refer, for instance, to a remark by F. Scott Fitzgerald, who claimed that there is a specific motive distinguishing human intelligence from all other natural or artificial intelligences: namely, its ability to simultaneously hold contradictory statements to be true, while preserving its own operating logic. Something similar can be said here too.[325]

Fitzgerald's statement helps Gaddis explore the two mindsets characteristic of a person devising a strategy to achieve some goal. Gaddis borrows his analogy from Isaiah Berlin, who divided people into two groups according to their preferred way of thinking: Berlin saw the world as being made up of "hedgehogs" and "foxes."[326] The key characteristic of the hedgehogs is that they evaluate every problem or phenomenon they come across in terms of a fundamental idea or concept, which is generally based on a strategic goal to be achieved in the distant future. Needless to say, such an approach can

---

325 Fitzgerald, 1936.
326 Berlin, 1953.

Figure 21: Fox and hedgehog in Samuel Howitt's drawing.
Source: Getty Images

lead to closed thinking, inflexibility of action, and thus to choosing less-than-optimal means of achieving goals. Foxes, by contrast, set themselves multiple independent or even contradictory goals at the same time, making them particularly good at recognizing opportunities, seizing tools, and taking the right action. However, they may perform poorly in terms of achieving their long-term goals, as they are prone to changing with the circumstances.

It is clear, therefore, that internal contradictions are a frequent occurrence in the mindset of foxes, and their goals may at times cancel each other out. However, Gaddis goes beyond this: after all, it would be short-sighted to label the approach of either foxes or hedgehogs as inherently superior or as more grounded in reality. Ultimately, he concludes that a good strategy must employ the approach of the hedgehog and the fox at the same time.[327] In other

---

327 Gaddis, 2018: 4.

words, we must be able to accept conflicting truths, not in setting our goals, but in shaping our own way of thinking. Only thus can we think effectively in a strategic sense.

The current Western concept of connectivity, whether in its former or current guises, essentially falls into the error that Gaddis attributes to the hedgehogs, namely that it examines every situation from a single perspective, a single principled conviction. When, at a given moment, our imaginary hedgehogs believe that the most favorable strategy is to link up the world's economic, cultural, and political systems, they relentlessly pursue it, but when they believe that the relative advantages lie elsewhere, they retreat no less determinedly behind their protective bristles. In other words, they lurch from one extreme to the other and back again.

However, if we accept the definition that the essence of resilience is that a system, having learned from the mistakes of the past, is able to redesign itself and return to a normal state, then the complete or partial eradication of systems that have been connected and intertwined through interdependency—or the declaration of such an outcome as a goal—by no means accords with resilience as understood here. After all, replacing one unquestioned principle (connectivity is good) with another (connectivity entails risks and is therefore bad) not only deprives us of the benefits of the synergies inherent in connectivity, but also forces us to pay the additional costs of disconnection. However, the concept of resilience that is currently emerging in the Western world (decoupling or de-risking) suggests just such an approach, and as such, in our view, is misguided.

True resilience means not uncritically celebrating the momentary benefits of interdependencies, but at the same time not unthinkingly foregoing these benefits in response to the risks associated with them. In this case, we must develop a concept of resilience that can simultaneously handle these two mutually contradictory principles: that is, it can take advantage of the beneficial synergies arising from connectivity and still minimize the risks associated with them. That is, we need to do as Gaddis suggested: we need to adopt the mindset of hedgehogs and foxes at the same time.

A similar approach is used by Peter Ping Li, who developed his own concept of resilience based partly on ancient Chinese principles of governance, and partly on the organizational management works of Douglas Orton and Karl E. Weick.[328] In his interpretation, a lack of resilience can be traced back to the fact that closely connected systems—be they interstate or corporate relations—simultaneously contain two mutually opposing elements.[329] On the one hand, these are highly rationalized systems, since such rationalization enables the exploitation of the potential inherent in synergies, while on the other hand, given the complexity involved, the functioning of the systems will never be fully predictable. Due to the high number of interconnections, these systems are also characterized by causal relationships of which we are unaware. This is why, from time to time, we tend to experience unexpected collapses similar to the so-called butterfly effect.[330] A system loses its resilience when its designers and operators focus on either the rational or the deterministic element exclusively. In the former case, they will be at the mercy of unexpected crises, but in the latter case, they will not be able to exploit the advantages inherent in connectivity.

In Li's interpretation, the previous concept of connectivity, which focused entirely on rationally exploitable advantages, created a "tightly coupled system" which, on account of its lack of resilience, would be unable to withstand unexpected crises.[331] He argues that only "loosely coupled systems" have sufficient resilience.[332] These are systems based on interconnectedness, aware not only of potentially rationalizable processes but also of the existence of

---

328 Li also claims that these ancient principles reappeared in the operation of the Chinese state from the second half of the 1970s, when Deng Xiaoping came to power.
329 Li, 2020: 506.
330 Gleick, 1987.
331 Orton-Weick, 1990; Zhou, 2020.
332 Li, 2020: 506–7.

deterministic elements. As a result of all this, an organization is created that is "simultaneously open and closed, indeterminate and rational, spontaneous and deliberate."

In order to achieve such a state, it is necessary to arrive at a dialectical balance between two opposing principles, namely rationality and determinism. The author calls this—in Chinese terms—a yin-yang balance, and at one point compares his findings with the dialectical frameworks developed in Western philosophy. This can help us understand how a loosely coupled system works in practice. In Western thought, dialectics—though it has many divergent interpretations—primarily draws attention to the fact that the relational properties of certain things (properties derived from their relationships with each other) can change, and these properties belong to the given thing even if they are not currently present.[333] In Hegel's example, many believe that life and death are opposite qualities, even though they are closely related concepts: a person's life also includes his death, and vice versa—only someone who has lived can be dead. Thus, the object under scrutiny is both open and closed at the same time. It is closed in terms of which of its relational properties are currently realized, but open in terms of the relational properties the given thing can potentially take on. Note that this state of being simultaneously open and closed is also one of the characteristics of loosely connected systems. It is also worth noting here how much the above agrees with Gaddis's findings regarding strategic thinking—namely that a good strategist must have the mindset of both the hedgehog and the fox at the same time.

One of the reasons for the lack of resilience in the Western model of connectivity that has been accepted and implemented until now is precisely that it does not account for changes in relational properties, or possible changes in the wider world. Of course, one of the reasons for this is that it makes it difficult to rationalize a system or process

---

333 Hegel, 1979: 142–43.

if contingencies must constantly be examined.[334] This can be seen in action even as a consequence of the development of modern supply chains, which may be very efficient, but are also very vulnerable, and can collapse with the slightest change in circumstances—the relationship of individual elements to each other—or at least their performance may drop to a fraction of the optimal level. The key maxims for building a loosely connected and therefore resilient system can be gleaned from the works of Li and the already cited Orton and Weick. First, all these authors agree that the operation of a larger, loosely connected system must allow space for both rational and deterministic processes, but at the same time, which principle applies in which areas must be clearly defined.

Rational and deterministic processes must comprise the technical core of the system, meaning that the decision-making procedures must be overseen primarily by the actors who create and operate the system. On the other hand, at the level of the individual elements that make up the system, room must be left for uncertainty and openness so that these elements are able to respond to changed circumstances.[335] These two levels—the technical core and the institutional framework—must be loosely connected, so the decision-makers at the technical center must only formulate guidelines and expectations for the institutional level, and not interfere in institutional decision-making and adaptation processes.

On the other hand, the authors also all agree that such a system should not be operated by completely automated processes: management is needed to override processes arising from the inertia of the system in the event of new phenomena and changes in relational properties.[336] Li calls this "threat-vigilant leadership,"

---

334 According to J. D. Thompson, Western culture initially has difficulty coping with situations in which mutually contradictory principles must be implemented simultaneously (Thompson, 1967).
335 Li-Zhou-Yang, 2020.
336 Orton-Weick, 1990: 204.

the essence of which is that the decision-makers in the technical core must constantly examine which changes are affecting the operation of the system, and in which direction. They must make the appropriate decisions with these factors in mind.

During the decision-making process, three factors must be considered: modularity, the necessary degree of variety, and the decision-making autonomy of individual non-core actors. Modularity should be understood as the interchangeability of individual elements in the system.[337] "Necessary variety" refers to a peculiarity of the loosely connected system, whereby elements of a different nature are able to deliver incoming information to the technical, decision-making core in a different way. Thus, a certain level of diversity in the elements of the system is necessary to keep the decision-making processes sufficiently grounded.[338] Finally, decision-making autonomy[339] is necessary to ensure that the individual elements of the system are able by themselves to deal with any problems that arise, and to proactively collect information from the wider environment.[340]

What is Connectivity? And How Can it be Turned into a Strategy?

After all this—i.e., after explaining the different elements and interpretations of connectivity, and, no less importantly, exploring the concept of resilience and possible ways of interpreting it—we must ask the key question: how do we define the essence of connectivity for ourselves?

Connectivity is primarily a capability. Or more precisely, it is several simultaneous capabilities: it is the capacity to think in a

---

337 For more on this, see Page-Jones, 1980.

338 For more on this, see Beekun-Glick, 2007.

339 For more on this, see Day-Schoemaker, 2006.

340 Consider, if we think of the human body as a loosely connected system, how the attention of our eyes is indeed at times directed by our conscious selves, but our eyes are also capable of autonomous (instinctive) focusing and, if danger is perceived, they will look that way of their own accord.

certain way and to act on that basis. Thus, politically speaking, it is the ability to manage the mutual dependencies we inevitably accrue, while increasing their number in order to maximize the relative benefits. In economic terms, meanwhile, it means increasing the economic performance of a country or organization through openness, improving its position in supply chains, and making the most advanced technologies available to it. In other words, connectivity means the ability to seize opportunities—and at the same time to recognize dangers. Connectivity can only benefit a country or organization in the long term if it is able to handle the unpredictability associated with a high degree of connectivity.

These general principles can be further broken down into specific, practical goals. If we take the discipline of organization building as an example, we find the following:[341]

- increasing the degree of regionalization, localizing some supply chains
- purchasing from two or more different sources
- balancing domestic and foreign purchases
- retraining the workforce for flexibility
- creating an operational structure that typically consists of three basic elements:
  - an extensive and modularized control node
  - autonomous external institutions
  - open-minded and far-seeing background institutions

If we apply all this more specifically to the functioning of a state, we can begin to see more clearly the elements necessary for a connectivity-based strategy. Above all, it is necessary to make the operation of the state fit for purpose, in the broadest sense. Based on the fifth point on the list above, this involves not only institutional but

---

341 Li, 2020: 507.

also personal factors. The balancing of opposing principles can never happen solely because of institutionalized and mechanistic processes. There is a need for a decision-maker—for "enhanced leadership"—to override automatic processes when the need arises.[342] In order to do this, decision-making itself must have a particular structure. There needs to be a control center that can perceive the overall functioning of the state, but also autonomous subunits capable of independent decision-making, as well as background institutions with analytical capacity that constantly warn decision-makers of potential dangers, as well as helping them find opportunities.

More specifically, for a connectivity-based strategy to work effectively, the state needs the following:

- stable political leadership
- help from economic actors in implementing the strategy (autonomous external actors)
- internationally relevant and connected institutions that help decision-making (institutes, universities, think tanks, etc.)
- strong regional embeddedness
- a balance of domestic and foreign procurement sources
- well-educated citizens

These requirements can be applied to any country that seeks to pursue a connectivity strategy. But it is only a framework, which Hungary must fill with content. Are we Hungarians capable of it?

---

342 Orton-Weick, 1990: 212.

3.2. The Hussar Cut: The "Keystone State" Concept That Will Enable Hungary to Follow a Strategy Based on Connectivity

"Go West, but never forget that you came from the East."
(Sándor Márai)

Are we Hungarians capable of it? The question is a legitimate one. Considering the lessons of Chapter 2, we need a strategy that takes maximum advantage of our cultural, geographical, and economic characteristics. This means a connectivity-based strategy. However, Chapter 2 showed that the world is moving toward decoupling and a bloc-based world, and even if there is clear evidence that such developments would serve neither the interests of the broader Western world or Hungary specifically, our country it is certainly not sufficiently powerful to significantly influence the direction of such global processes. This is where a hussar cut is needed: an attitude, self-image, or posture that would allow us to make maximum use of our strengths, and especially the ability to build connectivity. Fortunately, the literature on the subject does contain a theoretical description of countries that adopt such a posture—this is the concept of the "keystone state."

This is a relatively new concept. The prerequisite for its development was that in recent years, researchers began to realize that traditional methods were no longer sufficient to adequately describe the role of individual states in the international system. The traditional classification system of international relations is based on the understanding that there is an international hierarchy in terms of economic, political, and military power, and we can plot independent states on a linear scale of power, prestige, and influence, ranging from superpowers to microstates.

During the Cold War, the term "superpower" came to be widely used in both public discourse and technical jargon. Before the Cold War, analysis tended to focus on the model of the balance of power, the "concert" of the great powers, and a primarily Eurocentric international system.[343] In the postwar world, the functioning of the bipolar Cold War global order made the term "superpower" relatively logical and clearly understandable. According to Fox, a superpower is a state whose strength exceeds that of most countries, which has the right of veto in all major international decisions, and which can directly influence even geographically distant regions.[344] This is an acquired right of superpowers, resulting from their absolute superfluity of power.[345] According to another definition, a superpower is a state that cannot be prevented by any third country from asserting its will over others[346]—that is, superpowers have a well-defined sphere of influence in which they alone have the final say.

---

343 There can be no doubt that non-European episodes of the competition between the great European powers (for instance, the era of the "great game" between the British and Russian empires in Central Asia) and conflicts between non-European countries that, in some cases, cherished imperial dreams (the first Sino-Japanese War, for example) are under-researched topics. However, there is a stream of historical scholarship, underpinned by strong arguments, that argues that the conflicts of the ninteenth century and the first half of the twentieth century (up until around 1941) were in fact a European civil war. In other words, competition between the great European powers determined the world order. For more on this, see Preston, 1996; Payne, 2011; Nolte, 1997.

344 Fox, 1944.

345 Bull (2002: 221–22) complements Fox's insights by arguing that the rights of superpowers are limited by a complex network of obligations that require careful balancing. According to Bull, the primary reason for this is that while superpowers have an absolute surplus of power, in order to maintain the international system that they envision, they also need to appear legitimate in the eyes of other countries— not all issues can be settled simply by force and coercion. In addition, superpowers unquestionably need the support of powers of different strengths, including middle powers and regional powers. In other words, the absolute superiority of superpowers does not mean that their power is infinite, and the necessity to cooperate and balance is a "brake on the arrogance of superpowers."

346 Morgenthau, 1972: 130.

In the case of great powers—bearing in mind how difficult it is to define the term[347]—the main criterion is that their power-projection capabilities are significant and greater than those of most other countries.[348] Another important characteristic of the great powers is that they primarily care about regional processes, while possessing (and seeking) less influence over global processes. In this context, they have only a moderate degree of influence on the world order, and do not dominate it—in contrast to superpowers. Depending on the definition, the great powers are typically defined as the non-superpower G7 and BRICS countries.

Middle powers typically have relatively substantial influence in their own region. Their defining characteristic is that they are capable of taking unilateral steps in the international system, but are frequently compelled to form alliances, and in international conflicts

---

347 When it comes to defining what we mean by a "great power," we encounter several difficulties in examining the regularity of change in the international system. Here, we come across several theories that analyze the relative strength of states and changes in power; that is, the relative rise and decline of great powers. To understand the concept of great powers, it is therefore necessary to understand such explanatory models as the theory of power transition (Organski-Kugler, 1980), the theory of hegemonic wars (Gilpin, 1981), or the model of long-term cycles (Modelski, 1987).

348 According to Waltz (1993: 50), six aspects must be considered in determining great-power status: population and territory, efficient exploitation of resources, wealth performance, military strength, political stability, and political competence. Of course, a great power does not have to outperform other countries in all these domains equally. The given geopolitical situation determines which of the six variables a country must perform outstandingly in, but of course it cannot perform below average in the other areas either. According to Mearsheimer (1993), the most important characteristic of great powers is their ability to wage offensive wars against other states. In addition to military strength, the key characteristic of great powers is their ability to think at a truly strategic level, which entails minimizing costs. As an example of this, he cites the indisputable great power status of the United Kingdom in the nineteenth and early twentieth centuries. The country's economy allowed it to maintain the strongest military force (especially in terms of the Royal Navy), but instead of attempting to militarily conquer Europe, it turned the aspiring superpower states against one another. According to Mearsheimer, this is also the strategy of the USA: in the West it is clearly the hegemonic great power, and in the rest of the world it seeks to ensure that no similar hegemonic great power can arise.

they tend to seek diplomatic, consensus-based solutions.[349] "Soft" power and the regional influence it can confer are often key aspects of their overall political capital.[350] In the post-Cold War international order, their role has increased substantially, because the regional alliance networks they build are an important resource for both great powers and superpowers.[351] Regional powers represent a fourth level in the hierarchy. Such powers can play a leading economic role in their own region (for example, by helping to establish regional economic integration), and through their military power they can have significant regional influence in security matters. However, regional powers do not have the same overall impact on the international system as middle powers or great powers. Their influence is more local and regional. At this level, however, they are able to win the support of other states in the region by strengthening alliance systems and finding suitable regional partners, thus increasing their influence over regional affairs.

These, then, are the most important and established concepts in international relations regarding states and their relative power. However, as the world order is transformed, certain states come to occupy a situation or role not necessarily covered by these categories. The weakening of the validity of the old concepts is shown by the fact that certain foreign policy strategies no longer fall strictly within the above definitions. In relation to Russia and China, the term "revisionist power" appeared in the US 2017 security strategy, and reappears in the 2022 security strategy as "powers with revisionist

---

349 Cooper-Higgott-Nossal, 1993: 19.
350 Lyon-Tomlin, 1979: 12. This influence can be converted into political capital beyond the immediate region, though of course only to a limited degree. A good example of this is Canada, which with its political image as an "honest broker" has gained visible influence in several conflict resolution situations. Cf. Dewitt-Kirton, 1983: 403.
351 Sweijs-Mazarr, 2023. Taking advantage of this, several middle powers—such as Poland and the Netherlands—have more influence on the operation of the international system than their raw power status would seem to warrant. Cf. Moyer et al., 2018: 16.

foreign policy."[352] In these US documents, these new concepts are predominantly used to describe opponents,[353] and have only limited bearing on the small-state-to-superpower scale. By contrast, we find in the Chinese foreign policy framework the term "powerful state" (*chungeng xiangkuo*), which in this context we might translate as "a state with above-average capabilities."[354]

The signs of change are therefore already visible in foreign policy thinking. We believe that understanding and analysis should not shy away from considering the use of concepts that supplement the standard, established classifications.[355] One such possible framework is the category of regional middle power. This refers to states that are generally comparatively small but capable of exerting an influence on the international system similar to that of middle powers. Unlike middle powers, however, they do not seek hegemony. In comparison with regional powers, regional middle powers do not have a surplus of power covering all areas, even in their own region, and are therefore dependent on regional cooperation.

This is a very specific category, with characteristics of both regional and middle powers, and it fills a kind of intermediary role between these two. Compared to other states, the absolute advantage of regional middle powers lies in the fact that they have the densest network of connections—on a global level—in the international system. Regional middle powers thus perform outstandingly in the connectivity-based model.

Based on all this, it seems that the regional middle power may be a suitable model for describing Hungary's situation, and its

---

352 The White House, 2017; 2022.

353 The fact that the 2022 security strategy also uses the term "major autocratic powers" can be considered part of the framing of democracies versus autocracies as outlined in Chapter 2.

354 Gvosdev, 2015. We will return to this analysis later.

355 This position is shared by others. For example, Robertson-Carr, 2023, write about problems related to the applicability of concepts that can be considered "mainstream." Moeini et al., 2022, argue for the necessity of redefining the term "middle power" in contemporary international relations.

strategic ambitions. The advantages, capacities, and opportunities we enjoy cannot be encapsulated by traditional categories, and if we misidentify our situation, we may draw incorrect conclusions and formulate suboptimal plans of action. This, naturally, should be avoided as far as possible. Therefore, we recommend adopting the concept of the "keystone state" as a general interpretive framework in relation to Hungary, based on and inspired by the characteristics of the regional middle power.[356]

The Origin of the "Keystone State" Concept

The *Oxford English Dictionary* defines "keystone" as either "a central stone at the summit of an arch locking the whole together" or "the central principle of a system, policy, etc., on which the rest depends." Of course, like any definition, this one is not complete, but it will serve our purposes. It is interesting that the Oxford definition uses the term "locking"—as it happens, the Hungarian word for keystone is *"zárókő,"* or, roughly, "locking stone." But why does the English term refer to keys, rather than locks?

Converging arches exert force in opposite directions. We could almost see the two halves of an arch as wrestlers pushing against one another, though of course if they did not have the other half, they would simply fall over under their own unbalanced weight. These opposing forces, straining against each other and therefore pushing apart, are able to form a unity because the keystone forms them into a unity, a whole, holding together what would fall to pieces without it. The keystone is made of the same material as the other stones and does not necessarily differ much from them in size, so if we wanted to express the difference in mathematical terms, it would

---

356 Mišković (in publication) argues similarly, proposing the "keystone state" as a new power category. We also consider it worth mentioning that the problem outlined above also appears in Hungarian geostrategic and economic thinking. The Macronomic Institute (2023) uses a terminology different from ours, preferring the term "swing state," but also investigates and analyses the maneuvering room and bargaining position of middle powers, focusing largely on economic aspects.

be difficult to explain why the keystone is so different from the other elements of the arch. The difference is in the function, the goal, and the role it plays. The keystone must be a separate element from both halves of the arch for it to be able to create balance. But it also has to fit them, in order to fulfill its task. Difference in similarity, similarity in difference.

The situation is similar when we try to interpret the role of the keystone state in the international system. Such keystone states tend to be located along regional geopolitical fault lines, and these fault lines, where civilizations, cultures, and religions strain against each other, can put pressure on a region, and even threaten to fracture it into warring elements. This is where the keystone state comes into play, undertaking to mediate between opposing forces and thus stabilize its own region. It may be no larger than other states of the region in terms of population, landmass, etc., or in other key demographic indicators. Yet its goals, function, and self-perception may be markedly different.

The task of a keystone state is thus twofold. First, it must play a role in shaping its own region, and indeed it must help put its region on the map as an independent actor. Second, it must have connections to opposing forces—perhaps a little more in one direction, a little less in another, but broadly proportionally. It must be able to find common ground with both but also remain different from them. This is precisely why the significance of the keystone state—thanks to its own self-image—goes beyond itself: it is capable of more than its economy, military power, population, or other measurable indicators would suggest. This is an old strategic position, which—perhaps unsurprisingly—has only recently begun to be studied seriously and described in the requisite detail.

For a precise understanding of the keystone state's self-perception and strategy, we need to travel back into the past. Indeed, although the term only really took off in writings dealing with the study of international relations in the twenty-first century, there were states in earlier epochs to which it could have been applied. We might think, for instance, of the Ottoman Empire in the nineteenth century, which, due to its strategic location, was the unavoidable state of the "Eastern question" for both Great Britain and Russia.[357] And in scholarly works, we come across the first description of this concept at the very beginning of the twentieth century: the concept of so-called pivot regions was introduced by Halford J. Mackinder in an article entitled *The Geographical Pivot of History*, published in 1904.[358] However, it is only in recent decades that the concepts of keystone state and pivot state have returned to the forefront of scholarship in this area. This is probably not unrelated to the fact that, in the unipolar world order, it made less sense to think about how a given state could make use of its capabilities within the spheres of influence of two or more powers. With the ongoing transformation of the world order, this is no longer the case, and in consequence, a previously moribund field of discourse has been revived.[359]

In modern English, the word "pivot" has a double meaning, as it can be used as both a noun and a verb. In the former meaning, applied to international relations, it can be identified as a critical fulcrum around which the actions and activities of the great powers revolve. In the latter case, it describes a type of movement on the part of individual states, by which they are able to leave the sphere of one great power and enter that of another through their autonomous policies, changing their circumstances and situation within spheres of interest.[360]

---

357 Chase-Hill-Kennedy, 1996: 34.

358 Mackinder, 1904.

359 Brzezinski (1997) uses the term "geopolitical pivot." For more recent work on this issue, see, for example, Cha-Dumond, 2017; Panda, 2023; Tierney, 2016; Winrow, 2003. This is true not only for international political studies but also for foreign policy planning and practice. South Korea's 2022 Pacific strategy makes becoming a global pivotal state a direct and explicit objective. See The Government of the Republic of Korea, 2022.

360 Sweijs et al., 2014: 8–9. During the Cold War, the maneuvering room of pivot states was limited. Since what power and influence they had stemmed from the

Figure 22: A keystone that has stood for thousands of years:
Hadrian's Triumphal Arch (Ephesus, İzmir Province, Turkey).
Photo: Alex Tang

Ian Bremmer's book *Every Nation for Itself*, published in 2012, is virtually indispensable on this topic.[361] It was Bremmer who introduced the concept of G-zero. By this, he meant a new phase of globalization in which the old rules and regulatory institutions of the world order no longer apply but the rules and regulations that will characterize the new world order have not yet been formed. It is clear from the analyses of this book that we have now entered this phase. Such an intermediate state challenges states in terms of how they relate to the old order and how well they can prepare for unfamiliar conditions. It is difficult to find a balance between the

---

stability and prevailing conditions of the international order, their opportunities for independent action were decisively determined by the fact that they were interested in maintaining the status quo and less in changing the circumstances. Thus, their freedom of movement, which we identified above as the essential feature of "pivot" understood as a verb, was much more limited. Cf. Özkan, 2006: 79.

361 Bremmer, 2012.

two components. Those who cling too doggedly to the old order will be at a competitive disadvantage, while those who move too quickly toward a new order risk a deterioration of their relations with the status-quo states.

In this context, Bremmer also examined which states could be successful in G-zero conditions and with what strategy. Bremmer groups possible national strategies into several categories. In his view, the biggest winners of the changing world may be the so-called pivot states. This term is used by Bremmer to characterize countries that can establish beneficial relations with several great powers without relying excessively on any of them. Thus, a state following such a strategy can avoid having any single country—whether in economic or security terms—exerting an excessively large influence over it. Bremmer considers Brazil, Canada, Kazakhstan, Indonesia, and several African countries as possible pivot states. It is worth noting that Bremmer also examines how states could lose out from such processes. One group of countries that he believes have poor prospects are so-called shadow states, which are too unilaterally dependent on a single superpower or great power. He considers Mexico, for example, to be such a state, as its future depends excessively on its relationship with the United States.[362]

It can also be seen in the figure above that Bremmer examines the situation of a state based on two factors: the state's ability to mediate and act, and the extent to which it is exclusively dependent on a single power bloc.

---

362 It is worth noting that not only excessive unilateral dependence on a great power, but also the complete withdrawal of that great power can put a state in a disadvantageous position. This situation can come about when a great power completely withdraws from the pivot state, i.e., leaving it to fend for itself. As a result, the pivot state may "take revenge" on the great power, turning against it. Afghanistan is a good example. In the final proxy war of the Cold War, the USA provided substantial assistance to the Afghans against the invading Soviet Union. However, after the Cold War, the US no longer treated Afghanistan as a geopolitical priority and left the country to its own devices. Just a decade later, Afghanistan became one of the key loci of international terrorism against America.

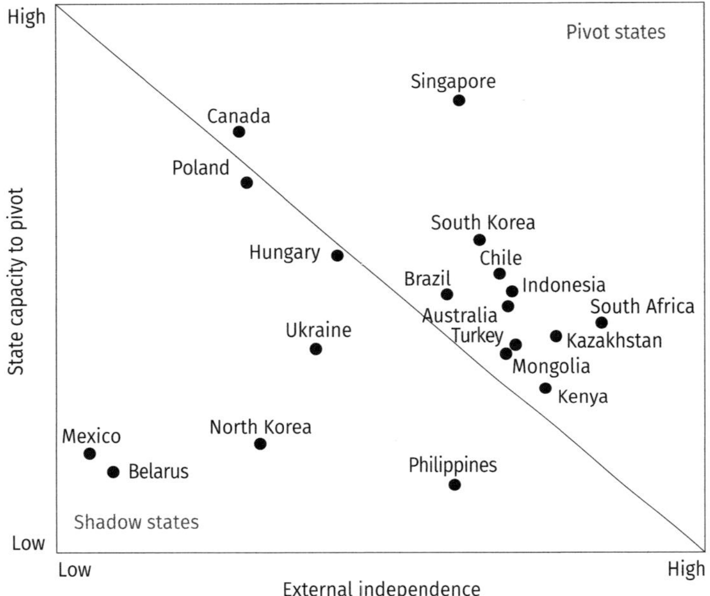

Figure 23: Pivot states that can build profitable relationships
with multiple countries and are not overly dependent on any one are likely
to win in a leaderless world; shadow states that become trapped
in the shadow of a single power are likely to lose out.
Source: Eurasia Group

Bremmer's description formulates general principles regarding only the kind of strategy and posture a country can take to be successful in a changing world, even though we have already learned that a successful mediating role requires a state capable of acting and the avoidance of unilateral dependencies. The table above shows that in 2015 Hungary was classified by Bremmer as a potential pivot state, on the verge of becoming a winner of these processes. Given this, the situation assessment and the task facing us are clear: we are ideally placed, but our relationships must be further strengthened and diversified.

Connectivity Strategies and Existing Keystone Roles

Changing times bring new concepts and new definitions. One sign of this is the fact that the term "keystone state" first shows up in the international relations context in 2015, and it is linked to the name of Nikolas K. Gvosdev.[363] Gvosdev first refers to Bremmer's theory of pivot states, which we have outlined above, and also notes that the Chinese state's foreign policy definition framework includes, in addition to the traditional categories of state power, a new element, namely the "state with above-average capabilities."[364] The essence of this category is that, although these states are typically small in size, they possess outsized international influence thanks to their military capabilities or economic power. In this context, Gvosdev argues that the available resources are only one component of the system for classifying states, and that the perception of the role of the states themselves and the narrative about them in the international system play at least as important a role in categorization. Among these, Gvosdev highlights the stabilization capacity of a given state within its own region. A country that can bring stability to its own region can play a greater role in the international system. Such states are keystone states. As Gvosdev puts it:

> *"As the name implies, a keystone state gives coherence to a regional order—or, if it is itself destabilized, contributes to the insecurity of its neighbors. Such countries are important because they are located at the seams of the global system and serve as critical mediators between different major powers, acting as gateways between different blocs of states, regional associations, and civilizational groupings. A keystone state, even if it is 'small' (xiaoquo in the Chinese*

---

363 Gvosdev, 2015. See also his later publication on the subject: Gvosdev, 2020. The issue was also addressed by Mišković, 2023.

364 Gvosdev, 2015.

taxonomy)—may nevertheless be important to regional or global security beyond what its own domestic capabilities may merit."[365]

Gvosdev formulates specific conditions that should be met by a state wishing to play the role of a keystone state in the international order and in its own region. These include

- suitable geographical features, and
- the ability to integrate.

Geographical location is a given and thus is not, or is only partially, a matter of choice. A country wishing to play a keystone role must be located on the border of regions with different geopolitical conditions. But there is some maneuvering room here too. Sometimes it is sufficient that there are certain trade, transport, or communication routes across the country in question.

The ability to integrate is a more difficult issue. In short, this means the ability to form positive relationships, which can be nourished from multiple sources.[366] If we adapt the aspects identified by Gvosdev to the thought process of this book, a state can acquire the ability to integrate if it fulfills the following preconditions:

- The ability to secure and maintain order is fundamental.
- In the same way, external security must be secured, which requires a strong, well-equipped army.
- Close multidirectional economic relations and substantial FDI must be maintained.

---

365 Gvosdev, 2015.

366 Gvosdev, 2015. By the way, Gvosdev relies on the communitarian foreign policy theory of Amitai Etzioni regarding the concept of integration capacity, on which he himself wrote separately: Gvosdev, 2014.

- In order to offset the vulnerability of the economic structure to external actors, domestic companies must invest—i.e., play an active role—in foreign markets.
- Robust infrastructure is needed to establish the physical foundations for becoming an economic and commercial transit hub.
- It is vital to have a pragmatic coalition-based foreign policy, organized around common interests.
- By playing a regional mediating role, a state can increase its own value in its region, guaranteeing its safety and stability.
- Hosting international events can give a state an outsized role in shaping diplomatic relations, relative to its economic or military strength.

In addition, Gvosdev also gives examples of states that have achieved a keystone role and how they did it:

- Jordan, by maintaining neutrality within its own region and staying out of conflicts.
- Kazakhstan, by diversifying its economic partners.
- Azerbaijan, through its good relationship with global powers and the fact that many transit routes pass through it.
- Indonesia, by participating in the multinational alliance systems of Southeast Asia.

3.3. Hungary as Keystone State

From the above, we can see that there are already successful keystone states in the world, with functioning strategies, breakout trajectories, and the mediating and stabilizing capacities that flow from the role they have adopted for themselves. All these countries have some advantageous feature that they can exploit to take advantage of the keystone-state role and the opportunities it affords. In theory, then, this is certainly a path that can be followed, and some actors have done so successfully. But can Hungary play such a role? Can it become a keystone state and follow a connectivity-based strategy?

We are convinced that Hungary is not only a viable keystone state but also an almost textbook case for such a role and for following a connectivity-based strategy, as a result of which it will soon become a developed country and a regional middle power. We base this claim on at least four factors: first, because of our geographical position and capabilities; secondly, because of our political values; thirdly, as a possible route to economic breakout through the rejection of bloc formation; and fourthly, because the operation of the Hungarian state virtually predestined us for such a role. In the following, we will examine these points in more detail.

Our Geographic Position in the World

Among the criteria necessary for becoming a keystone state, discussed in the previous subsection, one of the most important is geographical location. In this, Hungary is in a particularly advantageous position, which makes it a suitable candidate for regional keystone state.

Carlos Roa, the former editor-in-chief of the well-known American magazine *The National Interest*, who has conducted research in Hungary, came to the same conclusion. In an article in *The Hungarian Conservative*, Roa draws attention to the fact that the keystone role and strategy could prove particularly advantageous for Hungary, since it possesses certain key characteristics that already point in this direction.[367]

Geographically, Hungary occupies a strategic position at the intersection of the Western, Russian, and Turkish spheres of interest, and thus it can play the role of political intermediary and economic transfer hub. The country is a natural nexus of Eurasian trade and already plays an important role in this regard. Several investment projects have already been launched in Hungary to take advantage of this favorable situation.

Although, as discussed at length earlier in the book, the threat of geo-economic fragmentation seriously threatens the expansion of international trade, at present, after the shock caused by the global pandemic, the volume of global trade is increasing: this year, it is expected to increase by 2.4 percent and next year by 3.2 percent, which is well above pre-pandemic levels.[368] The volume of trade between Europe and Southeast Asia may almost double by 2030, with an annual growth of more than 6 percent.[369] Trade in Southeast Asia is dominated by the Chinese relationship, 70 percent of which is conducted through sea ports. This alone contains significant business opportunities.[370] Another 25 percent of the trade between

---

367 Cf. Roa (2022). At the same time, the following paragraphs rely on several points and fit the thought process of Roa's quoted article.

368 WTO, 2023: 3.

369 The estimate basically refers to Sino-German trade: according to Standard Chartered (2021: 64), trade between Germany and China will increase to more than 158 billion dollars by 2030 from the value of 87 billion dollars in 2020.

370 EEAS, 2018: 3.

Europe and China involves air transport, with railway responsible for the rest.

Hungary is also trying to maneuver itself into a favorable position in the field of sea, air, and railway transport. In 2020, Hungary bought one of the terminals at the port of Trieste. The Adriatic Sea is becoming more and more competitive in world trade, and the port of Trieste has almost doubled its commercial traffic in a decade; its major advantage is that it has rail connections to approximately ten countries.[371] The Hungarian terminal is scheduled to be fully operational from 2026, and it will have the capacity to handle up to 2.5 million tons of goods.[372] The giant Cargo City logistics center at Budapest International Airport is a good example of developments in air connectivity: after this expansion, it will handle approximately 240,000 tons of goods. The development of railway trade likewise has significant potential. In Hungary, primarily thanks to internal EU trade, railway freight is already significant by European standards: transnational transport accounts for more than 80 percent of the total traffic.[373] This year, railway transport connected with China recorded a 27 percent year-on-year increase,[374] while the volume of total foreign trade with BRICS countries increased by roughly 10 percent.[375] Furthermore, although railway transport with China currently takes place almost exclusively in the north, via Russia,[376] diversification of railway traffic through the countries of Central Asia and the Caucasus, i.e., by the so-called Middle Corridor, is currently under development, which, alongside ocean shipping, would enable goods to be brought to Europe from the south.[377] In terms of developing railway connectivity, there are two outstanding

---

371 Baniak, 2023.
372 Szabó, 2022.
373 Eurostat, 2022b: 32.
374 Blair, 2023.
375 Jingyi, 2023.
376 Jakóbowski et al., 2018: 35.
377 Chang, 2023.

Hungarian projects. One is the East-West Gate terminal, at the eastern tip of the country, which connects transportation on the northern route. Another factor increasing the competitiveness of this high-tech intermodal logistics center is the fact that the logistics center in Poland, which is the only entry point on the northern route, is currently dealing with many times its operational capacity.[378] The other, southern trade connects to the Budapest-Belgrade railway line, which in turn connects to the port of Piraeus in Greece, thus linking Mediterranean shipping with the Middle Corridor.[379] Of course, the logistics of goods arriving in Hungary—especially when it comes to regional foreign trade—would be unthinkable without connections based on a developed motorway network. Since 2010, we have opened thirty-five cross-border roads, and eleven border crossings have become motorways. At the same time, we have also improved the domestic road network: twenty-one of our twenty-five largest cities are now accessible by motorway, and less than 10 percent of the country's territory is more than one hour's drive from the motorway network.[380]

Our country is also able to function as an energy node, thanks to the Slovakian-Hungarian gas interconnector, the Arad-Szeged gas pipeline, the Turkish Stream gas pipeline, the connection to the Croatian LNG terminal,[381] our electricity network connections with almost all our neighbors,[382] and the Barátság oil pipeline. These energy infrastructure elements all either run through Hungary, or connect to other, larger energy systems on Hungarian territory.

Hungary is also trying to take advantage of its key diplomatic strengths, which are essential for fulfilling the role of keystone state. This can be seen primarily in Hungary's realistic attitude

---

378 K. Kiss, 2021.
379 GT, 2023.
380 Szabó, 2023.
381 IEA, 2023b.
382 IEA, 2023a.

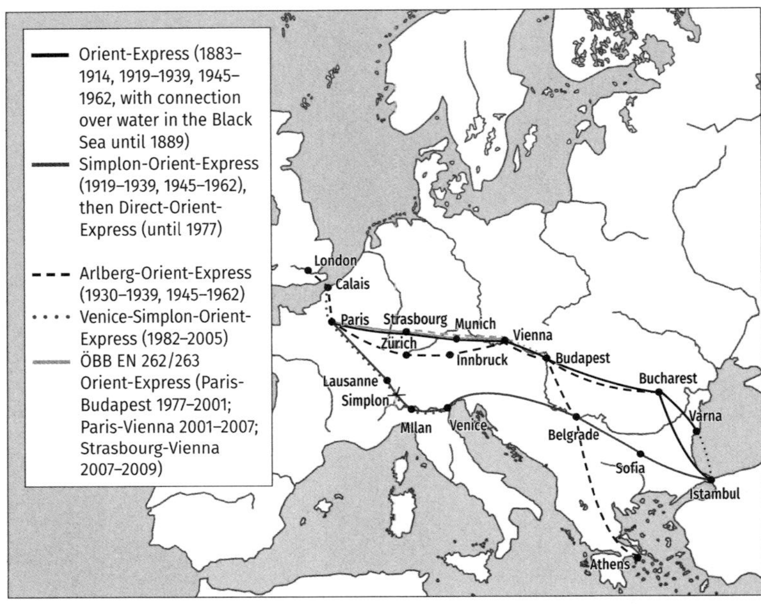

Figure 24: The stops of the iconic transport route of the early 20th century, the Orient-Express—Budapest lies halfway between London and Istanbul.
Source: Wikimedia Commons

Hungarian economy is an integral part of the Western economic system, and nearly 80 percent of Hungarian exports go to the West. But from a political standpoint, relations with the West are clouded by numerous points of controversy. If we are serious about our goals of both reducing unilateral dependence and maintaining good relations with major powers, our task when it comes to Hungary's relations with the West appears challenging. A large proportion of Western states are also unilaterally dependent, which can have political consequences (as we see in the discussions with the European Union). At the same time, attempts to reduce unilateral

---

383 Jeffrey D. Sachs, former chief advisor to the UN Secretary General, believes that the kind of connectivity strategy represented by Hungary is exemplary in the world, as it is how a normal economy can be operated (Kohán, 2023).

dependence (for example, openings to the East or South) can also give rise to political resistance from Western partners.

Representation of Traditional Values

One of the biggest rock bands of the post-1990 period in Hungary was *Tankcsapda*, or Tank Trap, and a line in their song "Mennyország Tourist" ("Tourist in Heaven") goes "The news is all about you, the press is full of you." Incidentally, not only this line but the meta-message of the whole song is related to the theme of this book: in a neoliberal world, even the divine act of grace is nothing but a service, and the result is not what was promised in the attached brochure. But the song proved prophetic in more than one respect. Taking a look at the Western media, we may observe that Hungary is in the news much more often and is the subject of more in-depth analyses than its size, economic weight, or military power would seem to warrant. The press is full of us.

So why is Hungary in the Western news so much? Because of its strong support for traditional Western values. These are the values that the progressive liberal forces of the West are weakening every day and want to erase.[384] That is why our country so often

---

384 According to Chris Rufo, senior researcher at the Manhattan Institute, the Hungarian government attracted the attention of American conservatives by maintaining the country's sense of cultural identity together with a democratic majority, and Hungarian family policy has already had a major influence in the United States (Bakodi, 2023). At the launch of the Hungarian edition of his book *The Parasitic Mind*, Gad Saad said that Hungarians should be very grateful that they had been inoculated against many of the harmful ideas currently on the rise around the world. The thesis of Saad's book is that harmful ideas infect the mind. Some of the ideas present in the Western world could only be described as parasites, so contrary are they to our rational shared interests. These parasitic ideas often start with noble intentions, and they have a common goal: to attain which they seek to destroy the truth (Hajdú, 2022). According to American constitutional lawyer Ilya Shapiro, despite Hungary's small size, it plays an extremely important in the American political discourse. After his visit to Hungary, he gave an account of the flourishing life of the Jewish community and the absence of anti-Semitism. In addition, he also emphasized that "cancel culture" has not spread to Hungary and, as a result, genuine academic freedom of speech prevails (Shapiro, 2022). Roger Köppel, editor-

features in the progressive Western press as a sort of villain. But the battle is not so one-sided. The fact that Hungary is high on the list of countries criticized by the liberal press does not mean that no one in the West shares the Hungarian position. Thus, the peculiar situation has arisen that, alongside the criticism, interested, appreciative, and supportive voices are becoming more and more prevalent.[385] Not to mention the curious phenomenon whereby certain organs of the press, in response to some international development, now wait on tenterhooks for the Hungarian response, because they will be able to build a "story" around that. So it seems that you can like or dislike Hungary's political standpoints and value commitments, but it would take a serious effort to avoid hearing about them. As such, it is precisely its embrace of traditional values that represents Hungary's most important point of potential connectivity in many directions worldwide.

---

in-chief of the Swiss weekly *Weltwoche*, has said that Hungary is an impressive nation that, like the Swiss, follows its own path and defends its own freedom. According to him, Hungary has undergone significant economic development in recent years, which is due to the work of the Orbán government (Köppel, 2023). We can also mention the conservative state- and institution-building successes, and even specific construction projects, currently taking place in the Hungarian capital. Thanks to these, the classical architecture of Budapest, destroyed during the Second World War and under Communism, is once again flourishing. Sholl (2021) considers the reconstruction work currently taking place in the Hungarian capital to be exemplary for Western countries. As he puts it, as an American he has always found European architecture fascinating, because it is the most substantial physical embodiment of Western cultural heritage. Whereas in Western Europe they have turned their backs on classical architecture, Hungary works hard in this domain to preserve its cultural roots, and at the same time strongly expresses its commitment to the Western world. American political scientist John Fonte draws attention to the fact that the bureaucracy and state administration must work with the government and not against it, meaning that the "deep state" cannot act against democratically elected political leaders. The deep state is very strong in the United States. In the long term, the right can act against this by building a parallel institutional system, headed by educated and talented leaders who are loyal to their country. And the Hungarian right, led by Viktor Orbán, is following that method (Szilvay, 2022).

385 According to Brent Buchanan, president of one of the most famous American polling companies, Cygnal, American conservatives now see Hungary as a laboratory for how to develop effective policies to defend traditional values (Dobozi, 2023).

Of course, it may seem strange that even this must be said in so many words. After all, these Classical values have traditionally served as the glue that binds together the Western world. But that, of course, poses an obvious question about when Western civilization began. Did it begin with the Greeks, or the Romans, or the canonization of the doctrines of the Judeo-Christian religions? Or perhaps, as Oswald Spengler believed, Western civilization originated later when these components were first assembled into an organic whole, i.e., at the end of the first millennium AD? In any case, throughout the history of Western civilization, at least until the last few decades, it was always true that these traditional values represented the common cultural and civilizational basis that made lasting cooperation between Western states possible—a kind of supranational cohesive force organizing the Western world.

It would be beyond the scope of this book to provide examples from all ages to support this, though it would be quite possible to do so. It is enough to think of the dawn of the West, the Middle Ages, when the universal church represented the shared forum and Christianity forged the values by which the states of the West were able to organize themselves. An example can also be given from the era of European reconstruction after the Second World War, when the principles of capitalism and the concept of democracy as developed by the English-speaking peoples were grafted onto the European principles of Christian democracy, and it was possible not just to rebuild the continent but to create a community of European states. This is also an important lesson for today's progressive liberals, who, while wishing to build a European empire, have in recent decades been unable to refrain from throwing these previously binding values out the window, replacing them with strange ideologies, abstract value commitments, a false constitutional identity, and distorted norms of the rule of law.[386] While this process has been going on, the

---

386 Adrian Vermeule, professor of constitutional law at Harvard Law School, stated in

Western world has experienced growing uncertainty and a gradual loss of global weight. As such, Hungary's efforts to represent these traditional values is not only logical from the point of view of its own cultural determination, but it can also be interpreted as a specific mission and a broader concern for Western civilization as a whole.

In any case, this Western-oriented stance is the second factor that makes Hungary suitable for the role of keystone state. It arouses interest, makes us relevant, differentiates us, and creates an excellent basis for building relationships with those who would like to do something analogous to the Hungarian approach in their own country. This can be done by taking a stand on specific issues, espousing political solutions, and organizing coalitions built around them. The first and most striking example of this was Hungary's conscious and very visible rejection of illegal and uncontrolled migration in 2015. At first, Western public opinion had no idea what to make of this stubborn resistance by "rebellious" Hungary, and progressive politicians and media outlets were up in arms, predominantly accusing Hungary of racism. However, as soon as the—quite foreseeable—disadvantages of illegal immigration (increased terrorism threat, higher crime rates, no-go zones, increasing anti-Semitism) became more and more obvious, the Hungarian position came to be seen more sympathetically by conservative Europeans and the American right, and more and more opportunities opened up for Hungary to develop especially close ties with these actors.[387]

---

an interview that liberalism as a political movement equates the rule of law with liberalism, just as it does with democracy and liberalism, meaning that democracy is seen as authentic only if it takes on a liberal character. He considers this to be a false equivalence because the rule of law is not necessarily liberal. An alternative to liberalism can be provided by the Christian-democratic constitutional system, which is in line with natural law and the natural foundations represented by, for example, family, marriage, and traditional morality. The Hungarian constitutional system is a good example of this (Dobozi, 2022).

387 According to Kevin D. Roberts, president of the famous Heritage Foundation, Hungary is not only *one* possible model of the conservative state system, but *the* model. He believes that all Western nations, including the Americans and the

Hungary's family policy, meanwhile, demonstrates an equally strong and concrete stance. Our country's efforts to solve demographic problems with the help of family support instead of migration have not gone unnoticed elsewhere. The progressive side—original as always—played the Nazi card again, after hearing about the Hungarian measures. However, this proved ineffective. The Hungarian family support system has not only had significant success, but it has attracted an increasing amount of international attention.[388] This is an area where the construction of international coalitions has already begun, and Hungary has also become a meeting point for those with pro-family views.

A similar picture emerges when we examine Hungary's stance in favor of national sovereignty. In Europe, the progressive liberal elites increasingly firmly represent the position that the future of Western civilization lies in supernational governance.[389] Many Western citizens experience this as an infringement of their own country's sovereignty, but within the EU, at the governmental level, Hungary stands out most markedly in favor of the idea of national sovereignty.[390]

British, could learn much from the Hungarian example (Orbán, 2022). It is perhaps no coincidence that the only place in Europe where the largest conservative political conference in the Western world, CPAC, has found a home is in Europe.

388 World-famous Canadian clinical psychologist Jordan Peterson spoke with data scientist Stephen Shaw. According to Shaw, there are no recent historical examples of a country having entered a downward spiral, reversing course. However, Peterson drew his attention to the fact that Hungary is precisely such an example, as, thanks to family subsidies, the decline in the birth rate has been stopped and reversed (Peterson, 2023).

389 According to American professor Daniel J. Mahoney, the Hungarian prime minister is trying to protect Europe from the postmodern steamroller that transcends states, and to prevent Hungary from losing its connection with its religious and cultural traditions. Viktor Orbán envisions a Hungary that is simultaneously able to enforce both tradition and freedom, and to resist such cultural madness as gender theory. What Viktor Orbán is doing to protect common sense, family, and traditions is nothing more than what every democracy sought for itself a generation or two ago (Híradó.hu, 2023).

390 According to Christopher DeMuth, a senior researcher at the Hudson Institute, America should pay attention to the Hungarian political culture and governmental

Today, therefore, alongside the many criticisms, the sympathetic voices are at least as loud, which shows that you can love or loathe Hungary, but you cannot ignore us.[391]

Equally, by definition, the point of connection with the Western world is the recognition and protection of the social role of Christianity. Progressives tend to see Christianity a kind of obsolete idea, whereas Hungary takes the view that it is impossible to talk about Western civilization while ignoring its Christian cultural foundations. And for a successful Western civilization, it is also necessary that the social teaching of the church—though not its religious activity, because that is a matter of conscience—should be present in political life, because this is precisely what once made Europe so successful.[392] Perhaps it is not solely the work of divine providence that His Holiness Pope Francis has already visited Hungary twice during the short period of his pontificate, and, for example, in the matter of peace, Budapest and the Vatican are singing from the same hymn sheet.

And, while we are on the topic of peace: Hungary has always stood for peace because it is impossible to build relations in times of war. Our country has consistently represented this position in the matter of the war raging on the territory of our neighbor Ukraine,

---

way of thinking. For the Hungarian government, the most important thing is for Hungary to be strong, sovereign, and resilient. According to DeMuth, increasing the proportion of national ownership in the economy is a legitimate goal, as are significant state investments in various strategic sectors. When it comes to certain products, it is better to become self-sufficient than to rely on global production chains (Papp, 2022).

391 American publicist Rod Dreher alludes to this. He states that Hungary is a "free, stable and peaceful country," with a sophisticated, cosmopolitan capital and a countryside that has not been flooded by migrants or the harmful effects of "Woke." In the words of a French citizen who lives here, Hungary is like the Europe in which he grew up (Dreher, 2023).

392 World-famous Israeli philosopher Yoram Hazony spoke on American commentator Dave Rubin's popular show, where they discussed the need for American conservatives to develop a sense of mission similar to that of Hungary, which is centered on building a better future, having children, and religion as a cultural heritage (Rubin, 2023).

Figure 25: On 20 August 2023, the day of Hungarian statehood,
a light show in the shape of a cross appeared in the sky over Budapest.
Source: MTVA, photo: Zoltán Balogh

which is why it has often been labeled as anti-Western.[393] However, it seems that public opinion in most Western countries is resonating more and more with the Hungarian position, and on the global political stage, demands for a cease-fire appear to be gaining ground. Unfortunately, it must be pointed out that had this happened a year earlier, hundreds of thousands of human lives could have been saved, since the front lines have not changed significantly since the summer-autumn of 2022, which only further illuminates the tragic nature of these events.

---

393 John Mearsheimer said about the Hungarian position regarding the war in Ukraine that Hungary has managed its relationship with the United States and Russia with its national interest in mind, balancing between the two great powers. The Hungarians have understood the need to maintain military and economic relations with the Western alliance system, but provoking Russia, which is close to its border, is not in the country's interest. Accordingly, Hungary also adopted the correct posture in the Russo-Ukrainian war and wisely opposed the conflict from the very beginning, urging instead the restoration of peace (Bráder, 2022).

The lesson of all this is that Hungary should remain faithful to the values stemming from its culture and history. Of course, some people will be upset by these values, but they are nonetheless the most foundational Western values, still dear to many Western political actors and social groups, for which the West has long been respected all over the world. Representing our values greatly helps us ensure that Hungary can act as a true keystone state.

Cooperation, Not Bloc Formation

We have already discussed the structure of the Hungarian economy, its export-oriented, investment-stimulating, complex nature, and its incompatibility with a bloc-based world. The real question, however, in a changing world order that may be forming into rival blocs is how to proceed so that Hungary is not the loser but one of the biggest winners. What do we need to do so that we can resist efforts to narrow our relations as a keystone state and to successfully implement our connectivity-based breakout strategy?

We have seen that the for the keystone states considered most successful in the literature, the most important elements in their strategies have been good relations with multiple great powers, "neutrality," and a diversity of economic partners. We have, in other words, the main ingredients of the recipe; we just need to prepare it to our own taste, with the means at our disposal. As such, the primary thing to do is to reject separation and decoupling on all fronts and forums—even when such a strategy is presented as de-risking.

We can easily see why it is not worthwhile for our country to separate itself from any economic powerhouse. In terms of Hungary's top ten import partners, the value of imports from non-EU countries was only 11.7 billion euros in 2010, but had risen to 30 billion euros in 2022—a significantly greater proportional expansion than the rise in total imports.[394] During the same period, we registered a threefold

---

394 Eurostat, 2023g.

rise in imports from India, eightfold from Serbia, fourfold from Turkey, and tenfold from Vietnam.[395] What is more, although the preponderant role of EU markets in terms of exports is self-evident, Hungary's exports to countries outside the EU have expanded spectacularly since 2010, especially to certain countries: Hungary's exports to Serbia increased by more than fourfold, as did exports to Mexico, while exports to Australia rose threefold, and those to Argentina registered a ninefold rise.[396] Based on this, we can say that spectacular growth in new markets can be experienced.

We have already noted that a significant part of the world's energy carriers and mineral resources are not under the control of the Western world. If the energy required to operate the economy, to cool and heat households, and for industrial production is not available in sufficient quantity, then it must be procured.[397] This is not just a matter of iron economic law of supply and demands, but a simple imperative of common sense. This is also why our country cannot support the sanctions imposed on energy carriers. Sanction

---

395 Ibid.
396 Ibid. In terms of trade and the risk of unilateral dependence, it is worth comparing our biggest European and Asian export partners: during the 2008 economic crisis, German imports fell by 20 percent, while Chinese imports fell by only 7 percent (KSH, 2023f; World Bank, 2023a).
397 Far from being an energy island in Europe, Hungary is an integral part of the EU energy network and market. Hungary's dependence on natural gas imports corresponds to the EU average, meaning that domestic consumption—which is typically around 10 billion cubic meters per year—is almost entirely covered by imports (Eurostat, 2023l). Most of the natural gas reaching our country (more than 8 billion cubic meters) enters the country from the south, through Turkey and Serbia, and from Austria in the West. In the past year, however, the value of natural gas from Slovakia, Romania, and Croatia has also increased: thanks to these interconnectors, in addition to Russian natural gas, LNG, Romanian, and Azeri natural gas have also appeared on the Hungarian market. In addition, Hungary also exports, including now to Ukraine, nearly 500 million cubic meters of natural gas per year (FGSZ, 2023). In terms of the electricity network, Hungary is connected to all neighboring states. We can cover our import demand of around 30 percent, and we can also trade with neighboring countries (Mavir, 2023). Thanks to the completion of the interconnector with Slovenia last year, a joint Hungarian-Serbian-Slovenian electricity exchange can finally be launched—it is scheduled to go online in early 2024 (*Világgazdaság*, 2023).

regimes not only lead the world in the direction of rival blocs, but also result in immeasurable economic losses and deterioration of competitiveness for Western economies.[398]

And the above findings are also true when it comes to investment from abroad. Self-isolation from technological developments elsewhere is a barrier to progress in production chains. Investment must come from both the East and the West so that we can be involved in production processes with the highest possible added value in as many areas as possible.[399] The trade data show that Western players are losing momentum, while non-Western states are gaining momentum in terms of their capacities. In addition, in many sectors currently undergoing a sea-change, the procedures, knowledge, raw materials, and resources required for production, i.e., the technological knowledge, are not (or at least are not only) in the hands of the West. As such, Hungary must face the fact that the extensive (that is, in terms of volume) and intensive (that is, in terms of added value) growth necessary to catch up successfully can only be achieved through relations maintained in all directions.

If we really aspire to the role of keystone state, we must become a hub for trade and economic relations. We must learn to transform contradictions and competition into cooperation, and separation into connectedness. Unilateral dependencies must be replaced and counterbalanced by a multidirectional, diversified network

---

398 Calculations suggest that separation would result in an almost 6 percent decrease in Germany's annual economic output, while real earnings would decrease by nearly 7 percent (Felbermayr et al., 2021: 8). Separation from China would cost Germany almost four times as much as Brexit. Cf. Fuest et al, 2022: 3.

399 According to data from the Hungarian Investment Promotion Agency (HIPA), in 2022, 48 percent of foreign direct investment came from the East and 42 percent from the West, which shows that the FDI inflow is roughly geographically balanced. Last year, for the third time, South Korea was the country that brought the most working capital to Hungary, while Germany, which contributed about a third of the investment volume, contributed the most projects (HIPA, 2023). Data from the OECD for 2021 show that capital inflows from the European Union and Asia were of roughly equal size in Hungary (OECD, 2023).

of relationships.[400] In addition to reducing the risk of conflicts in security terms, it is a driving force in achieving our goal of leveling up the Hungarian economy.

A Competent and Resilient State

So far, we have discussed in detail the external factors necessary to become a keystone state. In Hungary's case, these include the country's location, its value commitments towards Western civilization, and its intention to reduce its unilateral dependencies by rejecting the decoupling of the global economy. But we have not yet dealt with Hungary itself, and the peculiarities of its political and state operations. However, we know from our discussion of resilience that these internal elements are at least as essential to the success of a connectivity strategy as external factors. However, it seems that, here too, we possess singular advantages: the Hungarian state system and political structure make our country particularly suitable for the role of keystone state.

Two key issues for any political system are political legitimacy and the ability to operate effectively. Of course, these are quite separate elements, and they need not coexist: it is conceivable that a system of governance may work efficiently but not possess the necessary social support. On the other hand, fragmented and unstable political formations that nonetheless have broad popular backing are also entirely possible. Hungary has experienced this

---

400 This is also a lesson from Hungary's late-twentieth-century economic history. The significant Western exposure of the Hungarian economy (whether in terms of exports or FDI) can be largely traced back to the global economic events of the 1990s. First, with the transition to dollar transactions and the breakup of the Soviet Union, our Eastern markets collapsed. In 1991, the volume of Hungarian-Russian bilateral trade fell by 50 percent (Réthi, 2000: 11–12). At the same time, from 1991, Japan started to stagnate, and the country's "lost decade" began. Thirdly, in 1997, the crisis in Southeast Asia hit, which also affected China and the Little Tigers. Economic growth began again in 1999. In addition, the financial transformations that laid the foundations for subsequent growth in China started only after that point (Wang, 2007).

discrepancy. István Bibó, one of the greatest figures of twentieth-century Hungarian political thought, formulated the question in the most tangible way. In the mid-twentieth century, Bibó argued that all political systems since the 1867 Compromise had struggled with a legitimacy deficit. It had been possible to create efficient political systems, i.e., governmental structures capable of making and implementing decisions that could endure for decades (either as part of the Austro-Hungarian Monarchy, between the two world wars, or even in a sense under Communism), but all lacked broad democratic legitimacy. Under Austro-Hungarian Dualism, barely four percent of the overall Hungarian population were enfranchised, while in interwar Hungary there was no secret ballot in most regions, and during the Communist era, elections were a mere formality. According to Bibó, this ultimately led to a distorted political process in Hungary, which left its mark on both political decision-making and the thinking of citizens.[401]

In all of Hungarian history, true democratic legitimacy was only really achieved in the post-1990 period: in today's Hungary, 80 percent of the country's inhabitants, i.e., the entire adult population, has the right to vote, which they can exercise through a secret ballot. The integrity of the elections is checked every year by international organizations, and they typically find everything in order. However, in the twenty years following the end of Communism—i.e., until 2010—it was impossible to establish a stable political operation, as was most clearly demonstrated by the almost continuous political crises of the 2000s.[402] After 2010, Hungary managed to elect a stable

---

401 Bibó, 1990.

402 If we consider stability in terms of whether, during the post-1990 period, early elections had to be called (for example, following unsuccessful attempts to form a government due to the absence of a parliamentary majority), then we can say that the political system of post-1990 Hungary proved stable: all Parliaments completed their four-year terms. Moreover, until 2006, a new government was formed at every election. All true, but the balance of power in the parliament, which changed every four years, pointed to the volatility, variability, and contingency of both the party system and voter behavior. Cf. Szabó (2015). From the 2000s, these patterns

Figure 26: Ambrogio Lorenzetti's fresco The Allegory of Good Government—
resilience is primarily a matter of government performance.
Source: Wikimedia Commons

majority with a democratic mandate, thus meeting the requirements of both effective governance and democratic legitimacy.

We could say that this is the result of a happy accident, or more maliciously that it is the result of some devious political machination, but we are convinced that this is not the case. What is really at issue here is the problem of the relationship between leaders and the led. According to the American political philosopher

changed, and something like a two-party system began to emerge, which could have gone on to consolidate party structure and voter behavior. However, this process of partisanship and voter empowerment, input legitimacy, is only one side of the coin. The output side of efficiency and legitimacy concerns the acceptance by the community of the government's decisions. The political crises of the 2006 cycle (dissemination of the Öszöd speech, mass demonstrations, police excesses, the appearance of radical organizations) and economic governance during the financial crisis (austerity, unemployment), as well as overall governmental "degeneration" (Csizmadia, 2023), undermined the stability and acceptance of the political system.

Patrick J. Deneen, this is the issue that has defined Western political thinking since the beginnings of Western civilization, dating back to antiquity. In Deneen's account, the history of the concept can be reconstructed as follows. Until the emergence of progressive ideologies (i.e., Communism and liberalism), the task of leaders was to represent the whole political community and to enforce the goals and value commitments formulated by that community. Progressive ideologies changed this insofar as leaders who espoused this spirit no longer focused on representing the views of the led (cf. Plato's *The Statesman*), but on representing the goals of the ideology they espoused. Both progressive ideologies are teleological, designating a direction of historical progress (with either the coming of Communism or the victory of liberal democracy signaling the end of history) and members of the political community must fight for this goal. As such, the task of political leaders is not to represent the goals and values of the community and to shape them into action, but to put the resources of the community at the service of achieving the ultimate goal.[403] Deneen sees this as the reason why the liberal democracies in the West are struggling with an ever-increasing democratic deficit, because voters simply will not vote for the political and public policy programs offered to them by Western elites. According to Deneen, a regime change is therefore necessary. After the liberal age, the West must enter a so-called post-liberal age whose agenda is to restore the concept of the common good to its rightful place in the policy-making process (common-good conservatism).[404]

In this regard, Hungary, with its political history over the past thirty-four years, is a bright spot not only in the West but even in the whole world. It seems that the regime change Deneen sees as so desirable has already taken place here. As a result, the level of

---

403 Deneen, 2018.
404 Deneen, 2023.

democratic legitimacy in Hungary is so high that it does not come at the expense of political action. In this context, our country performs better in terms of efficiency and legitimacy than older, larger Western democracies, while in terms of legitimacy it outperforms the non-democratic states in the East. The latter can be effective, but—in the absence of fair and regular elections—it is impossible to really know how much legitimacy their political elite has. And this—as we saw in 1989-90 in Central and Eastern Europe—can ultimately lead to a sudden and complete collapse.

From this point of view, Hungary therefore has "best of both worlds." This is particularly important when it comes to connectivity and resilience. First, this approach combines the best elements of Western and Eastern political solutions, thus enabling Hungary to stand its ground in both environments. Secondly, as we have seen, true resilience can never come from an algorithmizable, automatic operating process. At times, it is necessary for human decisions to override automatic processes. And this necessitates the political willingness and ability to act.

In addition, Hungary is taking special measures to channel the opinions and preferences of voters into its political decision-making processes. Referendums are frequent on the most important issues, and regular questionnaires, known as National Consultations, allow citizens to express their views on key issues. Although these do not have the binding force of public law, 1.52 million Hungarian citizens have expressed their opinions through them.[405] The government typically acts on the basis of the results of these consultations, and even more importantly, the opinions of the Hungarian people

---

405 There were 3.4 million valid votes in the 2016 referendum on the mandatory resettlement quota, and 3.9 million in the 2022 referendum on child protection. As for the National Consultations, 1.7 million returned their questionnaires on EU leadership ("Stop Brussels!") in 2017, 2.3 million on immigration ("Stop Soros!") in the same year, 1.4 million on protecting families in 2018, 1.7 million in 2020 on measures to curb the impact of the pandemic, and 1.7 million in the 2022 consultation regarding sanctions.

serve as a reference point for the government during international negotiations on the most controversial issues.

It is only based on these foundations that Hungary can operate a connectivity-based strategy and fulfill its keystone role. The combination of democratic legitimacy and competent state leadership forms a rare and valuable combination in today's world, and it can set an example for other states as well.

3.4. The Twelve Rules of Hungarian Connectivity

*"It is better to have no system at all than one modelled upon another.
The Hungarian reality loses its shape and becomes unrecognizable if you force
it into a conceptual framework bearing the stamp 'made in Germany'."*
(Mihály Babits)

At this point, all that remains is to draw our conclusions. At some point in all our lives, there comes a moment when we must stand on our own two feet. The stabilizers are removed, and we have to stay upright on the bike without them. This is what Hungary is preparing for. The Hungarian connectivity strategy is an answer to the question of how to be independent in such a way that we do not close ourselves off from others but instead open up in all directions while preserving our own identity. The next decade will be about how Hungary can be an independent player in the international order. Actors who do not depend on the goodwill of others do not have to subordinate their own interests to the machinations of great powers, and they can generate their own well-being and the resources necessary for their rise. We went through the conceptual frameworks that can help us set our goals, what it means to be a developed country and a regional middle power, and how connectivity helps achieve this. We analyzed the international environment and found that, although the world is moving toward a multipolar order, giving up relations and forming blocs is a dead-end solution and thus is unacceptable for Hungary. We need both connectivity and resilience. We looked at how the operation of the Hungarian state needs to be transformed, what geopolitical role we want to play (keystone state), and how to build on our strengths. There is nothing left but to synthesize all this and formulate, as a kind of roadmap, the twelve rules of the Hungarian connectivity strategy:

I. *Don't give up your values, build on them!* The Hungarian language
and culture are unique. There is nothing quite like them in the
world. Although related languages do exist, they are such distant
cousins that it is difficult to find even vague resemblances. In
a cultural sense, Hungarians are an island in the middle of
Europe: all neighboring peoples have close relatives, but we only
have distant relatives who live far away. This may at first look
like a problem. What can a country do on its own? What can
give meaning to such a starkly separate identity? Moreover, if
Hungary is such a linguistic and cultural island, how can it aspire
to a relationship-building role? Fortunately, the opposite is true.
In order to connect, we have to be different. Those who identify
completely cannot connect, but rather copy, imitate, and thus
ultimately give up their values and themselves. True connection
requires differences as well as commonalities. This is why we
Hungarians are so lucky: Hungarian culture is both Western
and Eastern. It is both and neither. It is Western because more
than a thousand years ago the Hungarians decided to adopt
Western Christianity and settle permanently in the middle of
Europe. It is Eastern because our heritage from the great Asian
steppes still lives with us today. It is there in the fairy tales told
to every Hungarian child, in our folk songs we learn in school,
in our customs, our interactions, and our worldview, as well as
in the way we find solutions to shared problems. This is not a
hindrance but a help; it is our specialty. Being isolated in the
Carpathian Basin makes sense if we preserve our identity, build
on our unique culture, and thus walk the path of connectivity.

II. *Build coalitions!* Though Hungarian culture is unique, its
otherness hides the possibility of countless points of connection.
Hungary's connectivity-based strategy can work if it uses these
to create collaborations and participate in coalitions. One of
our most important points of connection is Christian culture.
Christianity is the shared culture of the Western world, of which

Hungarians are also a part. Christian culture is not just a matter of personal faith. It also shapes the way in which Hungarians, and Westerners more broadly, interact with one another. It is why we see unconditional, unique value in others. Christian culture is the force that always has and always will hold together the countries of the Western world. Today, this culture is under attack. If Christianity disappears from the West, the West too will cease to exist. As such, one of the most important points in the Hungarian connectivity strategy is to participate in a joint Western effort to safeguard the values of Christianity. Another point of connection is the issue of national independence. The history of mankind is replete with rivalries between empires and nations. The goal of empires is centralization and unification, while that of nations is self-determination and diversity. Hungarian culture and history are all about national self-determination. We Hungarians believe that the world can become a better place through cooperation between sovereign nations, just as we also believe that our world was most successful when it was organized based on free nations. Therefore, bringing together nationally minded forces all over the world is a priority of our connectivity strategy. It also follows from Hungarian culture that Hungarians are pro-family. The possibility of family life in all parts of our world is among the most pressing issues of our time—sometimes because of population decline, sometimes because of population growth. For this reason, Hungary must seek cooperation with all actors with a serious interest in population and family policy. This is also true of migration, which is closely related to population. We are convinced that, first, it is necessary to provide local help to parts of the world that are struggling, and secondly, that immigration is not a solution to the population problems of the Western world. Representing this conviction is another potential point of connection. Last but not least, there are the economic issues: in the modern world, investment, development, and innovation require connectivity. Therefore, Hungary must seek extensive opportunities for economic cooperation.

III. *Invite as many investors as possible!* The most obvious field of economic cooperation is the world of investment. Moreover, a country can only become permanently developed if levels of direct working capital investment are high. A connectivity-based strategy is specifically built around high levels of FDI. Diversifying investment from abroad increases a country's resilience and helps it stand on more feet in times of uncertainty. Thus, the task of the state is to facilitate and accelerate direct capital inflow. In addition, broad-based investment in priority industries should be encouraged. The global order is changing, and so is traditional, multilateral international engagement. This is why Hungary increasingly needs to independently build ways to increase capital inflow without depending on external approval or political pressure. This will enable Hungary to become an independent political actor and make effective use of its economic potential.

IV. *Let your national champions be decisive!* If more resources flow to Hungary, that will be a welcome development. But if we were to base our country's development on these alone, our economy would become one-sided, and we could easily find ourselves in a vulnerable position. Some of the resources that come here will eventually leave our country in the form of profits, so it is necessary that Hungarian companies also grow and become stronger thanks to the additional resources. Moreover, and even more importantly, Hungarian champions need to deploy their capital and thereby bring the ratio of investments into and withdrawals from the national economy as close to equilibrium as possible. In states as large as the United States and China—and this surely also goes for the larger European economies as well—these processes have already taken place. Hungary's economy is not large enough to spontaneously start moving in this direction. Without a sufficient critical mass, a catalyst is required. This catalyst is the Hungarian state. The task is for the state to help the most powerful Hungarian companies, which have a good chance of holding their own in regional and global competition. For this, the state must also develop new skills. We need to better understand the logic of the market, to be able to work smoothly and effectively with our national champions. But there is one more thing. The job of the champion is to lead the army in battle—but the battle can only be won by the whole army. Therefore, the task of the champions is to pull small and medium-sized Hungarian enterprises upwards, supporting them in their development and internationalization.

V. *Have sectors that serve as breakout points!* "Jack of all trades, master of none" is proverbial for a reason. If we want to aim for outstanding performance, we must specialize. Switzerland became known for its watches, Japan for its microelectronics, Israel for its arms industry, Szeged for its slippers, and Pécs for its gloves. It is good to have a trade. The Hungarian economy will only be successful if we focus on the sectors with the greatest potential growth. The state has a prominent role to play in this. The selection criteria are that these sectors should be future-oriented, have high added value, develop production chains, help connect Hungary and the Hungarian economy to the world, and last but not least, fit the profile of our national champions. We have identified several such sectors, including the military industry, which requires high-tech research and favors the logic of clustering; the food industry, which increases security of supply and resilience; information-communication, conceived in the spirit of connectedness; the vehicle industry, which has the most extensive supply chains; and the banking sector, which is outstanding in terms of financing and profitability. Finally, the great challenge of the future, which should also serve to reduce our unilateral dependence, is green energy.

VI. *Have developed infrastructure!* A good connectivity strategy requires connectivity not only in cultural and economic terms, but also in the physical world. Such is the case whether it be on land, sea or air, and whether it involves goods transport, travel, or energy. In other words, everything must be done to ensure that the developed infrastructure necessary for travel, goods traffic, and energy transfer is available in Hungary. Let there be roads. Let there be railways. Let there be airports. Let there be logistics, storage, and distribution centers. But it is not just about connecting the country to the world. We also need internal connectivity: the various regions of the country should have extensive connections with one another. Therefore, in the case of infrastructural development, special attention must be paid to ensuring that all parts of the country benefit proportionally from the developments, so that no areas are left out of the nation's arterial network. This enables the transport network to truly connect the entire country, and for economic activity to be evenly distributed among the various regions. Moreover, there is one other important aspect that relates to external and internal connectivity: redundancy. The goal is to ensure that every route connecting our country with the world can easily be replaced by another if sudden changes on the world stage make this necessary. In the same way, we seek to make connections within Hungary as decentralized as possible. If someone is traveling from Gyula to Villány, there is no reason why they should have to go via Budapest.

VII. *Participate actively in organizing your own region!* A connectivity-based strategy must be backed by a strong commitment to the local region. Regional commitment means that Hungary must focus not only on integration into global supply chains but also prioritize deeper involvement in regional supply chains. It is necessary to ensure that Hungary, as a key player in the region, participates actively in political decision-making affecting the future of the region, as well as in the development of plans that determine the future of the region. This means that Hungarians must have specific ideas and visions regarding the development of the region. However, a country interested in connectivity must not only keep its own success in mind but also strive to increase the global weight of the region. Therefore, it is essential for Hungary to use its connections, political influence, and economic power to strengthen the entire region. To this end, it must support regional trade and economic partnerships, as well as contributing to joint undertakings and infrastructure development projects. Politically, the country must take measures that promote the economic development and competitiveness of the entire region. Such active regional involvement not only contributes to the country's connectivity but also strengthens the region's stability and increases its weight on the international scene. The combination of a strong regional commitment and the benefits of connectivity will create an opportunity for the country to succeed in international competition with its competitive companies and strong economic position.

VIII. *Build for the next generation!* The success of Hungary's connectivity-based strategy depends on whether there are Hungarian citizens who can seize the opportunities inherent in it. Therefore, the state has a special responsibility to promote the development of the necessary skills in future generations. Education and talent management must be given special importance, so that the next generation has a thorough knowledge and understanding of the culture and operating logic of their own country. In addition, it is important that the next generation acquires not only theoretical knowledge but also valuable practical experience—skills that are useful in coordinating state and market players, training national leaders, and building foreign relations. As for the state, it is essential to build a professional civil service, while vocational schools and higher education courses must be harmonized with the needs of leading industries. The education system must prepare the next generation to be proud of their cultural roots and competitive on the international stage. We need a patriotic, knowledge- and performance-based educational culture that is open to the rest of the world, thus promoting connectivity. Only such an approach will enable us to take advantage of the buoyancy inherent in our own cultural values, and, through training and the knowledge and experience offered by the education system, give us the tools to effectively connect with other nations and cultures, thereby promoting common development and cooperation.

IX. *Make your country a meeting point!* One of the effective methods of building effective relationships is if Hungary can serve as a real meeting place, and this means we must attract and host international events. Major sporting events, economic conferences, cultural events, and exhibitions all provide an opportunity to showcase Hungary and catch the world's attention. Thanks to its hospitality and cultural heritage, our country can be an attractive destination for tourists, who will hopefully return home with positive memories. In addition, by hosting international events, Hungary can become an important meeting place for the scientific, political, economic, and cultural communities. All this contributes fundamentally to the effectiveness of relationship building, by creating an opportunity for dialogue and mutual understanding between different cultures. In this way, Hungary can not only promote its own culture and values but also contribute to strengthening the world's cultural diversity and connections. This strategy can promote the development of economic and diplomatic relations while enhancing Hungary's international reputation.

X. *Establish security!* You cannot grow without security. Disorder, confusion, and physical danger can ruin what a community has achieved and raise obstacles to further development. Today, we see that many factors threaten security in the world, and it is more than likely that challenges to security will only intensify. Wars are becoming more common, European countries are exposed to considerable terrorist threats, and migratory pressure on the European Union seems not only to be persisting but even increasing. Meanwhile, across Europe, we are seeing the decline of the middle class. As a result, traditional parties are eroding, political polarization and fragmentation are on the rise, and the distance between the political elite and the electorate is widening. In many places, this has meant a reduced ability to govern and not just a temporary but a permanent condition of instability. In such circumstances, a political community's success depends on being able to recognize such dangers in time and to guarantee security on all fronts. This requires a modern, well-trained army, strong police, strict border protection, and a stable political system serving the interests of the people. Without security, it is more difficult to build relationships. An uncertain region is never attractive in the eyes of the outside world: stability and public order are hard currencies that make a country a reliable partner, attract investment, and make trade dependable and predictable. Connectivity does not work without security.

XI. *Base your foreign policy on the national interest!* A fundamental element of a connectivity-based strategy is that countries can shape their foreign policy according to their own national interests. This also means that efforts to shepherd us into a state of unilateral dependency must be resisted. These trends are currently manifested in the process of bloc formation. During this process, a country fully integrates into one of several international blocs and, in doing so, severs or greatly reduces its relations with states outside that bloc. This would not be beneficial for Hungary, because it would reduce our country's resilience and make it vulnerable to the bloc's leading states. Instead, our connectivity-based strategy should be able to employ both an open and closed foreign policy. This means that Hungary must be able to manage its interdependencies in such a way as to gain relative advantages from them, but its further development should not depend on the existence or absence of any single relationship. This necessitates a foreign policy that effectively manages Hungary's dependencies and relations. The country must diversify its relations and connect to new partner countries and regions. This will enable our country to react flexibly to the changing international situation while maintaining our economic, political, and security independence. A connectivity-based strategy creates opportunities for Hungary to become an independent player in the international arena and effectively assert its national security and economic interests.

XII. *Support peace!* The world order is changing. The process has not only started, but we might even say we have passed the first act and are already approaching the climax. We can see from the war raging in Ukraine and the recently begun Israeli-Palestinian conflict that the realignment of world power is entailing armed conflicts that are increasingly bloody and demand ever more victims. We see also that these conflicts do not serve our interests. It is important to understand that there is no predetermined order in international politics, so the question of whether the transformation will continue to be violent or will take place peacefully depends on the key actors currently on the international stage. For Hungary, only the latter path is worth supporting. In addition to fundamental moral precepts, peace is in our national interest because connectivity works only if we place an emphasis on cooperation based on shared interests. The connectivity-based strategy seeks to find out where, in what areas, and in what form mutually beneficial relationships can be built. We must focus on what unites us, not on what separates us. But war builds strong and high walls. That is why we must seize every opportunity to advance the cause of a peaceful transition.

And the cause of peace is best served if we do not form economic blocs that promote isolation and the deepening or freezing of conflicts but strive for deeper trade relations. All this is based on the insight that extensive relations and cooperation beneficial to all parties based on intersecting interests can reduce the chances of war. For Hungary, this is a particularly important strategic precept arising from our geographical situation. Let us not forget the old wisdom, which, by some strange twist of fate, is also the last thought of this book: sometimes words can achieve what the sword cannot.

REFERENCES

Acemoğlu, D., S. Johnson, and J. A. Robinson. "The Rise of Europe: Atlantic Trade, Institutional Change, and Economic Growth." *The American Economic Review* 95/3 (2005): 546–79. https://doi.org/10.1257/0002828054201305

Acemoğlu, D. and J. A. Robinson. *Why Nations Fail: The Origins of Power, Prosperity, and Poverty.* New York: Crown Publishers, 2012.

Adhia, N. "The History of Economic Development in India since Independence." *Association for Asian Studies* 20/3 (2015). https://www.asianstudies.org/publications/eaa/archives/the-history-of-economic-development-in-india-since-independence/

Adler-Karlsson, G. *Western Economic Warfare, 1947–1967: A Case Study in Foreign Economic Policy.* Stockholm: Almqvist and Wiksell, 1968.

Agénor, P. "Caught in the Middle? The Economics of Middle-Income Traps." *Journal of Economic Surveys* 31/3 (2017): 771–91.

Ágh A. "A globalizáció rejtélyei" [The Riddles of Globalization]. *Educatio* 31 (2022): 951–53. https://mersz.hu/hivatkozas/matud202307_f89201/?fbclid=IwAR2Jdm788dSsEfVzp-DsZCVdx51kLRICHZh6SMzwfq3SY3sggL4niCAyY_Oo#matud202307_f89201

Ágh A. "Basic Democratic Values and Political Realities in East Central Europe." *Társadalom és Gazdaság Közép- és Kelet-Európában* 17/1 (1995): 75–94.

Ahlijian, C. "Congo's Cobalt Controversy" *globalEDGE,* April 20, 2022. https://globaledge.msu.edu/blog/post/57136/congos-cobalt-controversy

Ahmari, S. "Fukuyama's Blame Game." *Compact,* April 22, 2022. https://compactmag.com/article/francis-fukuyama-s-neoliberal-blame-game

Ahmari, S. *The Unbroken Thread: Discovering the Wisdom of Tradition in an Age of Chaos.* Colorado Springs: Convergent Books, 2021.

Aiyar, S. et al. "Geoeconomic Fragmentation and the Future of Multilateralism." *IMF Staff Discussion Notes,* January 15, 2023. https://www.imf.org/en/Publications/Staff-Discussion-Notes/Issues/2023/01/11/Geo-Economic-Fragmentation-and-the-Future-of-Multilateralism-527266

Albert, R. and A. Barabási. "Statistical Mechanics of Complex Networks." *Reviews of Modern Physics,* 74/1 (2002): 47–97.

Alfaro, L. et al. "FDI and Economic Growth: The Role of Local Financial Markets." *Journal of International Economics* 64/1 (2004): 89–112.

Allen, R. C. "The Rise and Decline of the Soviet Economy." *Canadian Journal of Economics / Revue Canadienne D'économique,* 34/4 (2001): 859–81.

Allison, G. "The Thucydides Trap: Are the US and China Headed for War?" *The Atlantic,* September 24, 2015.

Allison, G. "The New Spheres of Influence." *Foreign Affairs,* March/April 2020. https://www.foreignaffairs.com/articles/united-states/2020-02-10/new-spheres-influence

Amaro, S. "Biden's IRA has left Europe blindsided. And playing catch-up could lead to 2 big mistakes." *CNBC,* 2 February 2023. https://www.cnbc.com/2023/02/02/bidensira-has-left-europe-blind-sided-and- playing-catchup-could-lead-to-2-bigmistakes.html

Aristotle. *Politics.* Simpson, P. L. P. (ed.). University of North Carolina Press, 2000.

ASIS International. "ASIS SPC. 1-2009, Organizational Resilience Standard." https://www.ndsu.edu/ fileadmin/emgt/ASIS_SPC.1-2009_Item_No._1842.pdf

Association of Southeast Asian Nations (ASEAN): *Master Plan on ASEAN Connectivity 2025,* 2017. https://asean.org/wp-content/uploads/2018/01/47.-December-2017-MPAC2025-2nd-Reprint-.pdf

Bakodi P. "'Magyarország hihetetlen munkát végzett': amerikai konzervatív véleményvezér a Mandinernek" ["Hungary has done an incredible job": American conservative opinion leader speaks to Mandiner]. *Mandiner,* 30

March 2023. https://mandiner.hu/kulfold/2023/3/202303230-cristopher-f-rufo-interju

Baniak, S. "The Adriatic Ports: A Silent Expansion onto the Central European Markets." *Centre for Eastern Studies,* Number 541, October 10, 2023. https://www.osw.waw.pl/en/publikacje/osw-commentary/2023-10-02/adriatic-ports-a-silent-expansion-central-european-markets

Barabássy M. "A magyar Szent Korona szerkezeti egysége." [The structural unit of the Hungarian Holy Crown], *Országépítő* 29/1 (2018): 18–25.

Barber, J. "Economic Sanctions as a Policy Instrument." *International Affairs* 55/3 (1979): 367–84.

Bartlett, J. and E. Bae. "Sanctions by the Numbers: 2021 Year in Review." *Center for New American Security,* January 13, 2022. https://www.cnas.org/publications/reports/sanctions-by-the-numbers-2021-year-in-review

Bartoniek, E. *A magyar királykoronázások története* [A History of Hungarian Coronations]. Budapest: Akadémiai Kiadó, 1987.

Bateman, J. "U.S.-China Technological 'Decoupling': A Strategy and Policy Framework." *Carnegie Endowment for Peace,* April 25, 2022. https://carnegieendowment.org/2022/04/25/u.s.-china-technological-decoupling-strategy-and-policy-framework-pub-86897

Bathelt, H., A. Malmberg, and P. Maskell. "Clusters and Knowledge: Local Buzz, Global Pipelines and the Process of Knowledge Creation." *Progress in Human Geography* 28/1 (2004): 31–56.

Beckley, M. and H. Brands. *Danger Zone: The Coming Conflict with China,* New York, W. W. Norton & Company, 2022.

Beckley, M. "Delusions of Détente." *Foreign Affairs,* September/October 2023. https://www.foreignaffairs.com/united-states/china-delusions-detente-rivals

Beekun, R. I. and W. H. Glick. "Organization Structure from a Loose Coupling Perspective: A Multidimensional Approach." *Decision Sciences* 32/2 (2007): 227–50.

Bekkevold, J. I. "5 Ways the U.S.-China Cold War Will Be Different from the Last One." *Foreign Policy,* 29 December 2022. https://foreignpolicy.com/2022/12/29/us-china-cold-war-bipolar-global-order-stability-biden-xi/

Bélyácz I. *Privatizáció és gazdasági verseny.* Budapest: Prodinform, 1993.

Ben-Ari, R. H. *The Legal Status of International Non-Governmental Organizations.* Leiden: Martinus Nijhoff, 2013.

Benassy-Quere, A. et al. "Foreign Direct Investment and Company Taxation in Europe." *ENEPRI Working Paper* 4, April 2001. http://aei.pitt. edu/1864/1/ENEPRI_WP04.pdf

Bender, P. "America: The New Roman Empire?" *Orbis* 47/1 (2003): 145–59. https://www.sciencedirect.com/science/article/abs/pii/ S0030438702001801?via%3Dihub

Berlin, I. *The Hedgehog and the Fox: An Essay on Tolstoy's View of History.* London, Weidenfeld & Nicolson, 1953.

Beyer, S. and G. Molnar. "Accelerating Energy Diversification in Central and Eastern Europe." *IEA,* 2022. https://www.iea.org/commentaries/ accelerating-energy-diversification-in-central-and-eastern-europe

Bhattacharyay, B. N. "Institutions for Asian Connectivity." *ADBI Working Paper Series* 220 (2110). https://www.adb.org/sites/default/files/ publication/156075/adbi-wp220.pdf

Bibó I. *Válogatott tanulmányok* [Selected Studies]. Budapest: Magvető Könyvkiadó. 1990.

Biden, J. R. "Why America Must Lead Again." *Foreign Affairs.* March/ April 2020. https://www.foreignaffairs.com/articles/united-states/2020-01-23/why-america-must-lead-again

Bihari M. *Magyar politika, 1944–2004: Politikai és hatalmi viszonyok* [Hungarian Politics, 1944–2004: Political and Power Relations]. Budapest: Osiris Kiadó, 2005.

Binder, M. and Payton A. Lockwood. "With 'Frenemies' Like These: Rising Power Voting Behavior in the UN General Assembly." *British Journal of Political Science* 52/1 (2022): 381–98. https://centaur.reading. ac.uk/93690/3/02Nov2020frenemies_acceptedsubmission.pdf

Blair, A. "Signal: China-Europe Rail Freight Traffic Increases 27% in H1 2023." *Railway Technology,* August 28, 2023. https://www.railway-technology.com/deals-dashboards/china-europe-rail-freight-traffic-increases-by-27-in-2023/?cf-view

Blanchette, J. and C. Johnstone. "The Illusion of Great-Power Competition."
    Foreign Affairs, July 24, 2023. https://www.foreignaffairs.com/ united-
    states/illusion-great-power-competition

Bogdandy, A. von and S. Schill. "Die Achtung der nationalen Identität
    unter dem reformierten Unionsvertrag" [Respect for National Identity
    under the Reformed Union Treaty]. *Zeitschrift* 70 (2010): 710–34.
    https://www.zaoerv.de/70_2010/70_2010_4_a_701_734.pdf

Borvendég Zs. *Az "impexek" kora: Külkereskedelmi fedéssel folytatott
    pénzkivonás a „népgazdaságból" a Kádár-rendszer idején az
    állambiztonsági iratok tükrében* [The Age of "Impexes": Withdrawal of
    money from the "national economy" under the guise of foreign trade
    during the Kádár regime as revealed in state security documents].
    Budapest: Nemzeti Emlékezet Bizottsága, 2017.

Botos K. "A rendszerváltozás és a pénzügyi politika" [System change and
    financial policy]. In *Pénzügypolitika az ezredfordulón* [Fiscal Policy at the
    Turn of the Millennium], edited by K. Botos (Szeged: JATEPress, 2003),
    11–33.

Bourbeau, P. "Resilience and International Politics: Premises, Debates,
    Agenda." *International Studies Review* 17/3 (2015): 374–95.

Bown, C. P. and D. A. Irwin. "Trump's Assault on the Global Trading System:
    And Why Decoupling From China Will Change Everything." *Foreign
    Affairs* 98/5 (2019): 125–37.

Bozóki A. and D. Hegedűs. A kívülről korlátozott hibrid rendszer:
    Az Orbán-rezsim a rendszertipológia tükrében [The externally limited
    hybrid system: The Orbán regime in the light of system typology].
    Politikatudományi Szemle 2 (2017): 7–35. http://real-j.mtak.hu/9080/14/
    Poltud_Szemle_2017-02%20bel%C3%ADv%20nyomdai.pdf

Böckenförde, E. *Staat, Gesellschaft, Freiheit* [State, Society, Freedom].
    Frankfurt am Main: Suhrkamp Verlag, 1976.

Bráder, Á. "John J. Mearsheimer: Hungary Has Done a Great Job
    Navigating the Waters." *Hungarian Conservative,* November 16, 2022.
    https://www.hungarianconservative.com/articles/current/john-j-
    mearsheimer-hungary-has-done-a-great-job-navigating-the-waters/

Bradford, C. I. "Perspectives on the Future of the Global Order." *Brookings,* May 4, 2022. https://www.brookings.edu/articles/perspectives-on-the-future-of-the-global-order/

Brands, H. "The Last Chance for American Internationalism: Confronting Trump's Illiberal Legacy." *Foreign Affairs,* January 20, 2021. https://www.foreignaffairs.com/articles/united-states/2021-01-20/last-chance-american-internationalism

Brands, H. and J. L. Gaddis. "The New Cold War." *Foreign Affairs,* November/December 2021. https://www.foreignaffairs.com/articles/united-states/2021-10-19/new-cold-war

Bremmer, I. "The Next Global Superpower Isn't Who You Think." *Foreign Policy,* June 17 2023. https://foreignpolicy.com/2023/06/17/china-russia-us-multipolar-world-technology/

Bremmer, I. *Every Nation for Itself: Winners and Losers in a G-Zero World.* New York: Portfolio, 2012.

Brooks, S. G. and W. C. Wohlforth. "The Myth of Multipolarity." *Foreign Affairs,* May/June 2023. https://www.foreignaffairs.com/united-states/china-multipolarity-myth

Brzezinski, Z. *Strategic Vision: America and the Crisis of Global Power.* New York: Basic Books, 2012.

Brzezinski, Z. *The Grand Chessboard: American Primacy and its Geostrategic Imperatives.* New York: Basic Books, 1997.

Bull, H. *The Anarchical Society: A Study of Order in World Politics.* New York: Columbia University Press, 2002.

Bundeskanzler, der (website). *Regierungsbefragung im Deutschen Bundestag mit Bundeskanzlerin Merkel.* May 13, 2020. https://www.bundeskanzler.de/bk-de/aktuelles/regierungsbefragung-kanzlerin-1752666

Calderón, C. and L. Servén. "The Effects of Infrastructure Development on Growth and Income Distribution." *Policy Research Working Paper,* World Bank Group, September 2004.

Carothers, T. "The End of the Transition Paradigm." *Journal of Democracy* 13/1 (2002): 5–21. https://www.journalofdemocracy.org/wp-content/uploads/2012/02/Carothers-13-1.pdf

Carr, E. H. *The Twenty Years' Crisis, 1919-1939: An Introduction to the Study of International Relations.* New York: Harper & Row, 1964.

Cassani, A. "Hybrid What? Partial Consensus and Persistent Divergences in the Analysis of Hybrid Regimes." *International Political Science Review.* 35/5 (2014): 542–58.

Cave, D. "How 'Decoupling' from China Became 'De-risking'." *The New York Times,* May 20, 2023. https://www.nytimes.com/2023/05/20/world/decoupling-china-de-risking.html

Centraal Bureau voor de Statistiek. "Manufacturing Output Almost 8 Percent Down in June". Augustus 10, 2023. https://www.cbs.nl/en-gb/news/2023/32/manufacturing-output-almost-8-percent-down-in-june

Central Statistics Office (website). "Foreign Direct Investment in Ireland 2017." https://www.cso.ie/en/releasesandpublications/ep/p-fdi/foreigndirectinvestmentinireland2017/ae/

Cercas, J. "There is an Unprecedented Crisis because of the War: The Answer is a Powerful Europe." *El País,* January 19, 2023. https://english.elpais.com/international/2023-01-19/there-is-an-unprecedented-crisis-because-of-the-war-the-answer-is-a-strong-europe.html

Cerulus, L. and S. Wheaton. "How Washington Chased Huawei out of Europe." *Politico,* November 23, 2022. https://www.politico.eu/article/us-china-huawei-europe-market/

Cha, V. D. and M. Dumond, ed. *The Korean Pivot: The Study of South Korea as a Global Power.* Washington D.C.: Center for Strategic and International Studies, 2017.

Chang, F. K. "The Middle Corridor through Central Asia: Trade and Influence Ambitions." *Foreign Policy Research Institute,* February 21, 2023. https://www.fpri.org/article/2023/02/the-middle-corridor-through-central-asia-trade-and-influence-ambitions/

Chase, R., E. Hill, and P. Kennedy. "Pivotal States and U.S. Strategy." *Foreign Affairs,* January/February 1996. https://www.foreignaffairs.com/articles/algeria/1996-01-01/pivotal-states-and-us-strategy

Chenery, H. B. *Structural Change and Development Policy.* Oxford: Oxford University Press, 1979.

Chenoy, A. "Bypassing the Dollar: The Rise of Alternate Currency Systems." *The Wire,* 25 May 2020. https://thewire.in/trade/dollar-currency-trade

Chu, J. "The New Arms Race: Sanctions, Export Control Policy, and China." *CSIS,* March 25, 2022. https://www.csis.org/analysis/new-arms-race-sanctions-export-control-policy-and-china

Chung, S. "Innovation, Competitiveness, and Growth: Korean Experiences." In *Annual World Bank Conference on Development Economics, Global 2010: Lessons from East Asia and the Global Financial Crisis,* edited by J. Y. Lin and B. Pleskovic (2010). https://www.rrojasdatabank. info/wbdevecon10-22.pdf

CIA (website). *World Factbook: Country Comparisons—Population,* 2023. https://www.cia.gov/the-world-factbook/field/population/country-comparison/

Cianetti, L. and S. Hanley. "The End of the Backsliding Paradigm? Avoiding Reverse 'Transitology' in Central and Eastern Europe." *Journal of Democracy* 32/1 (2021). https://preprints.apsanet.org/engage/api-gateway/apsa/assets/orp/resource/item/5e859c0a37a5d600112072cd/original/the-end-of-the-backsliding-paradigm-avoiding-reverse-transitology-in-central-and-eastern-europe.pdf

Clarke, M. and A. Ricketts. "Donald Trump and American Foreign Policy: The Return of the Jacksonian Tradition." *Comparative Strategy* 36/4 (2017): 366–79.

Cliquennois, G. *European Human Rights Justice and Privatisation: The Growing Influence of Foreign Private Funds.* Cambridge: Cambridge University Press, 2020.

Clover, C. "Xi Jinping signals departure from low-profile policy." *Financial Times,* 20 October 2017. https://www.ft.com/content/05cd86a6-b552-11e7-a398-73d59db9e399

Colaresi, M. P. et al. *Strategic Rivalries in World Politics: Position, Space and Conflict Escalation.* Cambridge: Cambridge University Press, 2008.

Colin, C. *The Conditions of Economic Progress.* London: Macmillan, 1940.

Cooper, A. F., R. A. Higgott, and K. R. Nossal. *Relocating middle powers: Australia and Canada in a Changing World Order*. Vancouver: UBC Press, 1993.

Cox, M. "Empire by Denial: The Strange Case of the United States." *International Affairs* 81/1 (2005): 15–30.

Cui, Y., J. Jiao, and H. Jiao. "Technological Innovation in Brazil, Russia, India, China, and South Africa (BRICS): An organizational Ecology Perspective." *Technological Forecasting and Social Change* 107 (2016): 28–36.

Culbreath, J. "Rival Theories of Multipolarity: Aleksandr Dugin and Jiang Shigong." *European Conservative*, January 23, 2023. https://europeanconservative.com/articles/essay/rival-theories-of-multipolarity-alexander-dugin-and-jiang-shigong/

Csáky, V. et al. "Early Medieval Genetic Data from Ural Region Evaluated in the Light of Archaeological Evidence of Ancient Hungarians." *BioRxiv*, July 13, 2020. https://www.biorxiv.org/content/10.1101/2020.07.13.200154v1

Cseszka É.: Lefagyott a rendszer, a mechanizmus befejeződött: magyar gazdaságtörténet 1968–1978 között [The system is frozen, the mechanism is finished: Hungarian economic history between 1968–1978]. In *Alap és felépítmény: Gazdaságpolitika a Kádár-rendszerben* [Base and Superstructure: Economic Policy in the Kádár System], edited by A. Schlett. Budapest, Tarsoly Kiadó, 2008, 91–108.

Csizmadia E. "A kormányzati ciklusok mintázatának változásai 1990–2010 között: Külföldi példák és a magyar váltógazdálkodási ciklus módosulása 2006-ban" [Changes in the Pattern of Government Cycles Between 1990 and 2010: Foreign Examples and Changes in the Hungarian Transitional Government Cycle in 2006]. *Politikatudományi Szemle* 32/3 (2023): 55–77.

Csizmadia E. "Ellenzékiség, aktorok és a demokrácia nyitott kimenetele" [Opposition, actors and the open outcome of democracy]. *Politikatudományi Szemle* 28/4 (2019): 89–116.

Daalder, I. H. and J. M. Lindsay. "Bush's Revolution." In *Foreign Policy*, edited by R. J. Lieber. Abingdon: Routledge, 367–76.

Dadush, U. and B. Stancil. "The World Order in 2050." Carnegie Endowment for International Peace, 2010. https://carnegie-endowment.org/files/World_Order_in_2050.pdf?fbclid=IwAR2Jd-m788dSsEfVzpDsZCVdx51kLRICHZh6SMzwfq3SY3sggL4niCAyY_Oo

Damijan, J. P. et al. "Technology Transfer Through FDI in Top-10 Transition Countries: How Important are Direct Effects, Horizontal and Vertical Spillovers?" William Davidson Working Paper, Number 549. Rochester, NY: Social Science Research Network, 2003.

Dasgupta, S. and A. Singh. "Manufacturing, Services and Premature Deindustrialization in Developing Countries: A Kaldorian Analysis." In *Advancing Development: Core Themes in Global Economics*, edited by G. Mavrotas, G. and A. Shorrocks. London: Palgrave Macmillan, 2007, 435–54.

Datt, G. and A. Mahajan. *Datt & Sundharam Indian Economy.* New Delhi: S. Chand Limited, 2009.

Davies, N. *Europe: A History.* London: Random House, 2014.

Day, G. S. and P. J. H. Schoemaker. *Peripheral Vision: Detecting the Weak Signals that will Make or Break Your Company.* Brighton, MA: Harvard Business Review Press, 2006.

Delisle, J. and A. Goldstein. "China's Economic Reform and Opening at Forty: Past Accomplishments and Emerging Challenges." In *To Get Rich Is Glorious: Challenges Facing China's Economic Reform and Opening at Forty*, edited by Jacques de Lisle and Avery Goldstein. Washington D.C.: Brookings Institution, 2019, 1–26. https://www.brookings.edu/wp-content/uploads/2019/04/9780815737254_ch1.pdf

Demertzis, M. "De-risking as an Economic Strategy." *Bruegel*, June 6, 2023. https://www.bruegel.org/comment/de-risking-economic-strategy

Deneen, P. J. *Regime Change Toward a Postliberal.* New York: Sentinel, 2023.

Deneen, P. J. "The End of Fukuyama." *Postliberal Order*, May 23, 2022. https://www.postliberalorder.com/p/the-end-of-fukuyama

Deneen, P. J. *Why Liberalism Failed.* New Haven. CT: Yale University Press, 2018.

Deng, I., C. Pan, and B. Perez. "Huawei's 5G Smartphone Comeback, with Advanced Chip Wrapped in Secrecy, Releases Chokehold of US Sanctions on China Tech." *South China Morning Post,* September 30, 2023. https://www.scmp.com/tech/big-tech/article/3236295/huaweis-5g-smartphone-comeback-advanced-chip-wrapped-secrecy-releases-chokehold-us-sanctions-china

Denhardt, R. B. *Theories of Public Organization 5th California.* Belmont, CA: Thomson Wadsworth, 2010.

DerSimonian, A. "Europe Needs a Stable Russian-German Relationship." *Quincy Institute for Responsible Statecraft.* September 12, 2022. https://quincyinst.org/2022/09/12/europe-needs-a-stable-russian-german-relationship/

Desch, M. C. "America's Liberal Illiberalism: The Ideological Origins of Overreaction in U.S. Foreign Policy." *International Security* 32/3 (2007): 7–43.

Dewitt, D. and J. Kirton. *Canada as a Principal Power: A Study in Foreign Policy and International Relations.* Toronto: Wiley and Sons, 1983.

Di Maio, M. "Industrial Policy in the BRICS: Similarities, Differences, and Future Challenges." In *Structural Change and Industrial Development in the BRICS,* edited by W. Naude, A. Szirmai, and N. Haraguchi, Oxford: Oxford University Press, 2015, 429–53.

Diamond, L. "Elections Without Democracy: Thinking About Hybrid Regimes." *Journal of Democracy* 13/2 (2002): 21–35.

Dickel, R. et al. "Reducing European Dependence on Russian Gas: Distinguishing Natural Gas Security from Geopolitics." Oxford: The Oxford Institute for Energy Studies, 2014. https://www.oxfordenergy.org/wpcms/wp-content/uploads/2014/10/NG-92.pdf

DiPippo, G. I. Mazzocco, and S. Kennedy. "Red Ink: Estimating Chinese Industrial Policy Spending in Comparative Perspective." *Center for Strategic & International Studies,* May 2022. https://csis-website-prod.s3.amazonaws.com/s3fs-public/publication/220523_DiPippo_Red_Ink.pdf?VersionId=LH8ILLKWz4o.bjrwNScsuX_CO4FyEre

Dobozi G. "'Magyarország ellenáll a liberalizmus bomlasztásának': Harvardi professzor a Mandinernek" ["Hungary is resisting the chaos of liberalism": A Harvard professor speaks to Mandiner]. *Mandiner,* December 6, 2022. https://mandiner.hu/hirek/2022/12/kozelet-adrian-vermeule--liberalizmus?fbclid=IwAR34F3twF52o-Xfc-zgK2oORzImLkdlT95_nZ-8hjxOFK4xCf5S39QhBhHrA

Dobozi, G. "'A lot of my conservative friends in the US now look to Hungary as a blueprint': An Interview with Brent Buchanan of Cygnal Polling & Analytics." *Hungarian Conservative,* October 24, 2023. https://www.hungarianconservative.com/articles/interview/brent_buchanan_cygnal_polling_analytics_interview_us_hungary_conservatives/?fbclid=IwAR3SAYUQQ6_Aha4nqjexmePgyevv6QaCtVnSyDlxDu3cpxoT1NXvsHNWKSk

Dodds, K. "Both China and Russia Will Avoid the Arctic Ocean Becoming a 'NATO Ocean'" *Ankasam,* January 27, 2023. https://www.ankasam.org/royal-holloway-university-of-london-prof-klaus-dodds-both-china-and-russia-will-avoid-the-arctic-ocean-becoming-a-nato-ocean/?lang=en

Doner, R. F. and B. R. Schneider. "The Middle-Income Trap: More Politics than Economics." *World Politics* 68 (2016): 608–44. https://polisci.mit.edu/files/ps/imce/faculty/documents/SchneiderandDoner2017.pdf

Downes, A. B. and J. Monten. "Forced to be Free? Why Foreign-Imposed Regime Change Rarely Leads to Democratization." *International Security* 37/4 (2013): 90–131.

Doxey, M. *Economic Sanctions and International Enforcement.* Oxford: Oxford University Press, 1971.

Doyle, M. W. "Kant, Liberal Legacies, and Foreign Affairs." *Philosophy and Public Affairs* 12/3 (1983): 205–35.

Dreher, R. "Orbán: Guardian of Liberal Freedoms." *The Critic,* November 2023. https://thecritic.co.uk/issues/november-2023/orban-guardian-of-liberal-freedoms/?fbclid=IwAR38BbE83HHxH2IeRsNCMlWbrEEyjrDe2If2O1yBiqICvVIVREFVzdLb9jw

Duthoit, A. and M, Lemerle. "Missing Chips Cost EUR100bn to the European Auto Sector." *Allianz,* September 13, 2022. https://www.allianz-trade.

com/en_global/news-insights/economic-insights/european-automotive-semiconductor-shortage.html

Economy, E. "Xi Jinping's New World Order: Can China Remake the International System?" *Foreign Affairs* 101/1 (2022): 52–67.

Edwards, S. "Openness, Productivity and Growth: What Do We Really Know?" *The Economic Journal* 108/447 (1998): 383–98.

European External Action Service (website). *Joint Communication to the European Parliament, the Council, the European Economic and Social Committee, the Committee of the Regions and the European Investment Bank: The Global Gateway*, September 19, 2018. https://www.eeas.europa.eu/sites/default/files/joint_communication_-_connecting_europe_and_asia_-_building_blocks_for_an_eu_strategy_2018-09-19.pdf

Eldem, T. "Russia's War on Ukraine and the Rise of the Middle Corridor as a Third Vector of Eurasian Connectivity." *Stiftung Wissenschaft und Politik*, October 28, 2022. https://www.swp-berlin.org/en/publication/russias-war-on-ukraine-and-the-rise-of-the-middle-corridor-as-a-third-vector-of-eurasian-connectivity

Enterline, A. J. and J. M. Greig. "The History of Imposed Democracy and the Future of Iraq and Afghanistan." *Foreign Policy Analysis* 4/4 (2008): 321–47.

Erdős, P. and A. Rényi. "On Random Graphs, I." *Publicationes Mathematicae, Debrecen* 6/3–4 (1959): 290–97.

Essen, H. von. "Russia-China Economic Relations Since the Full-Scale Invasion of Ukraine." *The Stockholm Centre for Eastern European Studies (SCEEUS)*, 2023/2. https://sceeus.se/en/publications/russia-china-economic-relations-since-the-full-scale-invasion-of-ukraine/

Euractive (website). "Biden arrives in Europe for triple summits on Ukraine." March 24, 2022. https://www.euractiv.com/section/global-europe/news/biden-arrives-in-europe-for-triple-summits-on-ukraine/

Ewalt, J. A. G. and E. T. Jennings. "Administration, Governance, and Policy Tools in Welfare Policy Implementation." *Public Administration Review* 64/4 (2004): 449–62.

Fantappie, M. and V. Nasr. "A New Order in the Middle East? Iran and Saudi Arabia's Rapprochement Could Transform the Region." *Foreign Affairs,* March 22, 2023. https://www.foreignaffairs.com/china/iran-saudi-arabia-middle-east-relations

Fattal Jaef, R. N. "On the Welfare Costs of Premature Deindustrialization." *World Bank,* March 2023. https://openknowledge.worldbank.org/entities/publication/8f2c1a84-32cb-4f18-a4d0-9c01f6f0e0ea

Fazi, T. "Will America Win from De-dollarisation?" *UnHerd,* April 24, 2023. https://unherd.com/2023/04/will-america-win-from-de- dollarisation/

Felbermayr, G., H. Mahlkow, and A. Sandkamp. "Cutting Through the Value Chain: The Long-Run Effects of Decoupling the East from the West." *Empirica* 50 (2022): 75–108.

Felbermayr, G. et al. "Decoupling Europe." *Kiel Policy Brief* 153, 2021. https://www.econstor.eu/bitstream/10419/242494/1/KPB-153.pdf

Felbermayr, G. et al. "The Global Sanctions Data Base." *European Economic Review* 129 (2020).

Ferdinand, P. "Rising Powers at the UN: An Analysis of the Voting Behaviour of BRICS in the General Assembly." *Third World Quarterly* 35/3 (2014): 376–91.

Ferguson, N. "Biden Says Democracy Is Winning: It's Not That Simple." *Bloomberg,* 2023a. https://www.bloomberg.com/opinion/articles/2023-07-16/is-biden-right-that-us-democracy-is-beating-china-and-russia?sref=ojq9DljU

Ferguson, N. *Colossus: The Rise and Fall of the American Empire.* New York: Penguin Books, 2005.

Ferguson, N. "The Dollar's Demise May Come Gradually, But Not Suddenly." *Bloomberg,* 2023b. https://www.bloomberg.com/opinion/articles/2023-04-23/dollar-may-fall-to-yuan-crypto-but-not-soon-niall-ferguson

Fernández de Córdoba, S. and A. Bouhey. "Trade and the MDGs." *UN Chronicle* 45/1 (2008): 16–18.

Feulner, E. "What Are America's Vital Interests?" *The Heritage Foundation,* February 6, 1996. https://www.heritage.org/political-process/report/what-are-americas-vital-interests

Finnemore, M. *The Purpose of Intervention: Changing Beliefs about the Use of Force.* Ithaca, NY: Cornell University Press, 2013.

Fischer, S., R. Sahay, and C. A. Végh. "Economies in Transition: The Beginnings of Growth." *The American Economic Review* 86/2 (1996): 229–33. https://www.jstor.org/stable/2118128

Fisher, A. G. B. "Production, Primary, Secondary and Tertiary." *Economic Record* 15/1 (1939): 24–38.

Fitzgerald, F. S. "The Crack-Up." *Esquire,* February 1936.

Fodor I. "A keleten maradt ősmagyarok" [The early Hungarians who remained in the East]. *História* 34/2 (2012): 3–7.

Folke, C. "Resilience: The emergence of a perspective for social-ecological systems analyses." *Global Environmental Change* 16/3 (2006): 253–67.

Forbes, S. "Biden Says U.S. Must Lead New World Order: What America Needs If He's Serious." *Forbes,* 25 March 2022. https://www.forbes. com/sites/steveforbes/2022/03/25/biden-says-us-must-lead-new-world-order-what-america-needs-if-hes-serious/

Foroohar, R. "After Neoliberalism: All Economics Is Local." *Foreign Affairs* 101/6 (2022): 134–45.

Fox, W. T. R.: *The Super-Powers: The United States, Britain, and the Soviet Union: Their Responsibility for Peace.* New York: Harcourt, Brace and Co., 1944.

Frankel, J. A. and D. Romer. "Does Trade Cause Growth?" *The American Economic Review* 89/3 (1999): 379–99.

Franza, L. "Bone of Contention or Instrument of Peace?" *Clingendale Spectator* 72, 2018. https://spectator.clingendael.org/pub/2018/2/the-role-of-gas/

Friedberg, A. "A World of Blocs?" *War on the Rocks,* July 25, 2023. https://warontherocks.com/2023/07/a-world-of-blocs/

Friedman, G. "Still a Unipolar World." *Geopolitical Futures,* October 18, 2022. https://geopoliticalfutures.com/still-a-unipolar-world/

Friedman, M. "Neo-Liberalism and its Prospects." *Farmand,* February 17, 1951, 89–93. https://miltonfriedman.hoover.org/internal/media/dispatcher/214957/full

Friedman, S. "Beyond 'Democratic Consolidation': An Alternative Understanding of Democratic Progress." *Theoria (Pietermaritzburg)* 58/126 (2011): 27–55.

Frontex (website). "EU's External Borders in 2022: Number of Irregular Border Crossings Highest Since 2016." January 13, 2023. https://www.frontex.europa.eu/media-centre/news/news-release/eu-s-external-borders-in- 2022-number-of-irregular-border-crossings-highest-since-2016-YsAZ29

Fuest, C. et al. "Geopolitische Herausforderungen und ihre Folgen für das deutsche Wirtschaftsmodell." IFO Institute, August 2022. https:// www.ifo.de/en/publikationen/2022/monographie-autorenschaft/geopolitische-herausforderungen

Fukuyama, F. "More Proof That This Really Is the End of History." *The Atlantic,* October 17, 2022. https://www.theatlantic.com/ideas/archive/2022/10/francis-fukuyama-still-end-history/671761/

Fukuyama, F. *The End of History and the Last Man.* New York: The Free Press, 1992.

Funnell, A. "Joe Biden Wants a Global Democratic Alliance but Does He Risk Alienating Crucial US Allies?" *ABC News,* August 29, 2021. https://www.abc.net.au/news/2021-08-30/joe-bidens-belief-in-democracy-might-drive-allies-away/100411966

Gaddis, J. L. *On Grand Strategy.* New York: Penguin Press, 2018.

Galántai J. "Az Osztrák–Magyar Monarchia felbomlása" [The disintegration of the Austro-Hungarian Monarchy]. In *20. századi egyetemes történet,* 1. kötet, Európa, [Universal History of the Twentieth Century, Volume 1], edited by I. Németh. Budapest: Osiris Kiadó, 2006, 34–42.

Gan, N. et al. "China May Not Be a Member of the G7, But It's Dominating the Agenda." *CNN,* June 11, 2021. https://edition.cnn.com/2021/06/11/china/g7-summit-agenda-mic-intl-hnk/index.html

García-Herrero, A. and G. Ng. "China's State-owned Enterprises and Competitive Neutrality." *Policy Contribution,* 5, 2021. https://www.bruegel.org/sites/default/files/wp-content/uploads/2021/02/PC-05-2021.pdf

García-Herrero, A. and D. M. Turégano. "Europe Is Losing Competitiveness in Global Value Chains While China Surges." *Bruegel*, 2020. https://www.bruegel.org/blog-post/europe-losing-competitiveness-global-value-chains-while-china-surges

García-Herrero, A. "Resilience of Global Supply Chain: Facts and Implications." *ADBI Working Paper Series,* 1398, 2023. https://www.adb.org/sites/default/files/publication/891616/adbi-wp1398.pdf

García-Herrero, A. "The Geopolitics of Semiconductors and What Europe Can Expect." *Bruegel,* 2022. https://www.bruegel.org/newsletter/geopolitics-semiconductors-and-what-europe-can-expect

Geddes, B., J. Wright, and E. Frantz. *How Dictatorships Work: Power, Personalization, and Collapse.* Cambridge: Cambridge University Press, 2018.

Gehrke, T. and J. Ringhof. "The power of control: How the EU can shape the new era of strategic export restrictions." *ECFR,* May 17, 2023. https://ecfr.eu/publication/the-power-of-control-how-the-eu-can-shape-the-new-era-of-strategic-export-restrictions/

Georgieva, K. "Confronting Fragmentation Where It Matters Most: Trade, Debt, and Climate Action." *IMF Blog,* January 16, 2023. https://www.imf.org/en/Blogs/Articles/2023/01/16/Confronting-fragmentation-where-it-matters-most-trade-debt-and-climate-action

Georgieva, K. "Why We Must Resist Geoeconomic Fragmentation— And How." *IMF Blog,* May 22, 2022. https://www.imf.org/en/Blogs/Articles/2022/05/22/blog-why-we-must-resist-geoeconomic-fragmentation

Germuska, P. "Failed Eastern Integration and a Partly Successful Opening up to the West: The Economic Re-orientation of Hungary During the 1970s." *European Review of History: Revue europeenne d'histoire* 21/2 (2014): 271–91.

Gerő A. "1867 kiegyezése két látószögből" [The 1867 Compromise from two perspectives]. *Historia Critica,* 2014, 241–55. https://edit.elte.hu/xmlui/static/pdf-viewer-master/external/pdfjs-2.1.266-dist/web/viewer.html?file=https://edit.elte.hu/xmlui/ bitstream/

handle/10831/22380/Gero_Historia_critica_pdfa_241–55.
pdf?sequence=1&isAllowed=y

Gewirtz, J. *Unlikely Partners: Chinese Reformers, Western Economists,
and the Making of Global China.* Cambridge, MA: Harvard University
Press, 2017.

Gewirtz, P. "Words and Policies: 'De-risking' and China Policy." *Brookings,*
2023. https://www.brookings.edu/articles/words-and-policies-de-
risking-and-china-policy/

Gheribi, E. and N. Voytovych. "Prospects of Foreign Direct Investments in
Technology Transfer." *Economic and Environmental Studies* 18/46 (2018):
551–76.

Ghinamo, M., P. M. Panteghini and F. Revelli. "FDI Determination and
Corporate Tax Competition in a Volatile World." CESifo Working
Paper 1965, April 2007. https://www.ifo.de/DocDL/cesifo1_wp1965.
pdf

Gill, I. and P. Nagle. "Inflation Could Wreak Vengeance on the World's
Poor." *Brookings,* 2022. https://www.brookings.edu/articles/inflation-
could- wreak-vengeance-on-the-worlds-poor/

Gilpin, R. "No One Loves a Political Realist." *Security Studies* 53 (1996): 3–26.
https://www.tandfonline.com/doi/abs/10.1080/09636419608429275

Gilpin, R. *War and Change in World Politics.* Cambridge: Cambridge
University Press, 1981.

Giuliani, E. "The Selective Nature of Knowledge Networks in Clusters:
Evidence from the Wine Industry." *Journal of Economic Geography* 7/2
(2007): 139–68.

Glaeser, E. L. et al. "Do Institutions Cause Growth?" *Journal of Economic
Growth* 9/3 (2004): 271–303.

Glatz F. "Magyarország betagolása a szovjet zónába" [The integration of
Hungary into the Soviet zone]. *História* 28/6–7 (2006): 3–7.

Glawe, L. and H. Wagner. "The Middle-Income Trap: Definitions, Theories
and Countries Concerned—A Literature Survey." *Comparative Economic
Studies* 58/4 (2016): 507–38.

Gleick, J. *Chaos: Making a New Science.* New York: Viking, 1987.

Global Fire Power (website). "2023 Military Strength Ranking." 2023.
https://www.globalfirepower.com/countries-listing.php

Global Times (website). "GT Voice: US Chip Curbs Drive China's Acceptance
of Domestic Tech." November 8, 2023. https://www.globaltimes.cn/
page/202311/1301472.shtml

Gomart, T. and M. Hecker. "China/United States: Europe off Balance."
Études de l'Ifri. April 2023. https://www.ifri.org/sites/default/files/atoms/
files/gomart-hecker_china_usa_2023.pdf

Gorobets, K. "The International Rule of Law and the Idea of Normative
Authority." *Hague Journal on the Rule of Law*. 12/2 (2020): 227–49.
https://doi.org/10.1007/s40803-020-00141-3

Gould, D. M., D. Y. Kenett, and G. L. Panterov. "Multidimensional
Connectivity: Benefits, Risks, and Policy Implications for Europe and
Central Asia." Policy Research Working Paper 8483. Washington, D.C.:
World Bank, 2018.

Götz, E. and C. Merlen. "Russia and the Question of World Order." *European
Politics and Society* 20/2 (2019): 133–53.

Graf, H. and J. J. Krüger. "The Performance of Gatekeepers in Innovator
Networks." *Industry and Innovation* 18/1 (2011): 69–88.

Grinin, L., I. Ilyin, and A. Andreev. "Global History and Future World
Order." In *Globalistics and Globalization Studies: Global Transformations
and Global Future*, edited by L. Grinin et al. Volgográd: Uchitel Publishing
House, 2016, 93–110. https://www.ssoar.info/ssoar/bitstream/handle/
document/57584/ssoar-2016-grinin_et_al-Global_History_and_Future_
World.pdf?sequence=1&isAllowed=y&lnkname=ssoar-2016-grinin_et_
al-Global_History_and_Future_World.pdf

Gropp, R. and K. Kostial. "FDI and Corporate Tax Revenue: Tax
Harmonization or Competition?" *International Monetary Fund, Finance
and Development*, 38/2, 2001. https://www.imf.org/external/pubs/ft/
fandd/2001/06/gropp.htm

Grossman, G. M. and E. Helpman. "Endogenous Innovation in the Theory
of Growth." *The Journal of Economic Perspectives* 8/1 (1994): 23–44.
https://www.jstor.org/stable/2138149

Grygiel, J. J. and A. W. Mitchell. *The Unquiet Frontier: Rising Rivals, Vulnerable Allies, and the Crisis of American Power.* Princeton, NJ: Princeton University Press, 2017.

Gustafson, T. *The Bridge: Natural Gas in a Redivided Europe.* Cambridge, MA: Harvard University Press, 2020.

Guyer, J. "Why Some Countries Don't Want to Pick a Side in Russia's War in Ukraine." *Vox,* June 9, 2022. https://www.vox.com/23156512/ russia-ukraine-war-global-south-nonaligned-movement

Gvosdev, N. K. "Geopolitical Keystone: Azerbaijan and the Global Position of the Silk Road Region." *Baku Dialogues* 4/1 (2020): 26–39.

Gvosdev, N. K. "Keystone States: A New Category of Power." *Horizons* 5 (2015): 104–23. https://www.cirsd.org/en/horizons/horizons-autumn-2015--issue-no5/keystone-states---a-new-category-of-power

Gvosdev, N. K. "The Communitarian Foreign Policy of Amitai Etzioni." *Society* 51 (2014): 372–79.

Gyarmati E. "Az Osztrák–Magyar Monarchia az I. világháború centenáriumának angolszász történeti szakirodalmában" [The Austro-Hungarian Monarchy in the Anglo-Saxon historical literature of the centenary of World War I]. *Világtörténet* 5/2 (2015): 193–215.

Haass, R. N. "Libya: Too Much, Too Late." *Politico,* 2011. https://www. politico.com/story/2011/03/libya-too-much-too-late-051647

Haass, R. N. "Liberal World Order, R.I.P." *Project Syndicate,* March 21, 2018. https://www.project-syndicate.org/commentary/end-of-liberal-world-order-by-richard-n--haass-2018-03?barrier=accesspaylog

Haass, R. N. "The Dangerous Decade: A Foreign Policy for a World in Crisis." *Foreign Affairs,* September/October 2022. https://www.foreignaffairs. com/united-states/dangerous-decade-foreign-policy- world-crisis-richard-haass

Haass, R. N. and C. A. Kupchan. "The New Concert of Powers." *Foreign Affairs,* March 23, 2021. https://www.foreignaffairs.com/articles/ world/2021-03-23/new-concert-powers

Hajdú T. "Gad Saad: A woke ideológusok a cél érdekében elpusztítják az igazságot" [Woke ideologues are destroying the truth in pursuit of their goal]. *Neokohn*, April 29, 2022. https://neokohn.hu/2022/04/29/gad-saad-a-woke-ideologusok-a-cel-erdekeben-elpusztitjak-az-igazsagot/

Hall, R. E. and C. I. Jones. "Why Do Some Countries Produce So Much More Output Per Worker than Others?" *The Quarterly Journal of Economics* 114/1 (1999): 83–116.

Hamadeh, N., C. Van Rompaey, and E. Metreau. "World Bank Group Country Classifications by Income Level for FY24 (July 1, 2023 – June 30, 2024)." *World Bank Blogs*, June 30, 2023. https://blogs.worldbank.org/opendata/new-world-bank-group-country-classifications-income-level-fy24

Hamel, G. and L. Välikangas. "The Quest for Resilience." *Harvard Business Review* 81/9 (2003): 52–63.

Harrison, M. "The Soviet Economy, 1917–1991: Its Life and Afterlife." *CEPR*, November 7, 2017. https://cepr.org/voxeu/columns/soviet-economy-1917-1991-its-life-and-afterlife

Hartman, K. and L. Béraud-Sudreau. "Arming Autocracies: Arms Transfers and the Emerging Biden Doctrine." *SIPRI*, June 6, 2023. https://www.sipri.org/commentary/blog/2023/arming-autocracies-arms-transfers-and-emerging-biden-doctrine

Hausmann R. "Az osztrák 'rejtett bajnok' vállalkozások: Jó példa a magyar kkv-k számára is" [The Austrian "hidden champion" enterprises: A good example for Hungarian SMEs as well]. *Portfolio*, 2020. https://www.portfolio.hu/uzlet/20201218/az-osztrak-rejtett-bajnok-vallalkozasok-jo-pelda-a-magyar-kkv-k-szamara-is-461836

Havass R. "Magyar gazdasági és hatalmi törekvések a tengeren" [Hungarian economic and power aspirations at sea]. *Földrajzi Közlemények*, 40/8 (1912): 185–93.

Hazony, Y. *The Virtue of Nationalism*. New York: Basic Books, 2018.

Hazony, Y. *Conservatism: A Rediscovery*. London: Swift Press, 2022.

Heath, R. "Blinken: I press Saudis on LGBTQI issues 'in every conversation.'" *Politico*, June 16, 2022. https://www.politico.com/news/2022/06/16/blinken-i-press-saudis-on-lgbtqi-issues-every-time-00040325

Heather, P. and J. Rapley. *Why Empires Fall: Rome, America, and the Future of the West.* New York: Apollo, 2023.

Hegel, G. W. F. *The Phenomenology of Spirit.* Oxford: Oxford University Press, 2018.

Hegel, G. W. F. *The Encyclopaedia Logic, with Zusätze: Part I of the Encyclopaedia of Philosophical Sciences with the Zusätze (Vol. 1).* Indianapolis, IN: Hackett Publishing, 1991.

Heller M. and A. Nyekrics. *Orosz történelem: A Szovjetunió története* [Russian History: The History of the Soviet Union]. Budapest: Osiris, 2001.

Helpman, E. *The Mystery of Economic Growth.* Cambridge MA: Belknap Press, 2004.

Hémond, Y. and B. Robert. "Evaluation of state of Resilience for a Critical Infrastructure in a Context of Interdependencies." *International Journal of Critical Infrastructures* 8/2–3 (2012): 95–106.

Henderson, D. R. "Globalization and Its Discontents." *Hoover Institution*, March 2023. https://www.hoover.org/research/globalization-and-its-discontents

Hendrickson, D. C. *Republic in Peril: American Empire and the Liberal Tradition.* Oxford: Oxford University Press, 2018.

Hirado.hu (website). "Amerikai politikatudós: Az FBI politikailag elfogult módon használta hatósági jogkörét Donald Trump ügyében" [American political scientist: The FBI used its authority in the case of Donald Trump in a politically biased way]. May 21, 2023. https://hirado.hu/kulfold/cikk/2023/05/21/amerikai-politikatudos-az-fbi-politikailag-elfogult-modon-hasznalta-hatosagi-jogkoret-donald-trump-ugyeben

Hjerppe, R. *The Finnish Economy, 1860-1985: Growth and Structural Change.* Helsinki: Bank of Finland, 1989.

Holling, C. S. "Resilience and Stability of Ecological Systems." *Annual Review of Ecology and Systematics* 4/1 (1973): 1–23.

Holmes, S. and I. Krastev. *The Light That Failed: Why the West Is Losing the Fight for Democracy.* New York: Penguin Books, 2019.

Hóman B. *Magyar középkor,* II. kötet [Hungarian Middle Ages, Vol. II].
Gödöllő: Attraktor, 1936.

Honneth, A. and H. Joas. *Communicative Action: Essays on Jürgen
Habermas's The Theory of Communicative Action.* Cambridge, MA: MIT
Press, 1991.

Horváth L. *A kínai geopolitikai gondolkodás: „Egy övezet, egy út" kínai
szemszögből* [China's geopolitical thinking: "One Belt, One Road" from
a Chinese perspective]. Budapest: Pallas Athéné Könyvkiadó Kft.,
2022.

Hufbauer, G. C. et al. *Economic Sanctions Reconsidered: History and Current
Policy.* Washington D.C.: Peterson Institute, 1990.

Huntington, S. P. *The Third Wave: Democratization in the Late Twentieth
Century.* Norman, OK: University of Oklahoma Press, 1993a.

Huntington, S. P. "Why International Primacy Matters." *International
Security* 17/4 (1993b): 68–83.

Haass, R. N. "World Order 2.0." *Project Syndicate,* January 24, 2017.
https://www.project-syndicate.org/commentary/globalized-
world-order-sovereign-obligations-by-richard-n--haass-2017-
01?barrier=accesspaylog

Ikenberry, G. J. "Institutions, Strategic Restraint, and the Persistence of
American Postwar Order." *International Security* 23/3 (1998): 43–78.

Ikenberry, G. J. *Liberal Leviathan: The Origins, Crisis, and Transformation
of the American World Order.* Princeton, NJ: Princeton University Press,
2012.

Ikenberry, G. J. *A World Safe for Democracy: Liberal Internationalism and the
Crises of Global Order.* New Haven, CT: Yale University Press, 2020.

Ikenberry, J. G. Why American Power Endures: The U.S.-Led Order Isn't in
Decline." *Foreign Affairs* 101/6 (2022): 56–73.

Jakóbowski, J. et al. "The Silk Railroad: The EU-China Rail Connections:
Background, Actors, Interests." *Centre for Eastern Studies,* February,
2018. https://aei.pitt.edu/93477/1/studies_72_silk%2Drailroad_net_0.pdf

Janardhan, N. *The Arab Gulf's Pivot to Asia: From Transactional to Strategic
Partnerships.* Berlin: Gerlach Press, 2020.

Jansen, M., and M. S. Jallab, and M. Smeets. "Connecting to Global Markets: Challenges and Opportunities: Case Studies Presented by WTO Chair-holders." Lausanne, World Trade Organization, 2014, https://www.wto.org/english/res_e/booksp_e/cmark_full_e.pdf

Jennings, P. "AUKUS: New Opportunities for the United States and Its Closest Allies." 2023 Index Of U.S. Military Strength, Washington D.C., The Heritage Foundation, 2023, 23–35. https://www.heritage.org/sites/default/files/2022-10/2023_IndexOfUSMilitaryStrength_ESSAYS_JENNINGS.pdf

Jevtić, J. "Serbia Signs Free Trade Deal with China." *Euractiv,* October 18, 2023. https://www.euractiv.com/section/politics/news/serbia-signs-free-trade-deal-with-china/

Jingyi, C." China's Foreign Trade up 2.1% in H1 to Record High, Showing Resilience." *The Global Times,* July 13, 2023. https://www.globaltimes.cn/page/202307/1294322.shtml

Jisi, W. "China's Search for a Grand Strategy: A Rising Great Power Finds Its Way." *Foreign Affairs* 90/2 (2011): 68–79. https://www.jstor.org/stable/25800458

Jovanović, M. A. *The Nature of International Law.* Cambridge: Cambridge University Press, 2019.

K. Kiss G. "Példátlan beruházás került célegyenesbe, így lesz Magyarország Európa kapuja", *Economx.hu,* December 21, 2021. https://www.economx.hu/magyar-vallalatok/east-west-gate-ewg-intermodalis-terminal-east-west-intermodalis-logisztikai-szolgaltato-zrt-fenyeslitke-logisztikai-kozpont-vasuti-fejlesztes- logisztika-atrako.742547.html

Kagan, R. "The Benevolent Empire." *Foreign Policy* 111 (1998): 24–35.

Kagan, R. *The World America Made.* New York: Knopf, 2012.

Kagan, R. "A Superpower, Like It or Not: Why Americans Must Accept Their Global Role." *Foreign Affairs* 100/2 (2021): 28–38.

Kagan, R. and T. Piccone. "Reassert U.S. Leadership of a Liberal Global Order." *Brookings,* Janaury 23, 2014. https://www.brookings.edu/articles/ reassert-u-s-leadership-of-a-liberal-global-order/

Kahana, A. "Biden's New World Order Creates a New Era." *Israel Hayom*. https://www.israelhayom.com/2023/10/22/bidens-new-world-order-creates-a-new-era/

Kalmár G. *Magyar geopolitika*. Budapest: Stádium Sajtóvállalat, 1942.

Kanchana, K. and H. Unesaki. "ASEAN Energy Security: An Indicator-based Assessment." *Energy Procedia* 56 (2014): 163–71.

Kant, I. *Perpetual Peace and Other Essays*. Hackett Publishing, 1983.

Kant, I. and G. W. F. Hegel. *A tiszta ész (válogatott írások)* [Pure Reason (Selected Writings)], translated by Mihály Babits and Révai Gábor. Budapest: Interpopulárt, 2016. https://mek.oszk.hu/01300/01325/01325.pdf

Kaplan, R. D. *The Return of Marco Polo's World: War, Strategy, and American Interests in the Twenty-first Century*. New York: Random House, 2018.

Kaser, M. and R. Tölet. "East European Economies in Two World Crises." In *The Impact of the Depression of the 1930's and its Relevance for the Contemporary World*, edited by I. Berend and K. Borchardt. Budapest: Karl Marx University of Economics, 1986.

Katona H. "Kellő lökéssel a legszegényebbek is kitörhetnek a szegénységi csapdából" [With sufficient momentum, even the poorest can break out of the poverty trap]. *G7*, February 21, 2021. https://g7.hu/adat/20210221/kello-lokessel-a-legszegenyebbek-is-kitorhetnek-a-szegenysegi-csapdabol/

Katzenstein, P. J. and R. O. Keohane, ed. *Anti-Americanisms in World Politics*. Ithaca: Cornell University Press, 2007.

Keller, W. "International Trade, Foreign Direct Investment, and Technology Spillovers." *NBER Working Paper Series*. 2009/15442, https://www.nber.org/system/files/working_papers/w15442/w15442.pdf

Kennedy, P. M. *The Rise and Fall of the Great Powers: Economic Change and Military Conflict from 1500 to 2000*. New York: Vintage, 1989.

Kenney, C. M. "US Open to Expanding AUKUS, *Defense One*." June 26, 2023. https://www.defenseone.com/policy/2023/03/us-open-expand-ing-aukus/387948/

Keohane, R. O. and R. W. Grant. "Accountability and Abuses of Power in World Politics." *American Political Science Review* 99/1 (2005): 29–43.

Keohane, R. and J. S. Nye. *Power and Interdependence.* Harlow: Pearson Longman, 2011.

Khanna, P. *Connectography: Mapping the Future of Global Civilization.* New York: Random House, 2016.

Kharas, H. and H. Kohli. "What Is the Middle Income Trap, Why do Countries Fall into It, and How Can It Be Avoided?" *Global Journal of Emerging Market Economies* 3/3 (2011): 281–89. https://journals.sagepub.com/doi/dpf/10-1177/097491011100300302

Kirschner, J. "Globalization, American Power, and International Security." *Political Science Quarterly* 123/3 (2008): 363–89. https://www.jstor.org/stable/20203047

Kissinger, H. *On China.* New York: Penguin Books, 2012.

Kissinger, H. *World Order: Reflections on the Character of Nations and the Course of History.* New York: Penguin Books, 2014.

Klein, A., M. S. Schulze, and T. Vonyó. "How Peripheral was the Periphery? Industrialization in East Central Europe since 1870." In *The Spread of Modern Industry to the Periphery since 1871,* edited by K. O'Rourke and J. Williamson. Oxford: Oxford University Press, 2017.

Kohán, M. "Magyarország stratégiája jól mutatja, milyennek kellene lennie a világnak" – Jeffrey Sachs sztárközgazdászt kérdeztük ["Hungary's strategy clearly shows how the world should be"—we spoke to star economist Jeffrey Sachs]. *Mandiner,* June 17, 2023. https://mandiner.hu/belfold/2023/06/targyalas-nelkul-aligha-lehet-beke-jeffrey-sachs-a-mandinernek

Köppel, R. "Weltkrieg gegen Frieden und Wohlstand: Stoppt unsere Kriegstreiber – Mein Interview mit Viktor Orbán. Begeisterndes und inspirierenden Ungarn – Brotkorb-Terror: Uni Bonn schmeisst Ulrike Guérot raus – Jeff Sachs: Nord-Stream-Untersuchung veröffentlichen!" [World War against peace and prosperity: Stop our warmongers – My interview with Viktor Orbán. Inspiring and inspiring Hungary – breadbasket terror: University of Bonn throws Ulrike Guérot out – Jeff Sachs: Publish NordStream investigation!]. *Die Weltwoche,* February 24, 2023.

Körösényi A., G. Illés, and A. Gyulai. *Az Orbán-rezsim: A plebiszciter vezérdemokrácia elmélete és gyakorlata* [The Orbán Regime: Theory and Practice of Plebiscite Leadership Democracy]. Budapest: Osiris Kiadó, 2020.

Krauthammer, C. "The Unipolar Moment." *Foreign Affairs,* January 1, 1990. https://www.foreignaffairs.com/articles/1990-01-01/unipolar-moment

Krikke, J. "Till debt do us part." *Asia Times,* November 15, 2022. https://asiatimes.com/2022/11/till-debt-do-us-part-2/

Kuo, M. A. "NATO, China, and the Indo-Pacific." *The Diplomat,* June 5, 2023. https://thediplomat.com/2023/06/nato-china-and-the-indo-pacific/

Kupchan, C. "Bipolarity is Back: Why It Matters." *Eurasia Group,* February 2, 2022. https://www.eurasiagroup.net/live-post/bipolarity-is-back-why-it-matters

Lánczi A. *Konzervatív kiáltvány* [Conservative Manifesto]. Gödöllő: Attraktor, 2002.

Latawski, P. and M. A. Smith. *The Kosovo Crisis and the Evolution of Post-Cold War European Security.* New York: Manchester University Press, 2003.

Layne, C. "The Unipolar Illusion: Why New Great Powers Will Rise." *International Security* 174 (1993): 5–51.

Layne, C. "Coming Storms: The Return of Great-Power War." *Foreign Affairs* 99/6 (2020): 42–48.

Leigh, D., S. Fabrizio, and A. Mody. "The Second Transition: Eastern Europe in Perspective." *International Monetary Fund Working Papers,* March 1, 2009. https://www.imf.org/en/Publications/WP/Issues/2016/12/31/The-Second-Transition-Eastern-Europe-in-Perspective-22708

Lentzos, F. and N. Rose. "Governing Insecurity: Contingency Planning, Protection, Resilience." *Economy and Society* 38/2 (2009): 230–54.

Leonard, M. "Xi Jinping's Idea of World Order." *Project Syndicate,* March 30, 2023. https://www.project-syndicate.org/commentary/xi-jinping-idea-of-world-order-fragmented-sovereign-interests-over- western-domination-by-mark-leonard-2023-03?barrier=accesspaylog

Leonard, M., ed. *Connectivity Wars.* London: The European Council on Foreign Relations, 2016. https://ecfr.eu/wp-content/uploads/Connectivity_Wars.pdf

Leonard, M. *The Age of Unpeace: How Connectivity Causes Conflict.* New York: Random House, 2021.

Leonard, M. "What Does China Think?" *ECFR,* February 11, 2008. https://ecfr.eu/article/commentary_mark_leonard_what_does_china_think/

Levine, N. "A Clash of Worldviews." *Foreign Affairs,* August 30, 2023. https://www.foreignaffairs.com/china/clash-worldviews-united-states-ideological-impasse

Levitsky, S. and L. A. Way. "The Rise of Competitive Authoritarianism." *Journal of Democracy* 13/2 (2002): 51–65.

Lewis, J. A. "Learning the Superior Techniques of the Barbarians: China's Pursuit of Semiconductor Independence." *Center for Strategic & International Studies,* January 2019. https://csis-website-prod. s3.amazonaws.com/s3fs-public/publication/190115_Lewis_Semiconductor_v6.pdf

Lewis, W. A. "Economic Development with Unlimited Supplies of Labour." *The Manchester School* 22/2 (1954): 139–91.

Li, P. "The Unique Value of Yin-Yang Balancing: A Critical Response." *Management and Organizational Review* 10/2 (2014): 321–32.

Li, P. "Organizational Resilience for a New Normal: Balancing the Paradox of Global Interdependence." *Management and Organization Review* 16/3 (2020): 503–9.

Li, P., S. Zhou, and Z. Yang. "The Puzzle of Underdog's Victory: How Chinese Firms Achieve Stretch Goals Through Exploratory Bricolage." In *The Oxford Handbook of Innovation in China,* edited by X-L. Fu, J. Chen, B. McKern. Oxford: Oxford University Press, 2020.

Ligeti I. "A magyar gazdaság fejlődésének jellemzői – A makrogazdasági folyamatok alakulása (1990–2010)" [Characteristics of the development of the Hungarian economy – Evolution of macroeconomic processes (1990–2010)]. In *Két válság között* [Between Two Crises], edited by

M. Zádor. Budapest. M. Zádor and Ecostat, 2010. https://www.adko. hu/01_ files/adotanulmanyok/2010/ecostat-konyv.pdf

Lindsay, J. "Trade Sanctions as Policy Instruments." *International Studies Quarterly* 302 (1986): 153–73.

Lindseth, P. L. "Equilibrium, Demoi-cracy, and Delegation in the Crisis of European Integration." *German Law Journal* 154 (2014): 529–67.

Linz, J. J. and A. Stepan. *Problems of Democratic Transition and Consolidation: Southern Europe, South America, and Post-Communist Europe.* Baltimore: Johns Hopkins University Press, 1996.

Lippert, B., N. Von Ondarza, and V. Perthes, ed. "European Strategic Autonomy: Actors, Issues, Conflicts of Interests." SWP Research Paper 4, March 2019. https://www. swp-berlin.org/publications/products/ research_papers/2019RP04_lpt_ orz_prt_web.pdf

Low, L. and L. C. Salazar. *The Gulf Cooperation Council.* Singapore: Institute of Southeast Asian Studies, 2010.

Luttwak, E. N. "From Geopolitics to Geo-Economics: Logic of Conflict, Grammar of Commerce." *The National Interest* 20 (1990): 17–23.

Lyon, P. V. and B. W. Tomlin. *Canada as an International Actor.* Canadian Controversies Series, Toronto: Macmillan of Canada, 1979.

Mackinder, H. J. "The Geographical Pivot of History." *The Geographical Journal* 23/4 (1904): 421–37.

Macron, E. "Sorbonne Speech of Emmanuel Macron." *Ouest-France,* September 26, 2017. https://international.blogs.ouest-france.fr/ archive/2017/09/29/macron-sorbonne-verbatim-europe-18583.html

Magyarics T. and B. Mártonffy, ed. *Ütközőpályák* [Collision Courses]. Budapest: Ludovika Egyetemi Kiadó, 2023.

Makronóm Intézet (website). "Beköszöntött az ingaállamok és a középhatalmak korszaka" [The era of swing states and middle powers has arrived]. October 2023. https://makronomintezet.hu/public/ researches/documents/document-xRE9JaEJOk.pdf

Mamingi, N. and K. Martin. "Foreign Direct Investment and Growth in Developing Countries: Evidence from the Countries of the Organisation of Eastern Caribbean States." *CEPAL Review* 124 (2018): 79–98.

Maoz, Z. and B. Russett. "Normative and Structural Causes of
Democratic Peace, 1946–1986." *American Political Science Review* 87/3
(1993): 624–38.

Marrese, M. and J. Vanous. *Soviet Subsidization of Trade with Eastern
Europe: A Soviet Perspective.* Berkeley, CA: University of California
Press, 1983.

Martín, J. M. "Infrastructure Building, the New 'War' of the Great Powers."
Atalayar, September 7, 2021. https://www.atalayar.com/en/ articulo/
economy-and-business/infrastructure-building-new-war-great-
powers/20210907113806152820.html

Martin, W. "The US Could Lose Its Crown as the World's Most Powerful
Economy as Soon as Next Year, And It's Unlikely to Ever Get It Back."
Business Insider, January 10, 2019. https://www.businessinsider.com/
us-economy-to-fall-behind-china-within-a-year-standard-chartered-
says-2019-1

Mayne, Q. and B. Geißel. "Don't Good Democracies Need 'Good' Citizens?
Citizen Dispositions and the Study of Democratic Quality." *Politics and
Governance* 6/1 (2018): 33–47.

Mazarr, M. J. et al. *Understanding the Current International Order.* Santa
Monica, CA: RAND Corporation, 2016.

McMillan, M. S. and D. Rodrik. "Globalization, Structural Change
and Productivity Growth." *NBER Working Paper,* 2011 (17143).
https://www.nber.org/papers/w17143

Mead, W. R. "As India Rises, the G-20 Reveals a Shifting World Order."
Wall Street Journal, September 11, 2023. https://www.wsj.com/articles/
the-g-20-reveals-a-shifting-world-order-india-asia-china-geopolitics-
democracy-europe-russia-6604be20

Mearsheimer, J. J. "The Case for a Ukrainian Nuclear Deterrent." *Foreign
Affairs,* 72/3 (1993): 50.

Mearsheimer, J. J.: *The Tragedy of Great Power Politics.* New York: W. W.
Norton & Company, 2003.

Mearsheimer, J. J. "E.H. Carr vs. Idealism: The Battle Rages On."
International Relations, 19 (2005a): 139–52.

Mearsheimer, J. J. "Hans Morgenthau and the Iraq War: Realism Versus Neo-Conservatism." *OpenDemocracy,* April 21, 2005b. https://www.mearsheimer.com/wp-content/uploads/2019/07/A0037.pdf

Mearsheimer, J. J. "The Inevitable Rivalry." *Foreign Affairs,* October 19, 2021. https://www.foreignaffairs.com/articles/china/2021-10-19/inevitable-rivalry-cold-war

Mearsheimer, J. J. *A nagy téveszme.* Budapest: Századvég Közéleti Tudásközpont, 2022.

Menon, R. "The Quad Is a Delusion." *Foreign Policy,* June 28, 2021. https://foreignpolicy.com/2021/06/28/quad-delusion-china-power- containment/

Menon, S. "Nobody Wants the Current World Order: How All the Major Powers—Even the United States—Became Revisionists." *Foreign Affairs,* August 3, 2022. https://www.foreignaffairs.com/world/nobody-wants-current-world-order

Middelaar, L. van. *The Passage to Europe: How a Continent Became a Union.* New Haven: CT, Yale University Press, 2014.

Mika S. *Nagy képes világtörténet, V. kötet, A középkor, II. rész: A hűbériség és a keresztes hadjáratok kora* [Large Illustrated World History, Volume V, The Middle Ages, part 2: The Age of Feudalism and the Crusades]. Budapest: Franklin-Társulat and Révai Testvérek, 1900.

Miller, C. "The West's De-Risking Strategy Towards China Will Fail." *The Economist,* August 4, 2023. https://www.economist.com/by-invitation/2023/08/04/the-wests-de-risking-strategy-towards-china-will-fail-says-chris-miller

Ministry of Foreign Affairs of Japan (website). "G7 Hiroshima Leaders' Communiqué. May 19–21 2023." https://www.mofa.go.jp/ms/g7hs_s/page1e_000666.html

Mišković, D. K. *Superseding Middle Power Theory with the Keystone Concept* (submitted for publication).

Mišković, D. K. "On Some Conceptual Advantages of the Term 'Silk Road Region'." *Baku Dialogues* 6/4 (2023): 20–33. https://bakudialogues.ada.edu.az/articles/on-some-conceptual-advantages-of-the-term-silk-road-region-12-07-2023

Modelski, G. *Long Cycles in World Politics.* London: Palgrave Macmillan, 1987.

Moeini, A. et al. "Middle Powers in the Multipolar World." *The Institute for Peace and Diplomacy,* March 26, 2023. https://peacediplomacy. org/2022/03/26/middle-powers-in-the-multipolar-world/

Moravcsik, A. "Europe After the Crises: How to Sustain a Common Currency." *Foreign Affairs,* May/June 2012. https://www.princeton. edu/~amoravcs/library/after_crisis.pdf

Morgenthau, H. J. *Politics Among Nations: The Struggle for Power and Peace.* New York: A. A. Knopf, 1972.

Moura, G. N. P. et al. "South America Power Integration, Bolivian Electricity Export Potential and Bargaining Power: An OSeMOSYS SAMBA approach." *Energy Strategy Reviews* 17 (2016): 27–36.

Moyer, J. et al. "Power and Influence in a Globalized World." *CSS ETH Zürich,* March 5, 2018. https://css.ethz.ch/en/services/digital-library/ articles/article.html/c1718d5f-2dcf-4527-bf98-e7a8ca6aafe3

Muravchik, J. *Exporting Democracy: Fulfilling America's Destiny.* Washington, D.C.: AEI Press, 1991.

Murray, D. *The Strange Death of Europe.* London: Bloomsbury, 2017.

Nagel, T. *Mind and Cosmos: Why the Materialist Neo-Darwinian Conception of Nature Is Almost Certainly False.* Oxford: Oxford University Press, 2012.

Nair, C. "The West Must Prepare for a Long Overdue Reckoning." *The National Interest,* 8 June 2023, https://nationalinterest.org/feature/ west-must-prepare-long-overdue-reckoning-206538

Nekola, M. *Political Participation and Governance Effectiveness: Does Participation Matter?* Centre for Social and Economic Strategies (CESES). Prague: 2006.

Netchev, S. "Trade Networks in the Middle Ages, c. 1200." *World History Encyclopedia,* 24 May 2022. https://www.worldhistory.org/image/15923/ trade-networks-in-the-middle-ages-c-1200/

New Development Bank (website). *New Development Bank General Strategy for 2022–2026: Scaling Up Development Finance for a Sustainable*

Future, 2022. https://www.ndb.int/wp-content/uploads/2022/07/NDB_
StrategyDocument_eVersion_07.pdf

Nielsen, L. "How to Classify Countries Based on Their Level of
Development." *Social Indicators Research* 114/3 (2013): 1087–1107.

Nietzsche, F. W. *The Gay Science.* New York: Vintage Books, 1974.

Nietzsche, F. W. *Thus Spoke Zarathustra.* Cambridge: Cambridge University
Press, 2006.

Nolte, E. *Der europäische Bürgerkrieg, 1917-1945: Nationalsozialismus und
Bolschewismus* [The European Civil War, 1917-1945: National-Socialism
and Bolshevism]. Munich: Herbig, 1997.

Nye, J. S. "The Changing Nature of World Power." *Political Science Quarterly*
1052 (1990): 177–92.

Nye, J. S. *The Future of Power.* New York: Public Affairs, 2011.

O'Leary, E. "Reflecting on the 'Celtic Tiger': Before, During and After."
Irish Economic and Social History 38 (2011): 73–88.

O'Neil, S. K. "The Myth of the Global." *Foreign Affairs,* July/August 2022.
https://www.foreignaffairs.com/articles/united- states/2022-06-21/
myth-global-regional-ties-win

O'Rourke, K. H. "Independent Ireland in Comparative Perspective."
Irish Economic and Social History 441 (2017): 19–45.

O'Sullivan, J. and T. Orbán. "AUKUS Shuffles the Blocs." *The National
Review,* 1 November 2021. https://www.nationalreview.com/
magazine/2021/11/01/aukus-shuffles-the-blocs/

Okonjo-Iweala, N. "Why the World Still Needs Trade: The Case for
Reimagining—Not Abandoning—Globalization." *Foreign Affairs,* July/
August 2023. https://www.foreignaffairs.com/world/why-world-still-
needs-trade

Orbán, T. "'Politicians Don't Like Doing the Right Thing' — Interview with
Kevin Roberts." *Hungarian Conservative,* December 5, 2022. https://
www.hungarianconservative.com/articles/interview/politicians-dont-
like-doing-the-right-thing-interview-with-kevin-roberts/

Organski, A. F. K. and J. Kugler. *The War Ledger.* Chicago: University of
Chicago Press, 1980.

Orton, J. D. and K. E. Weick. "Loosely Coupled Systems:
A Reconceptualization." *Academy of Management Review* 15/2 (1990):
203–23.

Osborne, D. and T. Gaebler. *Reinventing Government: How the
Entrepreneurial Spirit is Transforming the Public Sector.* New York:
Plume, 1993.

Özkan, M. "A New Approach to Global Security: Pivotal Middle Powers and
Global Politics." *Perceptions: Journal of International Affairs.* 11/1 (2006):
77–95.

Page-Jones, M. *The Practical Guide to Structured Systems Design.* New York:
Yourdon Press, 1980.

Panda, J. "Awaiting a Pivotal Partnership? The Case of India and South
Korea." *Institute for Security and Development Policy – Focus Asia,* June 2,
2023, 1–16.

Pape, R. A. "Why Economic Sanctions Do Not Work." *International Security*
22/2 (1997): 90–136.

Papp, L. "Many of Us in the Ranks of the Conservatives and Intellectuals
Have Come to Look Upon Hungary as a Great Leader: Interview with
Christopher DeMuth." *Hungarian Conservative,* 2022.

Patnaik, S. and J. Kunhardt. "Biden Could Reduce Inflation, Mitigate
a Recession, and Strengthen Democracy with a New EU-US Trade
Agreement." *Brookings,* August 30, 2022. https://www.brookings.
edu/articles/biden-could-reduce-inflation-mitigate-a-recession-and-
strengthen-democracy-with-a-new-eu-us-trade-agreement/

Payne, S. G. *Civil War in Europe, 1905–1949.* Cambridge: Cambridge
University Press, 2011.

Peck, J. and A. Tickell. "Making Global Rules: Globalisation or
Neoliberalisation?" In *Remaking the Global Economy: Economic-
Geographical Perspectives,* edited by J. Peck and H. Yeung. London: Sage,
2003, 163–82.

Peck, J. *Constructions of Neoliberal Reason.* Oxford: Oxford University Press,
2010.

Péri J. "Időszaki jelentés a Szent Korona ötvösvizsgálatáról" [Interim report on the goldsmith's examination of the Holy Crown]. *Magyar Iparművészet* 1 (1994): 2–6.

Perović, J. and D. Krempin. "The Key is in Our Hands: Soviet Energy Strategy during Détente and the Global Oil Crises of the 1970s." *Historical Social Research / Historische Sozialforschung* 39/4 (2014): 113–44.

Peterson, J. B. "The Epidemic That Dare Not Speak Its Name." YouTube, March 9, 2023. https://www.youtube.com/watch?v=Qrg8t34yXR-s&t=615s

Phillips, N., ed. *Global Political Economy.* Oxford: Oxford University Press, 2020.

Pieterse, J. N. "Periodizing Globalization: Histories of Globalization." *New Global Studies* 6/2 (2012). https://www.academia.edu/7657053/Histories_of_globalization

Pintér L. and M. Santo. "Sem az USA, sem Kína nem tudja már irányítani a világot, az orosz–ukrán háború mindent átalakít – Abishur Prakash a Mandinernek" [Neither the USA nor China can control the world anymore, the Russian-Ukrainian war is changing everything – Abishur Prakash speaks to Mandiner]. *Mandiner* June 26, 2023. https://mandiner.hu/hirek/2023/06/abishur-prakash-interju

Plato. *The Sophist.* BoD–Books on Demand, 2019.

Plehwe, D. and P. Mirowski, ed. *The Road from Mont Pèlerin: The Making of the Neoliberal Thought Collective.* Cambridge, MA: Harvard University Press, 2009.

Posen, B. R. "From Unipolarity to Multipolarity: Transition in Sight?" In *International Relations Theory and the Consequences of Unipolarity,* edited by G. J. Ikenberry, M. Mastanduno, and W. C. Wohlforth. Cambridge: Cambridge University Press, 2012.

Prakash, A. "New Geopolitical Blocs Will Govern the Future." *Politico,* October 9, 2022. https://www.politico.eu/article/new-geopolitical-blocs-govern-future/

Prakash, A. "The U.S.-China Faceoff Is Not Halting Globalization." *Nikkei Asia,* April 5, 2023. https://asia.nikkei.com/Opinion/The-U.S.-China-faceoff-is-not-halting-globalization

Preston, P. P. *Republic Besieged: Civil War in Spain, 1936–1939.* Edinburgh: Edinburgh University Press, 1996.

Priest, D. and W. M. Arkin. *Top Secret America: The Rise of the New American Security State.* Boston: Little, Brown and Company, 2011.

Prior, T. J. and J. Hagmann. "Measuring Resilience: Methodological and Political Challenges of a Trend Security Concept." *Journal of Risk Research* 17/3 (2013): 281–98.

PricewaterhouseCoopers (website). "Shift of Global Economic Power to Emerging Economies Set to Continue in Long Run, with India, Indonesia and Vietnam among Star Performers." 2017. https://www.pwc.com/id/en/not-migrated/shift-of-global-economic-power-to-emerging-economies-set-to-cont.html

Pritz P. "A magyar nemzeti érdekek első világháború alatti érvényesítésének lehetőségei és vaskos korlátai" [Possibilities for and substantial limitations on the assertion of Hungarian national interests during the First World War]. In *Sorsok, frontok, eszmék: Tanulmányok az első világháború 100. évfordulójára* [Fates, Fronts, Ideas: Studies for the 100th Anniversary of the First World War], edited by I. Majoros. Budapest: ELTE BTK, 2015, 283–92.

Rada P. and P. Stepper. "A liberális rend szürrealizmusa: Amerikai belpolitikai trendek, választások és külpolitikai várakozások." *KKI Elemzések* 3, 2023. http://real.mtak.hu/165219/1/KE_2023_03_US_A_liberalis_rend_RBSP.pdf

Radelet, S. and J. D. Sachs. "Shipping Costs, Manufactured Exports, and Economic Growth." *The annual meeting of the American Economic Association.* Chicago: Columbia University, 1998.

Ramo, J. C. *The Beijing Consensus.* London: Foreign Policy Centre, 2004. https://www.files.ethz.ch/isn/23013/Beijing_Consensus.pdf

Ray, S. "BlackRock's Larry Fink Defends Stakeholder Capitalism in Annual Letter to CEOs." *Forbes,* January 18, 2022. https://www.forbes.com/

sites/siladityaray/2022/01/18/blackrocks-larry-fink-defends-stakeholder-capitalism-in-annual-letter-to-ceos/

Reinsch, W. A. "So Long, Globalization?" *CSIS*, May 1, 2023. https://www.csis.org/analysis/so-long-globalization

Réti, T. "East Central European Economic Transition and the West." *Macalester International* 2 (1995): 53–75. https://digitalcommons.macalester.edu/cgi/viewcontent.cgi?referer=&httpsredir=1&referer=-&httpsredir=1&article=1031&context=macintl

Réthi S. A magyar–orosz külkereskedelem az 1998. augusztusi orosz válság előtt és után [Hungarian-Russian foreign trade before and after the August 1998 Russian crisis]. *Külgazdaság* 44 (2000): 11–30. http://real-j.mtak.hu/17436/11/Kulg_2000_12_beliv.pdf

Reveel, P. "Russian President Vladimir Putin Says US Dominance Is Ending After Mistakes 'Typical of an Empire." *ABC News,* October 19, 2018. https://abcnews.go.com/International/putin-us-dominance-ending-mistakes-typical-empire/story?id=58611354

Riecke, T. "Resilience and Decoupling in the Era of Great Power Competition." *Mercator Institute for China Studies,* August 20, 2020. https://merics.org/sites/default/files/2020-08/Merics_ChinaMonitor_PowerCompetition.pdf

Riordan, P. "China Targets Consumption in Bid to Drive Growth." *The Financial Times,* 2023. https://www.ft.com/content/851f52d5-9423-419f-aecd-e0c7bf4908ef

Risen, J. "*State of War: The Secret History of the CIA and the Bush Administration.*" New York: Free Press, 2006.

Risen, J. *Pay any Price: Greed, Power, and Endless War.* Boston: Houghton Mifflin Harcourt, 2014.

Roa, C. "Between East and West: The Prospect of Hungary as a Keystone State." *Hungarian Conservative,* December 4, 2022. https://www.hungarianconservative.com/articles/current/between-east-and-west-the-prospect-of-hungary-as-a-keystone-state/

Roa, C. "Realists Have Problems with Realism." *The National Interest,* June 12, 2023. https://nationalinterest.org/feature/realists-have-problems-realism-206549

Robertson, J. and A. Carr. "Is anyone a middle power? The case for historicization." *International Theory* 15/3 (2023): 1–25.

Rodrik, D. *The Globalization Paradox.* Oxford: Oxford University Press, 2011.

Rodrik, D. "Premature Deindustrialization." *Journal of Economic Growth* 211 (2016). https://econpapers.repec.org/article/kapjecgro/v_3a21_3ay_3a201 6_3ai_3a1_3ad_3a10.1007_5fs10887-015-9122-3.htm

Rodrik, D. "Why Does Globalization Fuel Populism? Economics, Culture, and the Rise of Right-Wing Populism." *Annual Review of Economics* 13/1 (2021): 133–70.

Rodrik, D. and S. M. Walt. "How to Build a Better Order: Limiting Great Power Rivalry in an Anarchic World." *Foreign Affairs,* September/October 2022. https://www.foreignaffairs.com/world/build-better-order-great-power-rivalry-dani-rodrik-stephen-walt

Rolland, N. "China's Vision for a New World Order." *NBR Special Report,* 83, 2020. https://www.nbr.org/wp-content/uploads/pdfs/publications/sr83_chinasvision_jan2020.pdf

Roşu, I. "Post-Socialist Transition: A Comparison Between Romania and Poland." *HEC Paris,* 2020. https://people.hec.edu/rosu/wp-content/uploads/sites/43/2020/03/kornai.pdf

Rödder, A. *Wer hat Angst vor Deutschland? Geschichte eines europäischen Problems* [Who is Afraid of Germany? History of a European Problem]. Frankfurt am Main, S. Fischer Verlage, 2019.

Rubin, D. "How Israel Turned Division into a Strength." YouTube, June 15, 2023. https://www.youtube.com/watch?v=vfMepfTipHs

Russet, B. *Grasping the Democratic Peace: Principles for a Post-Cold War World.* Princeton, NJ: Princeton University Press, 1993.

Rustow, D. A. "Transitions to Democracy: Towards a Dynamic Model." *Comparative Politics* 23 (1970): 337–63.

Sabatini, C. "America's Love of Sanctions Will Be Its Downfall." *Foreign Policy,* July 24, 2023. https://foreignpolicy.com/2023/07/24/united-states-sanctions-debt-china-venezuela/

Sachs, J. D. *The Ages of Globalization: Geography, Technology, and Institutions.* New York: Columbia University Press, 2020.

Sachs, J. D. and A. M. Warner. "Natural Resource Abundance and Economic Growth." *NBER Working Paper,* 5398, 1995. https://www.nber.org/papers/w5398

Santiago, F. "Innovation Policy and Industrial Policy at the Crossroads: A Review of Recent Experiences in Advanced Developing Countries." *UNIDO Inclusive and Sustainable Development Working Paper Series,* 9, 2015.

Sauer, P. and A. Hawkins. "Xi Jinping Says China Ready to 'Stand Guard Over World Order' on Moscow Visit." *The Guardian,* March 21, 2023. https://www.theguardian.com/world/2023/mar/20/xi-jinping-vladimir-putin-moscow-ukraine-war

Savage, J. D. "Military Size and the Effectiveness of Democracy Assistance." *Journal of Conflict Resolution* 61/4 (, 2017): 839–68.

Schmidt, D. R. and J. Williams. "The Normativity of Global Ordering Practices." *International Studies Quarterly,* April 8, 2023. https://academic.oup.com/isq/article/67/2/sqad021/7111122

Schöttli, U. "The New Geopolitics of Trade in Asia" *GIS,* October 11, 2023. https://www.gisreportsonline.com/r/geopolitics-trade-asia/

Schweitzer I. "A hazai beruházások alakulásának főbb tendenciái az elmúlt évtizedekben és néhány tanulság I. rész." *Külgazdaság* 7–8 (2002): 4–32. http://real-j.mtak.hu/17434/7/Kulg_2002_07-08_beliv.pdf

Scruton, R. *Hogyan legyünk konzervatívok* [How to be Conservatives]. Budapest: Osiris Kiadó and MCC Press, 2023.

Seligman, M. E. P. "Learned Helplessness." *Annual Review of Medicine* 23 (1972): 407–12.

Seville, E. et al. "Building Organisational Resilience: A New Zealand Approach." 2006. https://ir.canterbury.ac.nz/server/api/core/bitstreams/c2e89813-74d0-4d73-b91b-49b8335ab13a/content

Shapiro, I. "Lessons Learned from My Hungarian Adventure" *Shapiro's Gavel,* October 18, 2022. https://ilyashapiro.substack.com/p/lessons-learned-from-my-hungarian

Sharma, R. *The Rise and Fall of Nations: Forces of Change in the Post-Crisis World.* New York: W. W. Norton & Company, 2017.

Sharma, R. "The Comeback Nation: U.S. Economic Supremacy Has Repeatedly Proved Declinists Wrong." *Foreign Affairs* 99/3 (2020): 70–81.

Shearing, N. "World Economy is Fracturing, not Deglobalizing." *Chatham House,* February 8, 2023. https://www.chathamhouse.org/2023/02/world-economy-fracturing-not-deglobalizing

Shelton, D. L. "Normative Hierarchy in International Law" *American Journal of International Law* 100 (2006): 291–323. https://www. semanticscholar.org/paper/Normative-Hierarchy-in-International-Law-Shelton/de816db929d778756ddb39dca7ca68a84f842821

Shoebridge, M. "Why Did AUKUS Happen? Because the World Changed." The International Centre for Defence and Security, November 24, 2021. https://icds.ee/en/why-did-aukus-happen-because-the-world-changed/

Sholl, S. "What Happened When Hungary Revived Classical Architecture in Budapest." *The Federalist,* April 26, 2021. https://thefederalist.com/2021/04/26/what-happened-when-hungary-revived-classical-architecture-in-budapest/

Silva, J. A. and R. M. Leichenko. "Regional Income Inequality and International Trade." *Economic Geography* 803 (2004): 261–86.

Sinha, J. and S. Saran. "Gated Globalisation and Fragmented Supply Chains." *ORF,* April 27, 2020. https://www.orfonline.org/research/gated-globalisation-and-fragmented-supply-chains-65216/

Søreide, T. "FDI and Industrialisation: Why Technology Transfer and New Industrial Structures May Accelerate Economic Development." *CMI,* 2001. http://www.iese.ac.mz/lib/saber/oa_64.pdf

Standard Chartered (website). *Future of Trade 2030.* 2021. https://av.sc.com/corp-en/content/docs/Future-of-Trade-2021.pdf?time=1661498387

Startevic, S. "Into the Honey Pot: Serbia and China Ink Free Trade Deal." *Politico Europe,* October 18, 2023. https://www.politico.eu/article/serbia-and-china-sign-free-trade-deal/

Steger, M. B. and R. K. Roy. *Neoliberalism: A Very Short Introduction.* Oxford: Oxford University Press, 2010.

Stiglitz, J. E. "How the US Could Lose the New Cold War." *Project Syndicate,* June 17, 2022. https://www.project-syndicate.org/commentary/us-squandering-soft-power-appeal-in-cold-war-with-china-by-joseph-e-stiglitz-2022-06?barrier=accesspaylog

Street, S. "A Darwinian Dilemma for Realist Theories of Value." *Philosophical Studies* 1271 (2006): 109–66.

Stuenkel, O. *Post-Western World: How Emerging Powers Are Remaking Global Order.* Malden: Polity Press, 2016.

Sullivan, J. "The Sources of American Power." *Foreign Affairs* 102/6 (2023): 8–29.

Sweijs, T. et al. *Why are Pivot States so Pivotal? The Role of Pivot States in Regional and Global Security.* The Hague: The Hague Centre for Strategic Studies, 2014.

Sweijs, T. and M. J. Mazarr. "Mind the Middle Powers." *War on the Rocks,* April 4, 2023. https://warontherocks.com/2023/04/mind-the-middle-powers/

Swicord, E. "NATO's New Strategic Concept: What it is and Why it Matters." *NTI,* July 20, 2022. https://www.nti.org/atomic-pulse/natos-new-strategic-concept-what-it-is-and-why-it-matters/

Syropoulos C. et al. "The Global Sanctions Data Base—Release 3: Covid-19, Russia, and Multilateral Sanctions." *CESifo Working Paper,* 10101, 2022, 1–42.

Szabó A. "A választók" [The voters]. In *A magyar politikai rendszer: Negyedszázad után* [The Hungarian Political System: After a Quarter of a Century], edited by A. Körösényi Budapest: Osiris – MTA TK PTI, 2015, 279–305.

Szabó A. "Kiderült, hogyan áll a magyar tengeri kikötő Trieszben" [It has been revealed how the Hungarian sea port in Trieste is doing]. *Növekedés.hu,* December 21, 2022. https://novekedes.hu/elemzesek/kiderult-hogyan-all-a-magyar-tengeri-kikoto-triesztben

Szabó G. "A magyar államadósság keletkezése (1973–1989)" [The origin of the Hungarian national debt (1973–1989)]. *Pénzriport,* 2016.

http://www.penzriport.hu/letoltes/Magyar_allamadossag_
keletkezese_1973_1989.pdf

Szabó G. "Nagy Márton: Magyarország gazdasága jelentősen megváltozik"
[Hungary's economy is changing significantly]. *Index,* October 10, 2023.
https://index.hu/gazdasag/2023/10/10/nagy-marton-eloadas-logisztika-
fejlesztes-gazdasagi-novekedes/

Szalai Z. "'70-es évek cikksorozat VIII. – A külső egyensúlyi helyzet
alakulása Magyarországon az 1970-es években" ['70s Article Series VIII:
The evolution of the external equilibrium situation in Hungary in the
1970s]. *MNB,* 2022. https://www.mnb.hu/letoltes/szalai-zoltan-a-kulso-
egyensulyi-helyzet-alakulasa-magyarorszagon-az-1970-es-evekben.pdf

Széchenyi I. *Hitel* [Credit]. Budapest: Neumann Kht., 2002 [1830]. https://
mek.oszk.hu/06100/06132/html/index.htm (October 24, 2023).

Szenes Z. "Felkészülés a háborúra? A NATO új stratégiai koncepciójának
értékelése" [Preparing for War? Evaluation of NATO's New Strategic
Concept]. *KKI Elemzések,* 41, 2022. https://kki.hu/wp-content/
uploads/2022/08/KE_2022_41_NATO_felkeszules_a_haborura_
Szenes_0818.pdf

Szilágyi Zs. "A magyar–mongol kulturális kapcsolatok történeti vázlata"
[Historical outline of Hungarian-Mongolian cultural relations]. *Passages* 1
(2023): 367–405.
http://real.mtak.hu/166596/1/202301-a025-00.pdf

Szilvay G. "Fontos Magyarország a szuverenitásért való küzdelemben –
John Fonte a Mandinernek" [Hungary is important in the struggle for
sovereignty - John Fonte speaks to Mandiner]. *Mandiner,* June 20, 2022.
https://mandiner.hu/belfold/2022/06/john-fonte-interju-szuverenitas-
orban-usa

Tabellini, G. "Culture and Institutions: Economic Development in the
Regions of Europe." *Journal of the European Economic Association* 8/4
(2010): 677–716.

Taleb, N. N. *The Black Swan: The Impact of the Highly Improbable.* London:
Penguin UK, 2010.

Teleki P. *Európáról és Magyarországról* [About Europe and Hungary].
    Budapest: Athenaeum, 1934.

Telò, M. ed. *Reforming Multilateralism in Post-Covid Times.* Brussels:
    Foundation for European Progressive Studies, 2020. https://feps-europe.
    eu/wp-content/uploads/2021/01/Reforming-Multilateralism-in-Post-
    COVID-times-.pdf

The Economist. "A Chinese Vision of Free Trade." October 7, 2021. https://
    www.economist.com/china/2021/10/07/a-chinese-vision-of-free-trade

The Economist. "What America's Protectionist Turn Means for the World."
    January 9, 2023. https://www.economist.com/finance-and-economics/
    2023/01/09/what-americas-protectionist-turn-mean-for-the-world

The Global Times. "Hungary's Participation in the BRI a Testament to
    Its Commitment to Opening Up to the East." September 2, 2023.
    https://www.globaltimes.cn/page/202309/1297434.shtml

The White House. "National Security Strategy of the United States of
    America". December 2017. https://trumpwhitehouse.archives.gov/wp-
    content/uploads/2017/12/NSS-Final-12-18-2017-0905.pdf

The White House. "Remarks by President Biden Before the 76th Session
    of the United Nations General Assembly". September 21, 2021.
    https://www.whitehouse.gov/briefing-room/speeches-
    remarks/2021/09/21/remarks-by-president-biden-before-the-76th-session-
    of-the-united-nations-general-assembly/

The White House. "Indo-Pacific Strategy of the United States". 2022a.
    https://www.whitehouse.gov/wp-content/uploads/2022/02/U.S.-Indo-
    Pacific-Strategy.pdf

The White House. "National Security Strategy". 2022b. https://www.
    whitehouse.gov/wp-content/uploads/2022/10/Biden-Harris-
    Administrations-National-Security-Strategy-10.2022.pdf

The White House. "Remarks by President Biden Ahead of the One-Year
    Anniversary of Russia's Brutal and Unprovoked Invasion of Ukraine".
    2023a. https://www.whitehouse.gov/briefing-room/speeches-
    remarks/2023/02/21/remarks-by-president-biden-ahead-of-the-one-year-
    anniversary-of-russias-brutal-and-unprovoked-invasion-of-ukraine/

The White House. "Remarks by President Biden and President Zelenskyy
of Ukraine in Joint Statement." 2023b. https://www.whitehouse.gov/
briefing-room/speeches-remarks/2023/02/20/remarks-by-president-
biden-and-president-zelenskyy-of-ukraine-in-joint-statement/

The White House. "Remarks by President Biden at a Campaign Reception".
2023c. https://www.whitehouse.gov/briefing-room/speeches-
remarks/2023/10/20/remarks-by-president-biden-at-a-campaign-
reception-3/

The White House. "Remarks by President Biden on the United States'
Response to Hamas's Terrorist Attacks Against Israel and Russia's
Ongoing Brutal War Against Ukraine". 2023d. https://www.whitehouse.
gov/briefing-room/speeches-remarks/2023/10/20/remarks-by-president-
biden-on-the-unites-states-response-to-hamass-terrorist-attacks-against-
israel-and-russias-ongoing-brutal-war-against-ukraine/

Thirlwall, A. P. "Balance of Payments Constrained Growth Models: History
and Overview." *PSL Quarterly Review* 64/259 (2011): 307–51.

Thompson, J. D. *Organizations in Action: Social Science Bases of
Administrative Theory.* New York: McGraw-Hill, 1967.

Tierney, D. "Why It's Good for Europe to Argue with America." *Foreign
Affairs,* September 11, 2023. https://www.foreignaffairs.com/united-
states/why-its-good-europe-argue-america

Tierney, M. "Beyond the Central Eurasian Pivot." *Journal of Military and
Strategic Studies,* 17/1 (216): 5–33.

Tomka B. "Gazdasági növekedés és fogyasztás Magyarországon
a 20. Században" [Economic growth and consumption in Hungary
in the twentieth century]. *Korunk* 21/4 (2010): 30–45.

Tongsopit, S. et al. "Energy Security in ASEAN: A Quantitative Approach for
Sustainable Energy Policy." *Energy Policy* 90 (2016): 60–72.

Townshend, A. "The AUKUS Submarine Deal Highlights a Tectonic Shift
in the U.S.–Australia Alliance." *Carnegie Endowment for International
Peace,* March 27, 2023. https://carnegieendowment.org/2023/03/27/
aukus-submarine-deal-highlights-tectonic-shift-in-u.s.-australia-
alliance-pub-89383

Tseng, C. "China Wafer Production Capacity Growth Fastest in World." *SEMI*, January 7, 2019. https://www.semi.org/en/china-wafer-production-capacity-growth-fastest-world

Tseng, Z. H. "China's Multilateral Diplomacy: Not Quite a Beijing-Moscow Alliance." *The Politburo*, September 3, 2023. https://thepolitburo.org/2023/09/03/chinas-multilateral-diplomacy-not-quite-a-beijing-moscow-alliance/

Turchin, P. *War and Peace and War: The Rise and Fall of Empires.* New York: Plume, 2007.

Turner, A. "China vs. the Washington Consensus." *Project Syndicate,* October 23, 2017. https://www.project-syndicate.org/commentary/china-versus-washington-consensus-by-adair-turner-2017-10

Vázquez, S. T. and A. Sumner. "Revisiting the Meaning of Development: A Multidimensional Taxonomy of Developing Countries." *The Journal of Development Studies* 49/12 (2013): 1728–45.

Veszprémy L. "Újabb szempontok a tatárjárás történetéhez" [New Aspects of the History of the Tatar Invasions]. *Iskolakultúra* 4 (1994): 15–16, 28–35.

Világgazdaság (website). *Szijjártó Péter: jövőre közös magyar–szerb–szlovén áramtőzsde indul* [Péter Szijjártó: a joint Hungarian-Serbian-Slovenian electricity exchange will launch next year]. August 29, 2023. https://www.vg.hu/regio/2023/08/szijjarto-peter-jovore-kozos-magyar-szerb-szloven- aramtozsde-indul

Virmani, A. "A Tripolar century: USA, China and India." *ICRIER Working Paper* 160, 2005. https://www.econstor.eu/bitstream/10419/176182/1/icrier-wp-160.pdf

Vourlias, C. "'Dune' Proves Hungarian Biz 'Hard Act to Beat' as Production in Budapest Booms." *Variety,* March 30, 2022. https://variety. com/2022/film/global/dune-hungary-production-boom-2-1235218728/

Walker, B. et al. "Resilience, Adaptability and Transformability in Social-Ecological Systems." *Ecology and Society,* 9/2, 2004. https://www.ecologyandsociety.org/vol9/iss2/art5/

Wallensteen, P. "Characteristics of Economic Sanctions." *Journal of Peace Research* 5/3 (1968): 248–67.

Walt, S. M. "U.S. Rules-Based Order isn't as Principled as It Seems." *Foreign Policy,* March 28, 2023. https://foreignpolicy.com/2023/03/27/some-rules-of-global-politics-matter-more-than-others/

Waltz, K. N. "The Emerging Structure of International Politics." *International Security,* 18/2 (1993): 44–79.

Waltz, K. N. "Structural Realism after the Cold War." *International Security* 25/1 (2000): 5–41.

Waltz, K. N. *Theory of International Politics.* Long Grove, IL: Waveland Press, 2010.

Wang, H. "The Asian Financial Crisis and Financial Reforms in China." *The Pacific Review,* 12/4 (2007): 537–56. https://www.tandfonline.com/doi/abs/10.1080/09512749908719305

Wendt, A. *Social Theory of International Politics.* Cambridge: Cambridge University Press, 1999.

Weng, S. and W. Ai. "China's Vision for a Future World Order and Its Implications for Global Governance." In *China and World Politics in Transition,* edited by Y. Feng, Y. and F. Attinà. Switzerland: Springer, 2023, 13–29.

Wight, M. *Power Politics.* New York: Holmes & Meier, 1978.

Winokur, J. "The Cold War Trap: How the Memory of America's Era of Dominance Stunts U.S. Foreign Policy." *Foreign Affairs,* July 13, 2023. https://www.foreignaffairs.com/united-states/cold-war-trap-america-foreign-policy

Winrow, G. M. "Pivotal State or Energy Supplicant? Domestic Structure, External Actors, and Turkish Policy in the Caucasus." *Middle East Journal* 57/1 (2003): 76–92.

World Economic Forum (website). *The Global Risks Report 2023.* 2023. https://www3.weforum.org/docs/WEF_Global_Risks_Report_2023.pdf

Wright, T. "Trump Takes Allies Back to 19th Century Global Order." *Brookings,* March 21, 2017. https://www.brookings.edu/articles/ trump-takes-allies-back-to-19th-century-global-order/

Wright, T. "The Folly of Retrenchment: Why America Can't Withdraw from the World." *Foreign Affairs* 992 (2020): 10–18.

Yan, S. "China and European Strategic Autonomy." In *China and World Politics in Transition*, edited by Y. Feng and F. Attinà. Cham, Switzerland: Springer Nature, 2023, 181–94.

Yellen, J. "Remarks by Secretary of the Treasury Janet L. Yellen on Way Forward for the Global Economy." *U.S. Department of The Treasury*, April 13, 2022. https://home.treasury.gov/news/press-releases/jy0714

Yergin, D. *Változó világtérkép: Energia, klíma és a nemzetek közti konfliktusok* [A Changing World Map: Energy, Climate and Conflicts Between Nations]. Budapest: MCC Press, 2023.

Zaidi, A. "Top 20 Countries with Lowest Crime Rates." *Yahoo Finance*, April 11, 2023. https://finance.yahoo.com/news/top-20-countries-lowest-crime-083500316.html

Zakaria, F. *The Future of Freedom: Illiberal Democracy at Home and Abroad.* New York: W. W. Norton & Company, 2007.

Zakaria, F. "The Self-Destruction of American Power." *Foreign Affairs*, June 11, 2019. https://www.foreignaffairs.com/united-states/self-destruction-american-power

Zaniewicz, M. "New Gas Pipeline Geopolitics in Central and Eastern Europe." *Warsaw Institute*, December 21, 2019. https://warsawinstitute.org/new-gas-pipeline-geopolitics-in-central-and-eastern-europe/

Zeihan, P. *The End of the World is Just the Beginning: Mapping the Collapse of Globalization.* New York: HarperCollins, 2022.

Zemánek, L. "The Rise of Liberal Authoritarianism and Global Transition to Polycentrism" *Russia in Global Affairs* 213 (2023): 84–102. https://eng.globalaffairs.ru/articles/global-transition-to-polycentrism/

Zétényi, Zs. *Magyarország Szent Koronája* [The Holy Crown of Hungary]. Budapest: Kairosz Kiadó, 2002.

Zhou, X. "Organizational Response to COVID-19 Crisis: Reflections on the Chinese Bureaucracy and Its Resilience." *Management and Organization Review* 16/3 (2020): 473–84.

Databases

Államadósság Kezelő Központ [Public Debt Management Centre] (ÁKK).
A központi költségvetés adóssága, 2023 [Debt of the central budget,
2023]. https://www.akk.hu/statisztika/allamadossag-finanszirozas/
kozponti-koltsegvetes-adossaga (24 October 2023).

CSO [Hungarian Central Statistical Office, or KSH]. *Trianon mérlege* [The
Scales of Trianon], 1936. https://www.ksh.hu/statszemle_archive/all/193
8/1938_04/1938_04_0358_0367.pdf (July 7, 2023).

CSO. *Külföldi irányítású vállalkozások Magyarországon* [Foreign-
controlled enterprises in Hungary], 2020. https://www.
ksh.hu/docs/hun/xftp/idoszaki/kulf_irany_vall/2020/index.
html#aklfldisahazaiirnytsszervezetektermelkenysge (July 7, 2023).

CSO. *Bruttó államadósság a GDP arányában* [Gross public debt as a
proportion of GDP], 2020a. https://www.ksh.hu/ffi/4-5.html (July 7,
2023).

CSO. *A vállalkozások teljesítménymutatói kis- és középvállalkozási
kategória szerint* [Enterprise performance indicators in the small
and medium-sized enterprise category], 2021. https://www.ksh.hu/
stadat_files/gsz/hu/gsz0018.html (July 7, 2023).

CSO. *A költségvetés sport kiadásai* [Budgetary sport expenditure], 2022.
https://www.ksh.hu/stadat_files/ksp/hu/ksp0018.html (July 7, 2023).

CSO. *A foglalkoztatottak száma a foglalkoztatás jellege szerint, nemenként*
[The number of employees according to the nature of employment, by
gender], 2023. https://www.ksh.hu/stadat_files/mun/hu/mun0011.html
(July 7, 2023).

CSO. *A költségvetés kulturális kiadásai* [Budgetary cultural expenditure],
2023a. https://www.ksh.hu/ stadat_files/ksp/hu/ksp0003.html (July 7,
2023).

CSO. *Élveszületések és teljes termékenységi arányszám* [Live births and total
fertility rate]. 2023b. https://www.ksh.hu/stadat_files/nep/hu/nep0006.
html (July 7, 2023).

CSO. *Turizmus, vendéglátás* [Tourism, hospitality], 2023c, https://www.
ksh.hu/turizmus-vendeglatas KSH: *A 15–74 éves népesség gazdasági
aktivitása, nemenként* [Economic activity of the population aged 15–74,
by gender], 2023d. https://www.ksh.hu/stadat_files/mun/hu/mun0002.
html (October 24, 2023).

CSO. *A külföldre tett utazások száma, átlagos tartózkodási ideje és a külföldi
utakhoz kapcsolódó kiadások* [Number of trips abroad, average length of
stay and expenses related to foreign travel,], 2023e. https://www.ksh.
hu/stadat_files/tur/hu/tur0010.html (October 24, 2023).

CSO. *A külkereskedelmi termékforgalom értéke euróban és értékindexei a
fontosabb országok szerint* [The value of foreign trade product turnover in
euros and value indices, arranged in order of importance], 2023f. https://
www.ksh.hu/stadat_files/kkr/hu/kkr0003.html (November 8, 2023).

CSO. *A szabadalmi tevékenység* [Patent activity], 2023g.
https://www.ksh.hu/stadat_files/tte/hu/tte0014.html (June 29, 2023).

CSO. *Az egy főre jutó éves kiadások COICOP-főcsoportok és jövedelmi tizedek
(decilisek) szerint (forint/fő/év)* [Annual expenditure per capita by main
COICOP groups and income deciles (HUF/capita/year)], 2023h. https://
www.ksh.hu/stadat_files/jov/hu/jov0025.html (October 24, 2023).

CSO. *Felsőfokú végzettséggel rendelkező fiatalok aránya* [Proportion of young
people with higher education], 2023i. https://www.ksh.hu/oktatas
(July 7, 2023).

CSO. *Hozzájárulás a bruttó hazai termék (GDP) változásához (felhasználási
oldal), előző év azonos időszakához viszonyított negyedéves indexekből
számítva* [Contribution to the change in gross domestic product (GDP)
(consumption side), calculated from quarterly indices compared to the
same period of the previous year], 2023j. https://www.ksh.hu/stadat_
files/gdp/hu/gdp0105.html (July 7, 2023).

Department of State (DOS). *Report to Congress on Voting Practices in
the United Nations for 2021.* https://www.state.gov/wp-content/
uploads/2022/11/Report-Voting-Practices-in-the-United-Nations-2021.pdf
(July 14, 2023).

Energy Information Administration (EIA). *EIA Projects Nearly 50% Increase in World Energy Use by 2050, Led by Growth in Renewables,* October 2021. https://www.eia.gov/todayinenergy/detail. php?id=49876 (June 29, 2023).

European Commission, Directorate-General for Taxation and Customs Union. *Taxation trends in the European Union – Data for the EU Member States, Iceland, Norway – 2022 edition.* Publications Office of the European Union, 2022. https://data.europa.eu/doi/10.2778/417176

European Commission. Directorate-General for Taxation and Customs Union, Poniatowski, G., Bonch-Osmolovskiy, M., Śmietanka, A. et al., *VAT gap in the EU – Report 2022.* Publications Office of the European Union, 2022. https://data.europa.eu/doi/10.2778/109823

European Commission. "EU Regional Competitiveness Index 2.0, 2023." https://ec.europa.eu/regional_policy/information-sources/maps/ regional-competitiveness_en (July 6, 2023).

European Commission. "Data on Taxation Trends, 2023a." https://taxation-customs.ec.europa.eu/taxation-1/economic-analysis-taxation/data-taxation-trends_en (June 29, 2023).

European Commission. "SME Performance Review: Annual report on European SMEs, 2023b." https://single-market-economy.ec.europa.eu/ smes/sme-strategy/sme-performance-review_en (29 June 2023).

European Gas Hub. "The Rise and Fall of the Dutch Groningen Gas Field, 2018." https://www.europeangashub.com/the-rise-and-fall-of-the-dutch-groningen-gas-field.html (October 13, 2023).

Eurostat. "Translate Government Expenditure on Recreation, Culture and Religion, 2021." https://ec.europa.eu/eurostat/statistics-explained/index. php?title=Government_expenditure_on_recreation,_culture_and_ religion (May 23, 2023).

Eurostat. "Population by Age Group, 2022." https://ec.europa.eu/eurostat/ databrowser/view/tps00010/default/table?lang=en (May 23, 2023).

Eurostat. "GDP per capita in PPS – Data from 1st of June 2022." https://ec.europa.eu/eurostat/databrowser/view/tec00114/default/table (May 23, 2023.).

Eurostat. *Key Figures on European Transport, 2022* Edition.
   https://ec.europa.eu/eurostat/documents/15216629/15589759/KS-07-22-
   523-EN-N.pdf (November 8, 2023)

Eurostat. *Annual Net Earnings,* 2023.
   https://ec.europa.eu/eurostat/databrowser/view/EARN_NT_
   NETcustom_7227637/default/table?lang=en (July 6, 2023.).

Eurostat. "Consumption expenditure of households, 2005–2022."
   https://ec.europa.eu/eurostat/statistics-explained/
   index.php?title=File:Consumption_expenditure_of_
   households,_2005%E2%80%932022_NA2023.png (October 24, 2023)

Eurostat. "People at risk of poverty or social exclusion in 2022."
   https://ec.europa.eu/eurostat/web/products-eurostat-news/w/ddn-
   20230614-1 (October 24, 2023).

Eurostat. "Quarterly national accounts: GDP and employment."
   https://ec.europa.eu/eurostat/statistics-explained/index.
   php?title=Quarterly_national_accounts_-_GDP_and_employment
   (October 24, 2023).

Eurostat. "41% of young adults hold a tertiary degree."
   https://ec.europa.eu/eurostat/web/products-eurostat-news/-/ddn-
   20220524-2 (July 6, 2023).

Eurostat. "At most lower secondary educational attainment by age."
   https://ec.europa.eu/eurostat/databrowser/view/TPS00197/default/
   table?lang=en (June 29, 2023).

Eurostat. "Early leavers from education and training by sex."
   https://ec.europa.eu/eurostat/databrowser/view/SDG_04_10/default/
   table?lang=en (June 29, 2023).

Eurostat. "EU Trade since 1999 by SITC." 2023g. https://ec.europa.eu/
   eurostat/databrowser/view/DS-018995 custom_8240518/default/
   table?lang=en (November 11, 2023).

Eurostat. "GDP per capita, consumption per capita and price level indices."
   2023h. https://ec.europa.eu/eurostat/statistics-explained/index.
   php?title=GDP_per_capita,_consumption_per_capita_and_price_level_
   indices (July 6, 2023).

Eurostat. *General Government Debt*, 2023i. https://ec.europa.eu/eurostat/
databrowser/view/GOV_10DD_GGD__custom_8124914/default/
table?lang=en&page=time:2022 (October 24, 2023).

Eurostat. *Government Deficit/Surplus, Debt and Associated Data*, 2023j.
https://ec.europa.eu/eurostat/databrowser/view/gov_10dd_edpt1__
custom_8121902/default/table?lang=en (October 24, 2023).

Eurostat. *Gross Domestic Expenditure on R and D, 2011 and 2021
(%, relative to GDP)*, 2023k. https://ec.europa.eu/eurostat/statistics-
explained/index.php?title=File:Gross_domestic_expenditure_
on_R_and_D,_2011_and_2021_(%25,_relative_to_GDP)_04-10-
2022.png (June 29, 2023).

Eurostat. "Natural gas supply statistics." April. https://ec.europa.eu/
eurostat/statistics-explained/SEPDF/cache/10590.pdf (November 3,
2023).

Eurostat. "Population by educational attainment level, sex and age (%)."
https://ec.europa.eu/eurostat/databrowser/view/edat_lfs_9903/ default/
table?lang=en (July 6, 2023).

Eurostat. "R&D expenditure in the EU at 2.3% of GDP in 2020."
https://ec.europa.eu/eurostat/web/products-eurostat-news/-/ddn-
20211129-2 (July 6, 2023).

Eurostat. "Road, Rail and Navigable Inland Waterways Networks by NUTS
2 Regions", 2023o. https://ec.europa.eu/eurostat/databrowser/view/
TRAN_R_NET__custom_8053979/default/table?lang=en (October 24,
2023).

FGSZ. "A magyar földgázrendszer 2022. évi adatai." https://fgsz.hu/file/
documents/2/2607/fgr_2022.pdf (November 3, 2023).

Groupe international des importateurs de gaz naturel liquéfié (GIIGNL).
"GIIGNL Annual Report. 2022." https://giignl.org/wp-content/
uploads/2022/05/GIIGNL2022_Annual_Report_May24.pdf (April 5,
2023).

Hungarian Investment Promotion Agency (HIPA). "Új csúcson a
magyarországi működőtőke-beáramlás, 2021." https://hipa.hu/hir/uj-
csucson-a-magyarorszagi-mukodotoke-bearamlas/ (April 5, 2023)

International Energy Agency (IEA). "The Netherlands 2020: Energy Policy Review." September 2020. https://www.iea.org/reports/the-netherlands-2020 (April 5, 2023).

International Energy Agency (IEA). *World Energy Outlook, 2021.* https://iea.blob.core.windows.net/assets/4ed140c1-c3f3-4fd9-acae-789a4e14a23c/WorldEnergyOutlook2021.pdf (October 6, 2023).

International Energy Agency (IEA). *Share of Top Producing Countries in Extraction of Selected Minerals and Fossil Fuels, 2019,* May 5, 2021. https://www.iea.org/data-and-statistics/charts/share-of-top-producing-countries-in-extraction-of-selected-minerals-and-fossil-fuels-2019 (April 5, 2023).

International Energy Agency (IEA). *Special Report on Solar PV Global Supply Chains,* 2022. https://iea.blob.core.windows.net/assets/d2ee601d-6b1a-4cd2-a0e8-db02dc64332c/SpecialReportonSolarPVGlobalSupplyChains.pdf (April 5, 2023).

International Energy Agency (IEA): *Executive summary: China Currently Dominates Global Solar PV Supply Chains,* 2023a. https://www.iea.org/reports/solar-pv-global-supply-chains/executive-summary (May 30, 2023).

International Energy Agency (IEA). *Hungary Electricity Security Policy,* 2023b. https://prod.iea.org/articles/hungary-electricity-security-policy (November 8, 2023).

International Energy Agency (IEA). *Hungary Natural Gas Security Policy,* 2023c. https://www.iea.org/articles/hungary-natural-gas-security-policy (November 8, 2023).

International Labour Organization (ILO). *Labour Force Participation Rate Age: ILO Model Estimates, Nov. 2022 (%) – Annual,* 2023. https://www.ilo.org/shinyapps/bulkexplorer16/?lang=en&segment=indicator&id=EAP_2WAP_SEX_AGE_RT_A (July 6, 2023).

International Labour Organization (ILO). "Unemployment Rate by Sex and Age (%) – Annual." https://www.ilo.org/shinyapps/bulkexplorer24/?-lang=en&segment= indicator&id=UNE_2EAP_SEX_ AGE_RT_A (July 6, 2023).

International Monetary Fund (IMF). "Enhancing Surveillance: Interconnectedness and Clusters." 2012. https://www.imf.org/external/np/pp/eng/2012/031512.pdf (May 23, 2023).

International Monetary Fund (IMF). *Fiscal Monitor*, 2022. https://www.imf.org/en/Publications/FM (July 6, 2023).

International Monetary Fund (IMF). *GDP, current prices*, 2023. www.imf.org/en/Publications/SPROLLS/world-economic-outlook-databases#sort=%40imfdate%20descending (May 23, 2023).

International Monetary Fund (IMF). *Global Financial Stability Report: Safeguarding Financial Stability amid High Inflation and Geopolitical Risks,* 2023a. https://www.imf.org/en/Publications/GFSR/Issues/2023/04/11/global-financial-stability-report-april-2023?cid=bl-com-spring2023flagships-GFSREA2023001#Chapter-3:-Geopolitics-and-Financial-Fragmentation:-Implications-for-Macro-Financial-Stability (May 30, 2023).

International Monetary Fund (IMF). *IMF Datamapper: GDP based on PPP, Share of World,* 2023b. https://www.imf.org/external/datamapper/PPPSH@WEO/OEMDC/ADVEC/WEOWORLD (October 24, 2023).

Magyar Energetikai és Közmű-szabályozási Hivatal [Hungarian Energy and Utilities Regulatory Office] (MEKH) . *Nemzetközi árösszehasonlítás 2023. szeptember* [International price comparison, September 2023], October 3, 2023. https://www.mekh.hu/nemzetkozi-arosszehasonlitas-2023-szeptember (October 24, 2023).

Mavir. *A magyar villamosenergia-rendszer 2022. évi adatai,* 2023 [2022 Data of the Hungarian electricity system, 2023]. https://www.mavir.hu/documents/10258/239341959/A+magyar+villamosenergia-+%C3%A9s+f%C3%B6ldg%C3%A1zrendszer+2022.+%C3%A9vi+adatait+bemutat%C3%B3+kiadv%C3%A1ny.pdf/dd5b5343-f7ab-f57f-e3ce-8ee9f25f4783?t=1697181260471 (July 7, 2023).

OECD. "Quarterly International Trade Statistics (by partner country)." 2022. https://stats.oecd.org/Index.aspx?DataSetCode=QITS (July 6, 2023).

OECD: *FDI Flows: Inward, % of GDP, 2005–2022,* 2023, https://data.oecd.org/fdi/fdi-flows.htm#indicator-chart (July 6, 2023).

OECD. "FDI Flows: Outward, Million US dollars, 2005–2022." 2023a. https://data.oecd.org/fdi/fdi-flows.htm#indicator-chart (June 29, 2023).

OECD. "FDI stocks." 2023b. https://data.oecd.org/fdi/fdi-stocks.htm (July 6, 2023).

OECD. *OECD International Direct Investment Statistics 2022*, 2023c. https://read.oecd-ilibrary.org/finance-and-investment/oecd-international-direct-investment-statistics-2022_deedc307-en#page2 (November 8, 2023).

OECD. "Statutory Corporate Income Tax Rates." 2023d. https://stats.oecd.org/Index.aspx?DataSetCode=CTS_CIT# (May 23, 2023).

OECD. "Tax wedge." 2023e. https://data.oecd.org/tax/tax-wedge.htm (June 29, 2023).

Stockholm International Peace Research Institute (SIPRI). *SIPRI Yearbook 2022, Armaments, Disarmament and International Security.* Oxford: Oxford University Press, 2022. https://www.sipri.org/yearbook/2022 (July 6, 2023).

Stockholm International Peace Research Institute (SIPRI). SIPRI Military Expenditure Database, 2023. https://www.sipri.org/databases/milex (July 6, 2023).

The Atlas of Economic Complexity. "Country & Product Complexity Rankings." *Growth Lab,* 2023. https://atlas.cid.harvard.edu/ rankings (June 29, 2023).

World Bank. *China 2030: Building a Modern, Harmonious, and Creative Society,* 2013. https://www.worldbank.org/content/dam/Worldbank/document/China-2030-complete.pdf (May 30, 2023).

World Bank. *Exports of goods and services (constant 2015 US$),* 2022. https://data.worldbank.org/indicator/NE.EXP.GNFS.KD?most_recent_value_desc=true (May 30, 2023).

World Bank. *Industry (including construction), value added (% of GDP) – Germany,* 2022a. https://data.worldbank.org/indicator/NV.IND.TOTL.ZS?locations=DE (November 8, 2023).

World Bank. *High-technology Exports (current US$),* 2023. https://data.worldbank.org/indicator/TX.VAL.TECH.CD (July 6, 2023).

World Bank. *Imports of Goods and Services (BoP, current US$)*, 2023a. https://data.worldbank.org/indicator/BM.GSR.GNFS.CD (May 30, 2023).

World Bank. *Exports of Goods and Services (% of GDP)*, 2023b. https://data.worldbank.org/indicator/NE.EXP.GNFS.ZS?most_recent_value_desc=true (July 6, 2023).

World Bank. *Foreign Direct Investment, Net Inflows (% of GDP): Ireland*, 2023c. https://data.worldbank.org/indicator/BX.KLT.DINV.WD.GD.ZS?locations=IE (May 30, 2023).

World Bank. *GDP Growth (annual %): Ireland*, 2023d. https://data.worldbank.org/indicator/NY.GDP.MKTP.KD.ZG?end=2012&locations=IE&start=1995 (May 30, 2023).

World Bank. *GDP per capita, PPP (current international $)*, 2023e. https://data.worldbank.org/indicator/NY.GDP.PCAP.PP.CD?locations=HU (June 29, 2023).

World Bank. *GNI per capita, Atlas Method (current US$): Hungary, United States, United Kingdom, France, Japan, Canada, Germany, Italy*, 2023f. https://data.worldbank.org/indicator/NY.GNP.PCAP.CD?end=2022&-locations=HU-US-GB-FR-JP-CA-DE-IT&start=2022&view=bar (July 6, 2023).

World Bank. *GNI per capita, Atlas method (current US$) – Ireland*, 2023g. https://data.worldbank.org/indicator/NY.GNP.PCAP.CD?locations=IE (May 30, 2023).

World Bank. *World Development Indicators*, 2023h. https://databank.worldbank.org/source/world-development-indicators (May 30, 2023).

World Trade Organization (WTO). *Global Trade Outlook and Statistics*, 2023. https://www.wto.org/english/res_e/booksp_e/trade_outlook23_e.pdf (November 8, 2023).

World Trade Organization (WTO). *Reinforcing the Deliberative Function of the WTO to Respond to Global Trade Policy Challenges*, 2023a. https://docs.wto.org/dol2fe/Pages/FE_Search/FE_S_S009-DP. aspx?language=E&CatalogueIdList=292124,291828,291568,291484,290470,290419,290374,290307,290275,290304&CurrentCatalogueIdIndex=0&FullTextHash=&HasEnglishRecord=True&HasFrenchRecord=False&HasSpanishRecord=False (November 8, 2023).